CALVIN'S
OLD TESTAMENT
COMMENTARIES

p 72 OT mustn't dissolve into NT (in interp) but stand on its own (p.80 too)

p.74 Anagogé

p.83 childhood + manhood of Church

Parker sets out list context in intro.

Tom Balserak
Purchased at RTS bookstore
on June 19, 1993.

CALVIN'S
OLD TESTAMENT
COMMENTARIES

T. H. L. PARKER

T. & T. CLARK LTD.
59 GEORGE STREET, EDINBURGH

Copyright © T. & T. Clark Ltd 1986
Typeset by Pennart Typesetting (Edinburgh) Ltd, Edinburgh
printed and bound by Billing & Sons, Worcester.

for

T. & T. CLARK LTD, EDINBURGH

First printed in the U.K. 1986

British Library Cataloguing in Publication Data

Parker, T.H.L.
  Calvin's Old Testament commentaries.
  1. Calvin, Jean 2. Bible. O.T.—Theology
  I. Title
  230'.092'4   BS1192.5

ISBN 0-567-09365-4

Two things of principal moment there are which have deservedly procured him honour throughout the world: the one his exceeding pains in composing the Institutions of Christian religion; the other his no less industrious travails for exposition of holy Scripture according unto the same Institutions.
Richard Hooker: *Eccl. Pol.*, Pref.ii.8.

Calvin is a cataract, a primeval forest, a demonic power, something directly down from Himalaya, absolutely Chinese, strange, mythological; I lack completely the means, the suction cups, even to assimilate this phenomenon, not to speak of presenting it adequately. What I receive is only a thin little stream and what I can then give out again is only a yet thinner extract of this little stream. I could gladly and profitably set myself down and spend all the rest of my life just with Calvin.
Karl Barth to Eduard Thurneysen, June 8, 1922

CONTENTS

Abbreviations

OC *Ioannis Calvini Opera [Corpus Reformatorum]*
OS *Joannis Calvini Opera Selecta*
SC *Supplementa Calviniana*
CTS *Calvin Translation Society*
    [Individual commentaries indicated thus: CTS Gen[esis],
    CTS Mo[saic], CTS Mi[nor Prophets], etc.]
CC *Calvin's Commentaries* [Edinburgh, 1959ff.]
CP *A Commentary on the Psalms [London 1965]*

Introduction

In many respects the scope of this present book differs from that of its predecessor, *Calvin's New Testament Commentaries*, which was concerned more with textual and technical matters and had less room for the substance of his exposition. Here little or no heed is paid to his Old Testament text or the source of his historical or geographical information, and the substance forms the bulk of the work. Some things they have in common. As then I tried to give an historical account of the writing of the New Testament commentaries, so now with those of the Old Testament, but especially I have aimed at casting light on the lectures, a strangely neglected subject. Where, however, the earlier book investigated Calvin's methods and principles of interpretation in the context of those men of the Renaissance like Rudolf Agricola and Philip Melanchthon, this book concentrates on the relationship between the Old and New Testaments according to Calvin. The hermeneutics stated more fully on the New Testament are mentioned only briefly here or are taken as read.

The work is therefore more suited to the general reader than those lists of Greek and Latin readings and the careful bibliographies of *Calvin's New Testament Commentaries*. It is, indeed, intended as an introduction, to portray these Old Testament expositions and perhaps whet the reader's appetite to read some of them for himself.

For the scholar the book is more like an ice-breaker opening up a way for the scientific party. He will see that many questions have been raised and not answered, and that some pertinent topics have not been mentioned at all. There is nothing on Calvin's knowledge of Hebrew or on his opinion on the canon or on the edition of the text he used. Such subjects as his reconstruction of Pentateuchal history are not followed through to see whether we have here a piece of early Pentateuchal literary criticism, and if so, how it fits in with other sixteenth century attempts in that field. Nor, and this is highly important because it touches the nature of "Calvin and Calvinism" itself, is the influ-

1

ence of the Old Testament on his general theology and his pastoral practice considered. As is well-known, the Lutheran Hunnius attacked Calvin in a book called *Calvinus Judaizans* (1593), with the full title *Calvin the Judaizer, or Judaistic Glosses and Corruptions in expounding Testimonies in Holy Scripture on the Trinity*, etc. Hunnius's approach was clumsy and amateurish; but some might wish to raise the same question rather more subtly and enquire into the unconscious influence of Old Testament studies on Calvin's theology and practice. It is, however, a question which should not be answered on the basis of what appears in this book or, indeed, in the expositions themselves, but after a reading of the New Testament commentaries also, and especially of *Galatians* and *Hebrews*.

The questions are many: but I have not attempted to answer most of them. With Viola I say, 'Time, thou must unravel this, not I'. I have also refrained, though not without a serious struggle, from drawing comparisons and contrasts between Calvin and other writers. It was a great temptation, overcome only in later drafts, to compare him with Lefèvre and Augustine on the Psalms, with Luther on Genesis, with such predecessors as Nicolas of Lyra and Andrew of St Victor on various points. Had I yielded, the book would not only have been much bigger but it would also have changed its character. I have therefore kept very strictly to Calvin and refrained from even quoting anyone else, apart from one or two writers on matters Calvinian.

Calvin himself, however, I have quoted liberally, not only for the sake of arguments but also to bring those into direct contact with his writings who cannot easily find a set of the Calvin Translation Society. This is, unfortunately, the only full edition. I say "unfortunately" because the Old Testament volumes are in general badly edited. In few instances are the foot-notes at all helpful; often they are downright silly. The exceptions shine as rare gems. The editor of Genesis adds to the score against him that he omits anything that might bring a blush to the cheek of the young person – Gen. 19:31ff. and 38:10 are left out *in toto*. The translating in most of the volumes is unsatisfactory, not in the sense of gross incorrectness but in its imprecision. This was, it may be suspected, often deliberate, in their effort to make Calvin a good "Evangelical" of the mid-nineteenth century breed, one who, if unlikely to frighten much the enemy, the Oxford Movement, could be relied upon to strengthen the faithful by confirming what they already held. Translating alone, however, could not do the trick; Calvin still remained an awkward ally. The editors therefore resorted to foot-notes stating the "correct" interpretation of verses according to the fashionable authorities. Daniel only differs from the run of the commentaries in bringing in quite respectable writers as the criteria by which to correct Calvin. The truth was that the editors were not interested in presenting a sound edition of their author but only in supplying commentaries on the Bible that should carry the authority of Calvin's name and therefore be of polemical service. All that being said, however, this is, apart from a very few individual commentaries and the sixteenth and early seventeenth century translations, all that is available. It is greatly to be wished that the new translation now being designed in Edinburgh will be sucessfully launched.

In the original, the edition commonly in use is that in the *Corpus Reformatorum:*but I think that there is little to choose textually between that and the two previous *Opera omnia,* the Amsterdam of 1671 and the Geneva of 1617. Once again, a sound critical edition of the Old Testament expositions is to be desired.

That I have kept so strictly to Calvin himself has isolated him from his age, made him, perhaps, almost appear the only Old Testament commentator in the fifteen-fifties. We must now briefly rectify this and place him in his setting.

This was the period of the revival of Biblical studies in Europe. For it was not a new movement; it was a revival, a renewal of the Church's living engagement with Scripture in the earlier part of the Middle Ages and before.[1] Old Testament studies had flourished from the eleventh to the fourteenth centuries. After this there seems to have been a decline, not so much possibly in quantity as in originality. It seems that the creative study of the Bible was elbowed out of its earlier primacy by a number of forces. For one thing, the doctrines in Scripture

[1] For the following paragraph see especially B. Smalley, *The Study of the Bible in the Middle Ages* (Blackwell, 1952, 1983).

were systematized into dogmatic theology, so that Peter Lombard's *Four Books of Sentences* were elevated into an authority alongside the Bible. Then again, the persecution and separating of the Jews meant that the former interest in Hebrew and rabbinics disappeared and scholars confined themselves to the Latin, the Vulgate. And yet again, just as Lombard's *Sentences* was authoritative in doctrine, so a collection of expositions, mainly taken from the Church fathers, assumed a place of theological authority. Together with expositions from the fourteenth century Franciscan, Nicolas of Lyra, the *Glossa ordinaria* formed the staple diet in Biblical interpretation for scholars and preachers. But by its very authority it tended to stifle creative Bible study. When one saw that Augustine or Ambrose, or even Bede, had explained a passage thus, he needed some courage and independence to explain it another way. On the other hand, it helped to keep alive the patristic tradition; and Lyra not only supplied the lacking Jewish element by quoting some rabbinic sources, but also gave the literal sense at a time when spiritualising was the fashion. In the printed editions the Gloss and Lyra were usually amalgamated, together with some other material, as one undoubtedly *magnum opus* of six massive volumes. The fact that it was printed several times at the end of the fifteenth century and during the sixteenth shows how much it was used, in spite of attacks on it by humanists and Reformers.

The revival of New Testament studies was dominated by one man, Erasmus of Rotterdam. No such single figure bestrides the world of the Old Testament. The nearest we see is the German scholar Reuchlin, a strange, ambiguous person, who was, by a sort of religious romanticism, captivated by Hebrew, so that, as has been said, 'His study of Hebrew was almost as much a religious exercise as a scholarly preoccupation'.[2] He was a linguist and not a theologian, and it was his Hebrew grammar of 1506 rather than any expository work that furthered Old Testament studies. His cabalistic speculations found no favour either with sober Romanist or Evangelical commentators. After Reuchlin, the next Old Testament scholar was certainly

[2] L. W. Spitz: *Reuchlin's Philosophy: Pythagoras and Cabala for Christ. Archiv für Reformationsgeschichte*, 47 (1956) 1/2, pp. 1ff.

Sebastian Münster, one of the Basel Reformers, who may have taught Calvin Hebrew. Münster published an edition of the Hebrew Old Testament, with a Latin translation in parallel columns, and with annotations largely taken from rabbinic commentaries. There can be little doubt that Calvin made use of this work.

1534, the date of Münster's Bible, is quite late when we are talking about Hebrew Bibles. Portions had been published a good forty years previous to the first printed Greek New Testament of 1516, and the complete Old Testament had appeared in 1488. After this there were several editions by the mid-sixteenth century.

The Greek Old Testament, the Septuagint, made its appearance not long after the first New Testament, when Aldus at Venice published the whole Bible in Greek. Calvin certainly possessed a copy of this book.[3] Another Greek Old Testament had been printed before this, in fact, but its publication had been delayed until 1522. This was the magnificent Complutensian Polyglot, in six volumes. Its first part contained the Old Testament in parallel columns of Hebrew, Greek, and Latin.

As for Latin Bibles, a very large number had been published in print, of course, but the multiplicity of the different versions showed up in corrupt and confused texts, with none of them being treated as authoritative. The credit for trying to clean up the text by publishing good critical editions belongs to Robert Stephanus, the scholar printer of Paris who later migrated to Geneva. Starting in 1527/28, he published four or five editions of the Vulgate, giving increasingly valuable variant readings in the margins. Although he did not achieve his over-ambitious aim of restoring the text to its original state, he at any rate provided a respectable text. Besides the Vulgate, which had the authority of coming down from the early Church, there were a few "modern" translations in "purer" (i.e. more classical) Latin.

No doubt it was inevitable that, when Hebrew and Greek versions of the Old Testament had become easily obtainable, commentaries would follow. Scholars who could read Hebrew and Greek were continually being surprised by their new

---

[3] Parker: *Calvin's New Testament Commentaries*, p. 105 n. 1.

insights and understandings. They wanted to communicate their discoveries to others, and so, from about 1530 onwards there was a flood of commentaries in comparison with the previous trickle. Another cause was the religious controversy. The Evangelicals took their stand on Scripture alone as the source and criterion of all the Church's teaching. It was therefore a major part of the work of the Continental Reformation to expound Scripture. And, on the contrary side, it became necessary for the Romanists to write commentaries which showed the truth of their claims and the errors of the Evangelicals'. To follow the controversies only from the books and pamphlets of dogmatic theology is to miss a lot. The real workshops on both sides were the commentaries. Yet a third cause was straightforward edification and education, partly of literate laymen, but even more of parish clergy. From both sides there came commentaries, like those of the Reformer Conrad Pellican of Zürich, which had the primary aim of helping the less well educated clergy to understand Scripture and of showing them how to expound it in their sermons.

By the time Calvin began publishing his Old Testament commentaries, therefore, the pioneering work had been done and there was a fairly solid body of material at his disposal – quite good texts of the Hebrew, Greek, and Latin Bibles, some grammars and lexicons and concordances, and several "modern" commentaries, besides those of the Church fathers which had been edited and printed. Even when there were no modern works and scholars had to rely on classical or early Christian authors, these were now available in print. The weakest technical part of Old Testament studies lay in history and geography, particularly geography.

But we must approach any of these older Biblical writers in a spirit of sympathy and humility, not judging them ignorant and backward because they seem strange to us. To approach them in such a spirit of sympathy will mean, I think, that we shall be surprised, not only at their intellectual energy, their insights, their incredible knowledge of the Bible, but also at their whole approach of submissive reverence for Scripture, of eager search for truth, of confidence and certainty.

Of course, this was not true of all sixteenth century commentators. There were the barren rascals then just as now. But it is true of Calvin, all round the greatest of them all. Yet what a strange medley we are going to meet in the following pages. Barth called Calvin 'a cataract, a primeval forest, a demonic power, something directly down from Himalaya, absolutely Chinese, strange, mythological'. That is one side, and nowhere is it more true than in the Old Testament expositions. But there is another Calvin, a bourgeois, down to earth, common-sensical Calvin, and this Calvin, too, is very evident in the expositions. Indeed, the Calvin we encounter there is a bundle of contradictions. He will say the loveliest and the ugliest things ('the Lord went to prison with him' – 'God never suffered any babies to be killed save those whom he had already reprobated and destined to eternal death'); he can be highly subtle (in literary criticism, say, or theological understanding) and unbelievably naive (Noah's Ark); he can interpret one passage with profound insight and another in the most mundane of ways; for page after page he can look like *Calvinus Judaeus* and then suddenly show that, in his voluntary exile among the men of the Old Covenant, living with them in shades and shadows, he has not forgotten the Sun of righteousness who, as he himself already knows, will in their future rise with healing in his wings.

* * * *

The impetus to provide this companion volume to my *Calvin's New Testament Commentaries* came when I was asked to give four lectures at the Central Readers' Conference in 1983. Looking round for a subject, I decided that the Old Testament expositions would both be suitable and would also get the obligation off my conscience, where it had lain, not very heavily, for too long. This book is a greatly expanded version of the lectures. The Conference itself at Selwyn College, Cambridge, proved a most pleasant occasion, and I would thank the Principal of the Conference, Professor W. O. Chadwick, for inviting me, and the Readers who were present, and especially their secretaries, Canon T. G. King and Mr. C. J. Ball, for their warm and friendly welcome.

I am also grateful to the publishers of *Calvinus Reformator*

(Potchefstroom University for Christian Higher Education, 1982) for permission to use a revision of my paper *The shadow and the sketch*, which was read at the First South African Congress for Calvin Research in 1980 and appeared in *Calvinus Reformator*, pp. 142-8.

Chapter One

The Three Forms of Exposition

We usually speak of Calvin's Old Testament "Commentaries", but, in fact, if by "commentary" we mean a work written or dictated by an author, then only three of these books are genuine commentaries. Most of the so-called commentaries are transcripts of expository lectures, differing formally from the commentaries in not unimportant respects. To the lectures must also be added the great mass of sermons, themselves connected expositions of Biblical books. It is for this reason that we have used the word "exposition" in our chapter title. If we are to offer a comprehensive introduction to Calvin's Old Testament work, we must describe not only the commentaries proper but also the lectures and sermons; otherwise we should have to confine ourselves to the *Mosaic, Psalms,* and *Joshua* and neglect the larger part of the Old Testament expositions.

Calvin's Old Testament activity falls within the last fifteen years or so of his life. Between 1540 and 1551 were published all his commentaries on the New Testament epistles. Only towards 1550 did he begin to write and lecture on the Old Testament; but even then for six or seven years he continued this in connection with the writing of commentaries on the Gospels and Acts.[1] After the publication of the definitive edition of the epistles in 1556/57, his Biblical work was confined to the Old Testament. It was halted only by his final illness.

1 The Sermons[2]

As the senior minister in Geneva, Calvin had charge of the parish and church of St Pierre, the former cathedral. This office

[1] So far as we know, all the NT commentaries were genuine commentaries in the sense I have given.

[2] For a full account of the sermons, see my book *The Oracles of God,* London and Redhill, 1947.

entailed a considerable amount of preaching. By the *Ordonnances Ecclésiastiques* of 1541, two Sunday services were ordered, with three weekday services. In 1549, however, these latter became a daily service, held first thing in the morning before most people had gone to work. Calvin himself preached at both the Sunday services every week and, from 1549, every weekday of alternate weeks. It is with the weekday sermons that we are now almost exclusively concerned, for his custom was to preach on the New Testament on Sundays (although occasionally on psalms in the afternoon) and on the Old Testament on weekdays. In these fifteen years, therefore, he had the opportunity of preaching over two thousand sermons on the Old Testament.

Calvin's extant sermons are, with very rare exceptions, connected expositions of books of the Bible. He began at Chapter 1, verse 1, of a book, taking one, or two, or many, verses and went on, day after day of alternate weeks, until he reached the end of that book. Then the next day he started another. He was in no hurry. He could devote a year to Job, fifteen months to Deuteronomy, even three years to Isaiah – it is true that he was ill and off-work for several months during the course of these sermons, but nevertheless the 342 sermons would need 57 fortnights, or two years and two months.

For the preservation of the sermons we have to thank, not Calvin himself, for he preached without even notes and therefore did not write his sermons, but a French refugee, Denis Raguenier. The refugees in Geneva had formed a society called *la Compagnie des Étrangers*, largely to look after those of their number that were in financial straits (and many, of course, had fled their native lands with neither adequate means nor prospect of work; some working-men had to learn a new trade, some gentlemen had to start working for a living for the first time in their lives). It was learned that Denis Raguenier was a skilful short-hand writer and that he was taking down Calvin's sermons verbatim, for his own spiritual profit. The value of the sermons had long been recognised and attempts had been made to record them, but without success. Here was an opportunity to succeed and at the same time to help the refugees.

The story is told in a preface to the sermons on Deuteronomy, published after Calvin's death. I will quote from the translation by Arthur Golding, whose prose is nearly always worth the reading. The writers must, they say, speak 'one word, concerning the printing of the sermons of our late good father M. Iohn Calvin. Nowe then, for the better understanding of the whole, you must consider that from the yere of our Lord 1549 forth on, the late M. Dennis Ragueneawe [a clumsy anglicising of Raguenier] being fled hither, gave himselfe to the gathering of the Sermons word for word, which M. Iohn Calvin did ordinarilie make: and that with such swiftnes and cunning, through the use of certain notes and shapes, as few words escaped him even from the beginning. Which thing when they saw which had the charge of the poor strangers at that time: although they had not any great sum of money wherewith to releeve the present needs: yet failed they not to take such order, that the said writer was intertained [i.e. supported] after a sort with some part of the same money, to the intent he might have wherewith to maintaine himselfe and his small familie, while he gave himself wholly to the gathering of these sermons, and to the ingrosing of them faire afterward, because he shoulde spare no time to any other businesse than that'.[3]

And indeed, it was a full-time task. Raguenier had to be there in church with his pen and ink and paper, not only twice on Sunday but also every morning of alternate weeks, at six o'clock in summer, seven in winter, taking down every word of Calvin's sermons, ranging from about three thousand to above six thousand words in length. He then had either to write them out in longhand himself or dictate them to another scribe, keep the sheets carefully in order until the series of sermons was completed and then get that set bound and delivered to the safe-keeping of the deacons. The sermons could be borrowed, or perhaps read on the premises, apparently on payment of a fee which went to the helping of the poor foreigners.

All the sermons which Calvin preached from 1549 were taken down in this way by Denis Raguenier until his death in 1560 and by other stenographers after that. The fact that others were involved provides us with a useful confirmation of the accuracy of the transmission, in that the style and vocabulary do not vary between Raguenier and his successors. That no little errors

[3] OC 25,587f.; Sermons...upon...Deuteronomie, sig. ¶v[r].

should be made would be asking too much of men writing short-hand with a quill and ink in an unheated church. Moreover, the transcripts were not checked by Calvin himself. But the errors are remarkably few, and are nearly always such as can be easily corrected by modern editors.[4] Thus the manuscripts can be taken as faithfully reproducing Calvin's own words.

Some sets were published in Calvin's own life-time;[5] others remained in manuscript. Two sets, those on I Samuel and Job, were translated into Latin some years after his death. Those which had remained unpublished, numbering over two thousand sermons, had a chequered history. They stayed in the library in Geneva until 1805, when they were sold, in effect as scrap paper, because it was said they were so hard to read. Some volumes have been recovered over the years, occasionally from unexpected places (one from an old-clothes shop, for example, another from a London auction room), so that in all, thirteen of the original forty-eight have been recovered and reassembled in the Bibliothèque publique et universitaire de Genève. The Bodleian Library revealed in the nineteen-sixties that they possessed a special set of Genesis sermons, written out fair and presented by the City of Geneva to Sir Thomas Bodley, who had studied there; another set, also on Genesis, was purchased by Lambeth Palace Library at about the same time. All the manuscript sermons are now in course of being edited and published under the title of *Supplementa Calviniana*.[6]

It is hard to see rhyme or reason in the order in which Calvin preached on the books. The first to be taken in this period was Jeremiah, from before 1549 into 1550, which was then, properly enough, followed by Lamentations. But then the canonical order, not only of the Old Testament in general, but of the

---

[4] For example, in the *Supplementa* volume of *Jeremiah*, we find the following editorial corrections to the MSS. of Sermon 7: Aprenons donc qu'il fault estre *for MS*. Aprenons donc qu'il faut donc estre (p.47[7]); nous cerchons *for MS*. nous cerchions (p.49[18]); c'en *for MS*. s'en (p.49[28]) – but this is probably only a spelling idiosyncrasy; Qu'ilz *for MS*. Qui (p.50[27]). Four trifling errors in one sermon; and only the last could mislead the reader for more than a moment.

[5] See *Oracles of God.*, pp. 167-70.

[6] See B. Gagnebin: *L'Histoire des Manuscrits des Sermons de Calvin,* in SC II, pp. XIV seq.

Minor Prophets, was broken; for he first preached on Micah and went on to Zephaniah. Only at this point was order observed with Hosea, Joel, Amos, Obadiah, Jonah, and Nahum. These have brought us to the early summer of 1552. He now went back to Daniel and then back to Ezekiel (November 21, 1552 – February 21, 1554). Job succeeded to Ezekiel and after Job, Deuteronomy until July 15, 1556. But at this point Calvin returned to the Prophets, with Isaiah from July 16, 1556 until September, 1559. Thereafter it was the turn of the historical books; Genesis (September 4, 1559 to February 1561), Judges, I and II Samuel (to February 3, 1563) and I Kings (the last sermon of which was preached on Wednesday, February 2, 1564. On the following Sunday, February 6, he preached his last sermon on the New Testament). It would be idle to speculate on the reasons for this erratic order. Translating it into the canonical order, we see that between 1549 and 1564 he preached on Genesis, Deuteronomy, Judges, I and II Samuel, I Kings, Job, some Psalms (on Sunday afternoons), and all the Prophets except Habakkuk, Haggai, Zechariah and Malachi, which were perhaps expounded before 1549, in the years for which we have no detailed records.

Of these many sermons less than a third are extant. Judges, I Kings, Lamentations (apart from the first two) and all the Minor Prophets except Micah 1-7.10 are missing, as are many of the Psalms, Isaiah 1-12, 52 (vv. 1-12), 54-66, Jeremiah 1-14, 19-52, Ezekiel 16-22, and Daniel 1-4. In Calvin's lifetime there were printed some of the Genesis sermons, all of Deuteronomy, Job, some of the Psalms, two extracts from Isaiah, and part of Daniel, and in Latin I Samuel and Job. In manuscript, and therefore in course of inclusion in *Supplementa Calviniana* we have the sermons on Genesis, II Samuel, some Psalms, Isaiah 13-51, Jeremiah 15-18, Ezekiel 1-15, 23-48, and Micah 1-7.12.[7]

2 The Lectures

As we have already seen, Calvin was originally appointed in Geneva as Biblical lecturer, shortly afterwards to become also a pastor. This dual role he maintained for the rest of his life. We

[7] See *Oracles of God*, pp.163-6.

possess only sketchy and infrequent references to his lecturing before 1549, but since we know he lectured on St Paul, (probably Romans) in the period 1536-38, and on St John's Gospel and I Corinthians in Strasbourg (1538ff.), it is a fair assumption that in the fifteen forties up to about 1546 or 1547, he lectured on books of the New Testament and that the commentaries arose out of the lectures – not that these were recorded as he spoke, but that he wrote the commentaries from his memory of what he had said. It is also a fair assumption that he finished lecturing on the epistles before he turned to the Old Testament.

Calvin's lecturing is an aspect of his activity which has largely escaped study. The history of his preaching is now well-known, but it would seem that no one has yet taken up the subject of his lectures. That his extant lectures were all expositions of the Old Testament is obvious enough, and we can very easily compile a chronological list of them. But to whom was he lecturing? How often did he lecture? What was the style of his lecturing? that is, did he follow the "modern" Renaissance manner, like his former professor at Bourges, Andreas Alciati? Did he divide his comments into *glossae* and *scholia*? And perhaps most important, what was the intention of the lectures? Were they intended as education or for edification?

The first question to answer concerns his audience. When we know the answer to that, many of the other questions can be understood more easily.

There is, however, a preliminary point to be made. The lectures (*leçons*) must not be confused with the *Congrégations*.[8]   The *Congrégations* were meetings of ministers and interested persons, held on Fridays, '*pour avoir conférence des Écritures*', 'for the study of the Bible'. Attendance was compulsory for the city ministers; the country clergy were urged to attend if they could. After one of the pastors had expounded the passage ('*chacun exposera à son tour*'), a discussion was held in which anyone might join. The *Congrégation* was conducted in French. Calvin usually was chairman of the meeting and also took his turn in delivering the exposition; but he certainly did not give the exposition every week.

Yet Colladon seems to suggest that Calvin as good as added

[8] See R.Peter: *Deux Congrégations...* pp.IX-XXIV (Paris, 1964).

his own lecture after the exposition: 'every Friday, in the conference on Scripture which we call *Congrégation*, what he added after the opening interpretation, was like a lecture'.[9] The only three Old Testament books expounded in the *Congrégations* after 1549 are the three on which Calvin wrote commentaries proper. In each case publication followed near or after the end of the *Congrégation* expositions on that book. Thus, Psalms was expounded from 1555 to August 1559 and Calvin's commentary appeared in 1557; his *Harmony of the Last Four Books of the Pentateuch* was used in the *Congrégations* from September 1559 until November 1562 and the commentary appeared in 1563; Joshua occupied the *Congrégations* from June 1563 to January 1564, and the commentary came out the following year. The most probable explanation is, not that the commentaries arose out of the *Congrégations*, but that the *Congrégations* were organized to fit in with a commentary that Calvin had begun to write, that he pushed ahead of the *Congrégation's* exposition, and that the *Congrégation* had the first benefit of Calvin's interpretation, no doubt delivered as a summary rather than read verbatim. Some at least of his own expositions as the leader were taken down in full; two on Galatians form the substance of Professor Peter's *Deux Congrégations*; two on Joshua remain in manuscript. But these quasi-lectures are quite distinct from the *leçons*.

We come to the hearers of the lectures, and it is again to Colladon that we turn first: 'in the theological lectures, he expounded to the scholars, ministers, and other auditors . . .'[10] And again: 'he expounded in the school the book of Genesis';[11] and in 1552 'he began to expound the Psalms in the school'.[12] The first point to make, therefore, is that the chief audience, that is, those for whom the lectures were primarily designed, were Genevan schoolboys. In the years before the establishment of the Academy in 1559 education had been organized according to the 1541 *Ordonnances,* which appear to demand school lectures on the Old and New Testaments and to make provision for preliminary teaching in languages and dialectic.

[9] OC 21,66.
[10] OC 21,71.
[11] OC 21,72.
[12] OC 21,75.

The Old Testament lectures, therefore, first in the school and from 1559 in the Academy, were being given by Calvin, at least from the late fifteen forties. But what was the age of these schoolboys? They had to be able already to understand Latin, for the lectures were delivered in that language. Certainly, it was, compared with the 1559 *Institutio,* a very simple Latin, and Calvin took pains to explain everything, without fearing repetition; but it was still Latin. In the universities students would be expected to understand Latin by the age of thirteen to fifteen, depending on their aptitude. These Genevan scholars were also, we see, expected to know Hebrew, for Calvin quoted his texts in Hebrew and discussed Hebrew words; but this fact does not necessarily demand that we increase their age. We shall probably not be far out if we think of an age-range of between twelve or thirteen and sixteen. For the rest, the lectures were attended by the ministers, no doubt voluntarily. The 'others' whom Colladon mentions will, of course, be restricted to those who had sufficient command of Latin and enough free time. We may suspect that they were mostly the refugees, who had, after all, fled to Geneva rather than to Basel or Strasbourg or Zürich precisely in order to benefit from 'the maist perfyt schoole of Chryst that ever was in the erth since the dayis of the Apostillis'.

The place of the lectures is not important, but we may briefly note that "in the school" is ambiguous. It could refer to the scholars (as we might say, "The whole school was given a holiday"), or to the building. In 1559, however, when describing Calvin's weakness after his severe illness, Colladon says that 'he came to the Temple [that is, St Pierre] to preach and to the *Auditoire* to lecture, sometimes walking unaided, sometimes supported and helped by someone; or, when he could do no other, being carried in a little chair or on horseback.'[13] (The *Auditoire* is beside St Pierre, at its south-east side; the two cannot be more than a couple of hundred yards from Calvin's house). It may be that the switch from the school to the *Auditoire* (if there was a switch) was connected with the establishment of the Academy. For a few days he lectured in his bedroom, for the start of an illness coincided with the completion of the lectures on the

[13] OC 21,89.

Minor Prophets: 'there were lacking only two or three lectures on Malachi. When the printer reached that point, Calvin, in order that the work should not remain unfinished, delivered these lectures in his room to whatever number could attend (because, on account of his fever and it being winter, it was not good for him to go into the open air); and so these lectures were taken down as he spoke them, just like the rest, and as they are printed'.[14]

We have seen that Calvin's sermons were preached daily in alternate weeks. It would seem that his lectures were intended to be held on three consecutive days each week, for Colladon writes of this as a historical fact: 'He preached ordinarily every day of one week in two; he lectured in theology three times every week'.[15] Colladon must have been confusing intention with reality. It is easy to prove that, although Calvin lectured three times a week, it was usually in alternate weeks. For the start and conclusion of some sets of lectures Colladon supplies firm dates. We are therefore able to compare the number of lectures with the number of weeks, and we find that 66 lectures on Daniel lasted up to 43 weeks, 193 on Jeremiah 72 weeks, 18 on Lamentations 17 weeks, and 65 on Ezekiel 54 weeks. If Calvin had lectured three times every week, the number of weeks would have been: Daniel, 22; Jeremiah, 65; Lamentations, 6; and Ezekiel 22. If, however, he lectured on alternate weeks, the figures become: Daniel, 44; Jeremiah, 130; Lamentations, 12; and Ezekiel, 44. The former are closer to the facts for Jeremiah, the latter for the others; for Daniel, indeed, it is almost exact.

We can be more precise if we take note of Calvin's own references to "yesterday" and "tomorrow". These occur frequently in most of the sets; in *Daniel* and *Lamentations* they allow us to date with certainty. It is clear that, with three lectures a week, he will refer to what he is going to say tomorrow in lectures A and B but not C, whereas he will refer to what he said yesterday in lectures B and C but not A. This will constitute a group of three lectures in one week. By this system, Daniel falls into the following groups (the numbers in brackets being lectures not indicated by "tomorrow" or "yesterday"):

[14] OC 21,88.
[15] OC 21,66.

1,2,3	24,25,26	46,47,48
4,5,6	27,28,29	49,50,51
7,8,(9)	30,31,32	52,53,54
10,11,12	33,34,(35)	55,56,57
13,14,15	36,37,38	(58),59,60
16,17,18	39,40,41	61,62,63
19,20	42,43,44	64,65,(66)
21,22,(23)	(45)	

The lectures in brackets will all fall easily into a three lecture sequence. Only 19-20 and 45 are isolated. Either in the seventh week he gave only two lectures and in the sixteenth one, or, more probably, during three weeks he lectured four times. We have established, therefore, that Calvin lectured on Daniel during at least twenty-three separate weeks, or, if 19, 20, and 45 were each the only lecture that Calvin managed in those three weeks, not more than twenty-four weeks. The twenty-three or twenty-four weeks could not have run consecutively from June 12, 1559 (when Colladon says he began on Daniel) and ended in mid-November, for Colladon expressly says that he finished Daniel in April 1560.[16] It is true that he fell ill on December 24, but this would not affect our calculations; for, apart from the fact that Colladon says that this did not prevent him from performing *'toutes les parties de son office'*,[17] the lectures would, as we have seen, have already been finished if they had been weekly. We conclude, then, that with Daniel the lectures were given every other week and that probably they ended the first week in April or the last week in March, 1560.

On Lamentations there were eighteen lectures given, according to Colladon, between September 20, 1562 and January 19, 1563. But Colladon must be wrong, for September 20 was a Sunday that year. Since Jeremiah was finished on Wednesday, September 9, we should expect the next lecture on the following Monday, (14th), if the lectures were weekly but Monday week (21st) if they were fortnightly. Since Colladon has put September 20, September 21 seems the more probable. The consecutive lectures ("yesterday" – "tomorrow") are 1-3, 7-9, 10-13, 14-15.

[16] OC 21,89-90.
[17] OC 21,89.

Lectures 10-13 demand explanation. Either Calvin lectured four times that week or perhaps his 'The rest tomorrow' at the end of lecture 12 was a slip, forgetting that there was no lecture the next day. Then we would have 10-12, 13-15. However that may be, we can supply a cross check on his activities from the concurrent sermons on II Samuel, which are dated daily. This shows that there were several gaps in his working weeks at this time.

Sept.	21-26	Sermons	48-53
Oct.	5		54
Oct.	12-15		55-58
Nov.	9-14		59-64
	23-24		65-66
Dec.	7-12		67-72
Jan.	4-9		73-78
	18-19		79-80

In each preaching week he was supposed to deliver six sermons. He achieved this only four times in this period. One week he preached only once, another only twice. Moreover, the timing is eccentric. Instead of the sermons being fortnightly, we twice have consecutive weeks, and twice have a four week gap. The cause lay in Calvin's illness: 'In the month of December he had gout for several days, so that on the 18th, the day of "censure of ministers" for the feast of Noël, they met in his room, he being in bed'.[18] To Sulzer Calvin wrote on Dec. 6: 'Pain so constricts me that I am slack at every sort of duty, except when necessity compels and so to say drags me unwillingly to my work'.[19] And to Bullinger on Sunday, Dec. 27: 'God holds me bound in shackles. The acute pains have gone, but I can hardly creep across my bedroom from the bed to the table. I did preach today, but I was carried to church'.[20] The number of weeks on which Calvin preached was eight. The groups of lectures number six or more, for Number 17 was delivered on a Monday and therefore Number 16 must either be joined to 13-15 or more probably stand alone. One could play around with the figures

[18] OC 21,93-4.
[19] OC 19,593.
[20] OC 19,602.

endlessly; the likeliest explanation is that these lectures followed the course of the sermons, and would have been delivered fortnightly. Jeremiah, however, cannot have been delivered fortnightly. Here it looks as if the lectures were given weekly, with a few interruptions. But with Ezekiel three lectures every other week, again with interruptions, seems more probable. We conclude that at some periods Calvin delivered his three lectures during alternate weeks, at others every week. I do not know the reason for this inconsistency.

Two accounts of his lecturing occur as prefaces to *Hosea* and the *Minor Prophets*, the one by Jean Budé and the other by the printer Jean Crispin. Crispin emphasizes the excellence of the transmission, that every single word Calvin uttered in his lectures was faithfully taken down. And this is the more remarkable when we consider the way he lectured: 'While he was publicly expounding Scripture, Calvin never dictated anything, as many do, or told his hearers to make any notes', then follows the puzzling parenthesis '(far less when the lecture was over or on the following day)'[21] - perhaps it refers only to the schoolboys, that he did not follow up his lecture by demanding notes from them. The general meaning, however, is clear enough; that he did not lecture at dictation speed and that he simply concentrated on lecturing without looking beyond the end of the hour. Crispin continues: 'but he kept on lecturing continuously for a full hour and did not write down one single word in his book to help his memory'.[22] The book in question was a Hebrew Old Testament, as a preface to *Daniel* tells us: 'Calvin is accustomed to read first each verse in Hebrew, and then turn it into Latin.'[23] As I quote Budé's own words, I will cut down his prolixity as far as I can: 'the author thought first of the school (as was right) and to some extent departed far from the accustomed grace of his other works and from the style of oratory ... He preferred to consult the edification and profit of his hearers by drawing out and clarifying the true sense rather than by an empty display of words to gratify their ears or to study ostentation and his own glory. Yet I cannot deny that these lectures were delivered more in the scholastic than

[21] OC 42,189-90; CTS Mi 1,xxx.
[22] OC 42,189-90; CTS Mi 1,xxx.
[23] OC 40,23-4; CTS Dan 1,lxii.

in the oratorical manner . . . The language here is bare and simple, very like that which, as we know, used to be common in lectures. He was not like many we have heard of, who from a script read to their hearers digests they have made at home'.[24]

Budè's main message is plain: Calvin lectured in a simple, understandable Latin. But when he goes on to call his lecturing manner "scholastic" , and the language such as was used in earlier days, what does he mean? Does "scholastic" refer to the school in Geneva, and therefore lessons? Or does the work bear its usual meaning, of "scholastic" as opposed to Renaissance humanist, and is he therefore saying that in some respects Calvin's lectures were closer to scholasticism than to the "modern" manner? This is a subject which would repay careful study. Crispin offers the hard facts that Calvin did not dictate any part of his lectures; that he did not tell his hearers to annotate; that he lectured extemporarily;[25] that he lectured for a full hour.

We may certainly accept that the lectures lasted a full hour, for it was very common for Calvin to have to break off when his hour was up. Thus: '*The mercies of God are not exhausted, and his loving kindness does not fail. Why? Because they occur new, or reborn, every day*, he says. He puts *morning*, but in the plural – I am surprised at the hour sounding so soon; I did not think I had been lecturing a whole hour'.[26] 'So there will be no delay, for the suitable time depends on God's will, and not on the judgment of men. It then follows – but the clock is striking, and I cannot go any further today'.[27] Occasionally he had to curtail a lecture because of some urgent duty: 'I wish I could proceed further, but I have some business to which I was called before the lecture'.[28] Again: 'I

---

[24] OC 42,185-8; CTS Mi 1,xxvi-xxvii.

[25] Colladon confirms this: 'When lecturing, he always had only the bare text of Scripture; and yet, see how well he ordered what he said! Even when (some years before his death) he was lecturing on Daniel, although at some places he had to narrate historical facts at length, as we see from the lectures, he never had any paper before him as an aide-mémoire. And it was not as if he had adequate time to prepare; for, whatever he may have wished, he simply had not the opportunity. To say the truth, he usually had less than an hour to prepare' (OC 21,108-9).

[26] OC 29,575; CTS Jer 5,407-8.

[27] OC 37,485; CTS Jer 1,51.

[28] OC 37,499; CTS Jer 1,75.

cannot proceed further, on account of some other business '.[29] In April 1561 it was *promotiones* that prevented a lecture: 'I shall not be lecturing tomorrow, for we shall be busy with promotions, as you know '.[30] On another occasion the lecture was put off because of a meeting of the Consistory, presumably an extraordinary meeting.[31] But the great moment came in the lecture on Jonah 3.10 - 4.4, when the clock stopped and Calvin not only went twenty minutes over his time but then apparently apologized for ending too soon, for a marginal note reads: 'The clock had stopped and he thought he had finished early'.[32] In Ezekiel, near the end of his life, comes the pathetic 'I feel too weak to go on'[33] – he was then ten minutes short of his hour. He began the lecture on Amos 3. 13ff. with an apology: 'One thing escaped me yesterday; my headache prevented me looking at my book '.[34] Had he then recited the Hebrew of 3.11-12 from memory?

If the reader will forgive me for introducing yet more arithmetic, we will pursue this question of the length of the lectures a little further. According to *The Writers' and Artists' Year Book, 1970*, the B.B.C. reckons 'one minute for every 120 words' (p.301) for radio talks. If Calvin lectured for an hour, therefore, we should expect each lecture to be about seven thousand words. I have taken samples from *Jonah* (lectures 1–7),*Ezekiel* (60–65), *Jeremiah* (1–5), and *Daniel* (1–10, 62–66) with rather surprising results. The average length of the lectures, with the approximate number of words a minute, are as follows:

[29] OC 37,665; CTS Jer 1,352.

[30] OC 38,428; CTS Jer 3,172. I take *promotiones* to be a ceremony at which the names of boys who had been moved into a higher class were read and prizes were given. A note in the *Registres du Conseil*, Monday, April 21, 1561, refers to the present occasion: '[Calvin and Beza come to invite *Messieurs* to attend the promotions in the College on the 27th] and ask that they will be pleased to donate some small gifts for those who have done best' (OC 21,747). The 27th cannot be correct if it refers to April, for that was a Sunday, and there would, in any case, have been no lecture on a Sunday.

[31] OC 38,616; CTS Jer 4,11.

[32] OC 43,271; CTS Mi 3,132.

[33] OC 40.389; CTS Ezek 2,167.

[34] OC 43,50; CTS Mi 2,221.

		Length	Words per minute
Jonah		3,217	58
Ezekiel		2,847	51
Jeremiah		2,939	49
Daniel	(a)	2,784	46
	(b)	3,346	56

These figures need modifying in that they do not include the recital of the text in Latin and Hebrew, for which we should add about two hundred words, and they take no account of curtailed or over-long lectures. The introductory and concluding prayers would last hardly a minute between them. If we reckon as much as 60 words a minute for Jonah and Daniel (b) and 50 or 58 for the others, it is still remarkably slow. The slowness may be attributed to two factors, Calvin's breathing difficulties and his audience of immature Latinists.[35]

We may add to Crispin's factual account the slight informality that is evident in the lecture transcripts. Calvin will put in an aside which suggests that the boys had preparatory lessons on the passage: 'But all these things have been explained to you better than I can do, so I have only just mentioned them in passing'.[36] This refers perhaps to a Hebrew class by the professor of Hebrew, Antoine Chevallier, who had been appointed to the Academy in March, 1559. Indeed, two other chance remarks suggest that Calvin and Chevallier worked together to some extent: 'another explanation, which our brother Dominus Antonius gave you, fits in better';[37] and, 'I shall now briefly state what our brother Dominus Antonius has suggested to me from a certain rabbi, Barbinel'.[38]

It is these lectures which form the bulk of the Old Testament expositions. The first to be published was on Isaiah, on which he

[35] On this subject, we may note that the sermons show an astonishing range of length. I have taken sermons from Isa. 13-29, II Samuel, Micah, and Jeremiah, all as printed in *Suppl. Calv.*, and found the average length to be: Isaiah, 6,700 words; II Samuel, 5,500; Micah, 6,000; Jeremiah, 3,980 – a range of over half as much again between the longest and shortest.

[36] OC 40,542; CTS Dan 1,96.

[37] OC 40,557; CTS Dan 1,116.

[38] OC 40,604; CTS Dan 1,183.

lectured from perhaps 1546 or 1547 until 1549. His secretary, Nicholas des Gallars, had attended the lectures, but, unable to write short-hand, had taken down only the main points. These notes, however, with the help of his memory, he wrote up into a connected commentary after each lecture. He read his version to Calvin who amended or added as he wished.

He described his method of working in a preface to the first edition. He had, he said, the enormous advantage of being admitted to close friendship with Calvin, and could therefore question him about difficulties in Isaiah practically every day. 'And especially in leisure hours, that is, when he had some free time from the more important affairs which almost overwhelmed him, I would read to him what I had written. He could not read it all carefully, but at any rate he was able, when necessary, to add, to delete, and to advise. This he did diligently – although sometimes I had scarcely read two or three verses before he was called away by importunate interruptions or by friends. However, I would go over all he had said as faithfully and diligently as I could and then, as soon as leisure and opportunity arose, I would again ask my questions. My work was lightened to some extent because I had already taken down notes from Calvin's preaching – this was four years ago in his public preaching, when he expounded this Prophet ... before he commented on him to us in the school ... When I got back home from the sermon I used to write in Latin [what Calvin had said], so far as my memory served and as I had time. This turned out very useful to me when it came to gathering together this Commentary. Not that I included everything I had written or even put it in the same order and manner; but I had already a sound grasp of his views (*sententias*) and was used to this style and method of interpretation'.[39] Calvin's own account suggests that he himself played a larger part in the composition of Isaiah than des Gallars had credited him with: 'You say', he wrote to Dryander in 1550, 'that you are waiting for my meditations on Isaiah. They will be coming out shortly. But they were written by des Gallars, because I have little time for writing. He takes down what I dictate to him and later arranges it at home. Then I read it over again and if anywhere he

[39] OC 36,11-4; CTS Isa 2, viii-ix.

has not followed my meaning I restore the sense'.[40] But against this must be set the opening sentence of the dedication of the first edition to Edward VI: 'I confess that this Commentary has been faithfully and skilfully compiled from my lectures and was written up(*expolitus*) by another hand'.[41] I think we may take it that the actual composition of the Commentary was done by des Gallars – as he says in a preface to the 1570 edition, 'using my own judgment and style'[42] – but that Calvin satisfied himself that what was written represented his own views. First published in 1551, it was revised by Calvin himself (thoroughly, as he said in his dedication to Queen Elizabeth of England)[43] for a second edition in 1559. It is safe to say, therefore, that, although even the second edition is still largely the work of des Gallars (in the sense that it is only a revision of the first) there is nothing in it that Calvin did not accept as representing his own views.

No sooner had he finished the lectures on Isaiah than he embarked on a series on Genesis. But at the same time he started to write a commentary on it, for we find in a letter to Farel in July 1550 that he had begun work on *Genesis* a week before.[44] That he meant a commentary and not the lectures is shown by his next letter, of August 19, when he promised 'as soon as the Lord grants that I get to the end of the third chapter of my commentary on Genesis, I will give you a taste of it'.[45] But on November 10 he had to write again, rather impatiently, 'Why do you remind me of *Acts* and *Genesis*? They are but embryos, hardly even conceived in the womb. I am ashamed to confess how slowly I am getting on with *Acts*. I have written only a third of it; and yet what I have written is so long that I can see it is going to add up to a big volume. I have had to give up *Genesis* for the time being. For the past four months I have been occupied with correcting the New Testament [that is, of a French translation published in Geneva]. Now I am unwillingly dragged into part of the Old Testament'.[46]

[40] OC 13,536.
[41] OC 14,30; CTS Isa 1,xix.
[42] OC 36,17-8; CTS Isa 2,xv.
[43] OC 17,413; CTS Isa 1,xvi.
[44] OC 13,606.
[45] OC 13,623.
[46] OC 13,655.

Acts, indeed, became so long that it had to be issued in two parts, in 1552 and 1554. *St John's Gospel*, which came out in 1553, caused a further delay, but *Genesis* was published at last in July 1554, two years after he had ended the lectures. That this commentary, like *Isaiah*, was the work of des Gallars is stated by the title-page of the 1572 French edition: '*recueilli soigneusement des leçons et sermons . . . par M. Nicholas des Gallars*'. I would suggest that Calvin wrote the first two or three chapters himself, was then held up by his other work, and in the end turned to des Gallars for help, at least to the extent of supplying him with notes of the lectures and of sermons which Calvin had preached before 1549.

The work was now piling up more and more. Besides his ordinary duties in Geneva (sufficient in themselves to make a man feel that he had done a good day's work) and the burden of his vast correspondence, he had in the space of six years written commentaries on the Acts, St John, and the Harmony of the Gospels, and thoroughly revised his commentaries on the Epistles. Therefore, when a few of his younger friends hit on an ingenious scheme, he was not sorry, after initial misgivings, to fall in with it. One or two of them had been taking notes of the lectures for their own benefit. They lacked Raguenier's skill in short-hand, but they circumvented this by forming a little syndicate, as one of them, Jean Budé, narrates in his preface to the commentaries on Hosea: 'When some years ago that most learned man Jean Calvin at the request and entreaty of his friends undertook to expound in the school the Psalms of David, some of us who were hearers from the beginning took some notes in our own way for our private study and according to our own mind and judgment. But then we began to think how great a loss it would be to many, and almost to the whole Church, that the benefit of such lectures should be confined to just a few hearers . . . It seemed possible to [rectify] this if we extended our usual practice of selecting and tried to take down the lectures verbatim, so far as we could. I at once joined myself as the third to two energetic brethren in this undertaking, and it came to pass, through God's kindness, that our labours were successful. For when the work of each of us was compared and the lectures written out, we found that so few things had escaped us that the gaps could easily be supplied'.[47] Jean Crispin fills in the details: 'in their writing, they followed this plan. Each had his paper ready in the most convenient form, and each took down as quickly as possible what was said. If any word escaped one of them (which sometimes happened, especially on controversial matters and places expounded more vehemently) it was caught by another; and when this happened the Author easily replaced it. For immediately after the lecture, Joinvillier took the papers of the other two, placed them before him, consulted his own, put them all together more accurately, and dictated to someone else what he had copied from their hasty writings. At the end he re-read it, so that he might repeat it the next day to M. Calvin at home. When sometimes any little word was wanting, this was supplied, or if anything did not seem explained sufficiently, it was easily made clearer'.[48]

The expositions thus composed may be regarded as accurate enough transcripts of the lectures and, since Calvin himself had a chance to revise them, as fully representative of his mind. Indeed, he says as much in his preface to the lectures on Hosea, which were the first he allowed to be published: 'I was not really free to withhold the publication of these expositions of Hosea – so let them appear! But it is important to say how they were taken down; not only that they who have laboured for the Church should not be defrauded of the praise their diligence, industry, and skill deserve, but that readers may be assured that the writers did not go beyond their brief, that they did not permit themselves to replace one single word by a better. How they worked together, one of them, my friend M. Jean Budé, who is dear to all good men on account of his virtues, will, I hope, explain more fully. But I would not have believed, unless I had seen it with my own eyes, how, when they read it back to me the next day, their transcriptions differed nothing from my spoken words. It might perhaps have been better if they had used greater liberty and deleted superfluities, arranged other things into a better order, and made yet others more distinct or more stylish – but that is

[47] OC 42,183–4; CTS Mi 1,xxiv.
[48] OC 42,189–90; CTS Mi 1,xxx-xxxi. Three secretaries are consistently mentioned, but only Budé and Joinvillier are ever named. Who was the third? And why was his name not given?

only my opinion. I just wanted to set to my solemn signature (*manu mea consignatum esse*) that they recorded so faithfully what they heard me say that I can see no alteration'.[49] Nevertheless, he did not give way without a struggle, as we shall see when we come to the *Psalms*; and even when he consented to the publication of the *Hosea* transcripts, it was with reservations, which he voiced in the earlier part of the preface in which he so praised his friends: 'I can truly and justly say, and have good witnesses to prove it, that the writings (*lucubrationes*) which I have hitherto published and which were perhaps polished with more care and application, have been pretty well forced out of me by importunity. These Annotations, therefore, which were bearable as lectures but not worthy, as I thought, to be read, would never have been published on my initiative. For if I can hardly succeed in being slightly useful to the Church by compositions well worked over, how foolish I should be to claim a place for my spoken words among my published works! Then, even with works which I write or dictate privately at home, when there is more leisure for thinking, and where I attain a definite brevity by care and diligence, my hard work is called a crime by malignant and envious people. So how shall I escape accusation of pride if I thrust on the wide world the reading of those thoughts which I freely poured out in the *Auditoire* for present use? But it was not in my power to suppress them, and I could only have prevented their publication by undertaking the labour of writing it all anew; and this my circumstances did not permit. And since many friends thought me too stern a critic of my own work, and clamoured that I was injuring the Church, I preferred to let this volume be published just as it is, taken down from my lips, rather than forbid it and so having the labour of writing. That, in fact, is what earlier I had to do with the *Psalms*, before I found out by that long and difficult task how unequal I am to so much writing'.[50]

It is clear from this that his misgivings did not arise from doubts of the accuracy of the transcripts, but only mistrust of his own extemporary lecturing. His oversight of the material was in no way a revision. He left in the many involutions, repetitions, and asides which a revision would have excised.

[49] OC 42,183–4; CTS Mi 1,xxiii.
[50] OC 42,183–4; CTS Mi 1,xxii–xxiii.

The order and dates of the lectures, with the date of their publication, can conveniently be seen in the following table.

	Lectures	Commentaries
Date unknown	Isaiah	*Isaiah* (1551/1559)
	⌐	
1550	Genesis	*Genesis* (1554)
	⌐	
1552	Psalms	*Psalms* (1557)
	⌐	
Date unknown	Hosea (38 lectures)	*Hosea* (1557)
	⌐	
Date unknown	Minor Prophets (134)	*Minor Prophets* (1559)
	⌐	
June 12, 1559	Daniel (66)	*Daniel* (1561)
	⌐	
April 15, 1560	Jeremiah (193)	*Jeremiah* (1563)
Sept. 9, 1562	⌐	
Sept. 21(?), 1562	Lamentations (18)	*Lamentations* (1563)
	⌐	
Jan. 19, 1563		
Jan. 20, 1563	Ezekiel (65)	*Ezekiel* (1565)
	⌐	
Feb. 2, 1564	Ezek. 20. 40–44	

3 The Commentaries

It remains to recount the story of the three commentaries proper, *Psalms*, the *Mosaic*, and *Joshua*. As we have already seen, each was being written concurrently with its exposition in the *Congréga-tion*. Some psalms and the whole of Deuteronomy had also been covered in sermons; and the Psalms as a whole were lectured on between 1552 and 1555 or 1556.

The lectures on the Psalms were not the source but they were certainly the stimulus for the commentary. It was early in the course of them that the project for recording the lectures was conceived, with the original purpose of starting with this book. Calvin, however, was unwilling to fall in with the scheme. The first reason he gave (and it was no doubt sincere) sprang from the rather naïve self-distrust that he often showed. Martin Bucer had already written a commentary on the Psalms, and how could he, John Calvin, hope to improve on Bucer? 'I expounded in our small school here the Book of Psalms about three years ago, and then decided not to publish abroad what I had familiarly deposited with my own household. In fact, even before I had undertaken the exposition at the request of my brethren, I spoke the truth in saying that I had refrained because that most faithful doctor of the Church of God, Martin Bucer, was pre-eminent in this work, with his outstanding learning, diligence, and fidelity; so there was, at any rate, not so much need for anything of mine'.[51] Similar praise, he says, is now due also to Wolfgang Musculus, but his commentary had not then been published. 'I had not reached the end of the work before they begged me again not to let my meditations perish; for they had been faithfully and skilfully taken down – a work of great labour. My decision still stood. But I did promise something that had been in my mind a long time – to write something in French, that my own countrymen might have the chance of being enabled to understand such a useful book.'[52] There was, however, another reason why Calvin was unwilling to allow the publication of lecture transcripts; quite simply that they were below the standards he set himself. For he went on in the preface to say that he had at last agreed to write a commentary out of 'anxiety lest at some future time the transcript of my lectures might be published against my wishes or even without my knowledge.'[53] The

[51] OC 31,13–4; CTS Ps 1,xxxv; CP 1,15.
[52] OC 31,13–4; CTS Ps 1,xxxv–xxxvi; CP 1,15.
[53] OC 31,15–6; CTS Ps 1,xxxvi; CP 1,15.

scheme to write a French commentary was superseded before it was even started: 'While I was thinking of attempting this, it suddenly and quite contrary to my plans occurred to me, by what impulse I do not know, to compose in Latin an exposition of one Psalm by way of experiment. I was encouraged to find that my hopes had succeeded more than I had dared expect and so began to try the same in a few more Psalms'.[54]

The *Psalms* commentary, then, was written from about 1553 until 1557. Calvin found it a heavy task, in spite of some help in the shape of lecture notes that had been taken. For example, Nicholas des Gallars wrote to him on June 16, 1555: 'I had meant to leave with you what I took down from your lectures on the Psalms of David; but I was very busy and just forgot. But now that I have recently seen on your bedside writing-table some things which you once wrote on the same Psalms, I thought you might like to consult this work. Therefore I did not want to postpone sending you also my own things (or rather, what I have from you!) if they can be of any use to you or lighten your task'.[55] It is possible, therefore, that Calvin also made use of the full transcript made by Budé and Joinvillier. The study of the Psalms in the *Congrégations* from 1555 until August 1559 could also have served as aids.[56]

The memory of the labour pains of bringing forth the *Psalms* soon faded, for by 1559 he must have conceived the scheme of the *Mosaic*. In September of this year, as Colladon reports, 'they began to expound in the Friday *Congrégation* the four last books of Moses in the form of a harmony, as Calvin has comprehended it in the Commentary that he afterwards published'.[57] Calvin therefore had arranged the harmony before September 1559,

[54] OC 31,15–8; CTS Ps 1,xxxvi; CP 1,15.

[55] OC 15,657. I have rendered very freely *ad spondam lecti in cathedra tua* (literally: "at the side [taking *sponde* as equivalent to older French *esponda*] of the bed in your chair". Calvin seems to have had a writing desk in his bedroom. See p. 19)

[56] The printer (R. Stephanus) and Calvin were rebuked by the Council for publishing *Psalms* without a licence. See entries for July 27–29, 1557 (OC 21,670–1). We learn incidentally that Calvin delivered his work to Stephanus in batches as it was finished: 'M. Calvin, qui luy avoit ballie de folles en folles pour mectre en impression' (OC 21,670).

[57] OC 21,90.

probably working on it over several months, for such a complicated piece of literary arrangement was not made in a hurry.[58]

As we have seen, the Calvin–des Gallars *Genesis* was published as a separate work in 1554. It was included in the *Mosaic,* for the sake of completeness, in a slightly revised form. Alone, it had been dedicated to John Frederick, John William, and John Frederick, Dukes of Saxony, and to the eternal memory of yet another John Frederick, Duke of Saxony; but by the time of the collected edition the political needs had shifted, and the four Dukes had to make way for the ten year old Duc de Navarre, afterwards to become Henri IV of France.

It would appear, then, that Calvin not having lectured on the *Mosaic*, the commentary was written or dictated privately, with no other preparation than the communal *Congrégations* from 1559. Calvin himself translated this vast work into French, (apparently after August 1563, when the Latin edition was published), partly in order to reach French readers, partly to correct 'many errors' – presumably misprints.

On November 30, 1563, he wrote in a letter: 'I have undertaken to translate my commentaries on Moses into French, partly that we may share the book with you in France; but I was not sorry on another account, for it was necessary to correct the many errors in it.'[59]

The letter went on: 'The brethren have urged me to explain the book of Joshua. So far I have hardly reached the third chapter, even though I am studying the greatest brevity'.[60] But if Calvin had reached only chapter three by November 30, could he really have written or dictated comments on the remaining twenty-one chapters in the four or five months left to him, taking into account, moreover, that he was also translating the *Mosaic*? On the other hand, *Joshua* is treated more sketchily than any other of Calvin's commentaries. The whole twenty-four chapters of the original call forth only some 42,500 words, very brief even by modern standards, let alone by sixteenth century.

[58] CR editors believed the plan of the *Mosaic* was made very soon after the publication of *Genesis* (OC 23,XV).
[59] OC 20,199.
[60] OC 20,199.

We may also take up the query raised by the editors of *Corpus Reformatorum*:[61] Why was Joshua first published in French when all the other commentaries appeared first in Latin? Neither of their two answers is satisfactory, that Beza wanted to get his panegyric on Calvin out as soon as possible after his death, and that he wished it to match the *Mosaic*, which would come out in Calvin's translation.

I would suggest a simpler solution: That Calvin himself wrote the commentary in French and that he did so because a large part of it consists of revised and integrated transcripts of his contributions to the *Congrégations*, in which he sometimes took part even after he had stopped lecturing and preaching.[62] He gave full expositions of passages on two recorded occasions (June 4, 1563 on Joshua 1. 1-5, and September –, 1563 on Joshua 11),[63] besides making apparently lengthy contributions as a participant, as we have seen. He may have given the exposition on other occasions, as there is no record for eleven Fridays.

How far finished he left it we do not know. *Corpus Reformatorum* editors said that it remained *"inachevé"*[64] at his death, but this may be only on the basis of Beza's lament that it lacked a preface: 'this commentary would not be published without being crowned, so to say, with an excellent Preface, like the others'.[65]

With the written commentaries, the lectures, and the sermons, Calvin expounded in one way or another, sometimes with duplication, about three-quarters of the books of the Old Testament; everything (except Ruth) from Genesis to I Kings, all the Prophets (apart from Ezekiel 21ff.), and Job, and the Psalms. He therefore did not expound II Kings to Esther or the rest of the canonical Wisdom Literature. The list should not be interpreted too subtly, as if it represented an absolute order of theological importance for Calvin. Its chief significance no doubt lies in its betraying his view (or that of his colleagues) of the needs of the Church at any particular time. According to Beza, he would have

[61] OC 23,XVII.
[62] OC 21,96.
[63] R. Peter: *Deux Congrégations*, XIX.
[64] OC 21,5-6.
[65] OC 21,21-22.

gone on to expound all the Old Testament if he had lived to man's allotted span. It is not therefore a question of his rejecting certain books as unimportant, far less as unnecessary, but of his judgment on which were most relevant at any time.

4 Characteristics of the three forms

The general pattern of Calvin's expositions is remarkably simple. It follows broadly the same lines in commentaries, lectures, and sermons. Having given the text for the section under discussion, he first explains what he takes it to mean and then applies its message to the readers or hearers. The first part will either begin with exegesis, linguistic or otherwise, or plunge at once into exposition. For example:

Isaiah 40. 10. 'Behold, the Lord Jehovah. He [the Prophet] fills out this short sentence with many beautiful words because it needs explanation. The demonstrative adverb [Behold] is again used for the sake of assurance, to make the minds of good men more trustful. He therefore shows more clearly how much the presence of God profits us; and first he says that he will come with strength – not mere otiose potentiality but power joined with effect, so that we shall feel it. Translators render לו "From himself". But some may prefer to translate it "He is powerful, or reigns, in himself". He means that God is sufficient to himself and does not need outside help. He repeats the same thing more clearly by the words "reward" and "work", for it is quite common in Hebrew to say the same thing twice. "Reward" is not debts owed to merits but the righteousness of God by which he testifies that he is the rewarder of all who truly and sincerely call upon him (Hebrews 11. 6). That this is what שכר means all who are even moderately acquainted with Hebrew know. The sum of it is that when God comes we shall not see him idle but exerting his strength, a strength that we shall experience. Hence "effect" would not be a bad substitute for "work". Many expound this more subtly and philosophize childishly on the words "work" and "reward", as if work were a merit to which a reward were paid. No such thing was in the Prophet's mind. For it is a repetition, as I have already said, declaring the fruit of the Lord's coming, which will be the greatest blessing to believers.'[66]

[66] OC 37,14; CTS Isa 3,215.

We see that the whole of this passage is dominated by exegesis, with only incidental exposition. In the next it is exposition that dominates, but around the exegesis.

Hab. 3. 6. 'He adds that *the ways of the age* are God's. Some translate it "the ways of the world". But 'olām properly means an age, or a lengthy time. The Prophet, I have no doubt, means by "ways of eternity" the wonderful means by which God is wont to work for the salvation of his Church. For we are always accustomed to reduce God's works to our own grasp; but he wills to accomplish the work of our salvation . . . in ways that surprise us. Therefore the Prophet here commands the faithful to lift up their minds on high and to conceive something greater of the power of God than we grasp by nature. If this way of understanding "ways of eternity" is accepted, it will stand in opposition to known ways and accustomed methods. Daily ways are when the sun rises and then sets, when spring succeeds to winter, when the earth brings forth her fruits. Although all these are miracles, they are common ways. But God has "ways of eternity"; that is, he has methods unknown to us, by which, when he pleases, he can rescue us from death. But if anyone prefers to take "ways of eternity" for the continuous power of God which, from the beginning, has always appeared, it will be a fit and useful interpretation. For it also avails much to the confirming of our faith when we reckon that the same has always been true from the time when God created heaven and earth; his power has never diminished nor his disposition changed. From the fact that God has continuously demonstrated his power in all ages we can infer that we have no cause for despair if at any time he shall hide his hand. This does not despoil him of his right; he keeps his rule over the world always. And so we should be attentive to "the ways of the age", that is, to the demonstration of the power which was revealed in the creation of the world and continues its course up till now',[67]

The comments on Psalms, as separate poems, very frequently begin with a discussion of authorship and historical circumstance or of the type of music intended in the rubric. Thus, Ps. 4; 'It is uncertain at what time this Psalm was made, saving that from the

[67] OC 43,572-3; CTS Mi 4,147-8.

tenor of it a probable argument is gathered, that he was then an outlaw and a banished person. I therefore refer it to the time that Saul persecuted him. And yet, if any man had rather understand it of his other exile, which he was driven to by the conspiracy of Absalom, I will not greatly strive with him'.[68] And Ps. 7: 'The Hebrew interpreters do not agree among themselves upon the word *Siggaion*, for some take it for an instrument of music. Unto some it seems to be a tune to sing a song by. Others think it to be the beginning of some common carol, to the tune of which it was David's will to have this Psalm sung. And others interpret the Hebrew word to signify delight. In my judgment, the second opinion seems most likely, namely that it was some kind of tune, or song; as if a man would speak of a Sapphic, or Phaleusian verse. However, I press not a matter of so light importance'.[69] Elsewhere he says impatiently, 'I like not these riddle-like titles'.[70] But the individual verses are treated in the same way as in other books.

This is the general pattern, then, of Calvin's expositions; but there are necessarily some minor differences of form between the three kinds that we are considering.

The commentaries first print Calvin's translation (Latin in all but *Joshua*) of a self-contained section of the text, the length depending on the context. This may be followed by a statement of the general theme of the passage (a sort of argument in particular) before he comes to the exposition of individual verses. The linguistic exegesis, where it occurs, may be no more than the translation of a Hebrew word or it may run to a detailed examination of a word or clause, making use perhaps also of the Septuagint and the Vulgate and referring to previous interpretations. Or the exegesis may be not linguistic but an elucidation of historical, geographical,[71] or cultural fact, or it may simply be the explanation of some point in a narrative.

[68] OC 31,57; CTS Ps 1,36-7; CP 1,50.
[69] OC 31,79; CTS Ps 1,75; CP 1,76.
[70] OC 31,65; CTS Ps 1,51; CP 1,59.
[71] But geography seems to have been one of Calvin's less strong points: 'I have already said that I shall not be very diligent in searching out and identifying the names of places, partly because I confess I am not trained in topography and geography (*in topographica scientia vel chorographica*), partly because a deal of hard work on my side would lead to little fruit for the reader' (on Josh. 15.1 OC 25,525; CTS Josh 200).

References to previous writers are usually made anonymously in some such terms as "Some . . . others . . . " The intention of this deliberate anonymity was to keep the reader's mind on the matter in hand instead of letting it stray to a particular person. Such references are usually brief but may occasionally run to considerable length and complexity.

After this, Calvin will draw together the points of exegesis and give what he thinks, with varying degrees of assurance, to be the meaning intended by the author. He is remarkably free in admitting ignorance of details, even sometimes ignorance of the meaning of a passage. He is also ready to admit the possible correctness of other interpretations than his own. Finally, he will usually apply the message of the verse to his readers.

The only formal difference between the three commentaries written by Calvin and the two compiled by des Gallars is that, instead of splitting up the chapters into smaller sections, the latter print Bible chapters as a whole followed by the comments on the chapter. But a careful study would quite probably show differences in style and in the use of words.

In substance and procedure the lectures are no different from the commentaries. Formally, however, they do present some new features, even apart from the lecture form which necessitated breaking up the Biblical material into sections which could be expounded in an hour, and in making each section only a verse or two rather than the several verses customary in the commentaries. Again, whereas the commentaries gave the text in only the one language (Latin or French), the later lectures faithfully reproduce Calvin's own practice by giving a Hebrew version alongside the Latin.[72]

But the most striking difference lies in his use of glosses to the

[72] The study of Calvin's OT text is not only extraordinarily difficult in itself, but it is also complicated by the differences mentioned above. In the commentaries he could make his translation carefully; in the lectures (and apparently also in the sermons) the translation was almost extemporary, and might vary every time he quoted a verse. Then again, what text did des Gallars print in *Genesis* and *Isaiah*? The one he had copied in Calvin's lectures? One he made himself? One from a printed edition? We should probably be looking for the original of three or even four texts – that in the commentaries, that in des Gallars, and that in the lectures and sermons.

text. By "gloss" I mean here a very short note by Calvin himself, inserted into the Bible text. This is something he never does in his commentaries proper, but only in the lectures. It is unfortunately obscured in the Calvin Translation Society volumes, where all the glosses are put as foot-notes or included in the exposition or even left out altogether.

Examples will elucidate the method better than a verbal explanation. Ezekiel 6. 6: '*In all your habitations* – that is, "In every habitable region," – *the cities shall be made desolate* – or "they shall be deserted." We have spoken about this word before. – *And the high places shall be reduced to waste, so that your altars may be laid waste and made desolate* – or, "shall be destroyed, shall perish" – *and that your idols may be cut down and cease* – or, "abolished". The same word [for idols] which is derived from heat – *and that your works may be blotted out.*'[73]

Daniel 3. 21. '*Then these men were bound with* – or, "tied in" – *their coats*, – some translate it "sandals" or "shoes", others, "hose"; but most take the second word for hose. But we need not trouble ourselves about the words so long as we agree on the substance. After that *and with their turbans* – for we know that the Orientals wore turbans then as they do now, for they wrap their heads in bandages; and though not many of them appear among us, yet we know what clothes the Turks wear. Then the general word is added – *and their other garments and they were thrown into the burning fiery furnace.*'[74]

We must 'make it clear that these "glosses" differ from the medieval *Glossae* in not being extracts from other writers, and from the sort of gloss that we are familiar with in Luther's earlier lectures, in that they are not doctrinal exposition, but almost invariably linguistic explanations.

The sermons stand in a rather different formal category again. They were not intended for academic instruction but for the teaching and training of the Church in Geneva; and they were, after all, addressed to a very mixed congregation, ranging perhaps from the great Robert Stephanus, who had done more than any man in his age to restore the text of the Vulgate and had edited the first genuinely critical Greek New Testament, to the

[73] OC 40,141; CTS Ezek 1,224.
[74] OC 40,636; CTS Dan 1,228.

little servant boy or girl who did not understand theology much but laughed at the jokes and enjoyed the way M. Calvin made the Bible seem just like their Geneva. In the sermons everything was in French, as clear and as easy as this master of French could make it, with a lot of homely proverbs and imaginary conversations to drive home what was being taught. The underlying pattern was the same – a passage (perhaps one verse, perhaps several) translated into French as the sermon text, then each part of it explained in turn, but at greater length and on a more elementary level, and finally the teaching applied to the preacher and the congregation – again, more fully and more urgently.

As we possess both commentaries or lectures and sermons on some books, it is possible to compare them and discover the resemblances and differences. For an example we take the early verses of Micah 1. The lecture was given in about 1556–7, the sermon on Wednesday, November 12, 1550.

The lecture[75] begins, like all the opening lectures on a book, with a brief Argument on the author and his circumstances. Then Calvin comes to his text.

1. 1. *The word of the Lord that came to Micah the Morasthite in the days of Jotham, Ahaz, and Hezekiah, kings of Judah, which he saw concerning Samaria and Jerusalem.*

(a) The information given here is necessary for us: 'his sermons would be useless to us today, or at any rate, frigid, unless we reckon with his times, so that we can compare and contrast our own circumstances with those of men of his age.'

(b) Micah had been a Prophet for probably thirty years or possibly over forty. [Calvin explains how he arrives at this figure, from the years of the reigns of kings as given in II Kings and II Chronicles.]

(c) Micah was the friend and colleague of the rather older Isaiah. They spoke as if with one mouth.

The sermon[76] also has an introductory paragraph, but this is an exhortation to obey the word which God speaks in Scripture and which is now to be expounded.

(a) Micah was contemporary with Isaiah. Why the need for two witnesses? Was not Isaiah's word sufficient? Certainly, but

[75] OC 43,281-3; CTS Mi 3,149-53.
[76] SC 5,1-4.

the Lord wanted to make the Jews quite inexcusable by publishing his message through more than one Prophet.

(b)   But their message was not only for their own times but also for us. Jesus Christ is the end of the Law; the teaching of the Law and the Prophets is revealed more clearly in the Gospel. So we must let Micah speak to us and confirm even more what we have already heard from Isaiah and Jeremiah [that is, in previous courses of sermons]. To say that we do not need the Prophets but have enough in the Gospel, 'C'est un blaspheme execrable'.

(c)   Micah prophesied for about thirty-eight years, during the reigns of three kings. [Later this becomes 38–40 years].

(d)   We note, therefore, Micah's constancy and perseverance, and we must be ready to be like him, instead of being like the Jews who would not listen to him.

(e)   How grateful we should be to have the book of Micah – a little book 'we can read in an hour', but containing the preaching of thirty-eight to forty years. Therefore we must pay good heed to it.

(2)   *Lecture*[77]

1.1.   *concerning Samaria and Jerusalem*

(a)   Micah was a Morasthite; that is, from Maresah in Judah. He was therefore being sent to his own people.

(b)   Then why also to Samaria? Just as Hosea was sent to Israel but also spoke words to Judah, so also Micah, but in the opposite order. Moreover, he was sent to Israel because the Covenant with Israel had not been annulled by their schism.

(c)   The inscription, strictly speaking, refers to only the first part of the book, which deals with threatenings, whereas joyful promises are given later.

(d)   His message must have been unpalatable to the Jews, who would not have liked being joined with Samaria. The Prophet, however, executed his office boldly, and spoke simply what God had commanded him.

Sermon:[78]

(a)   Calvin moves at once from the "fascheuse" message

[77] OC 43,283; CTS Mi 3,153-4.
[78] SC 5,4-7.

against Jerusalem and Samaria to an identification of "us" with "them". We, too, do not like to hear of God's wrath, but only of his kindness. But, if we are to know God's love, we must first feel his wrath and be wounded to the bottom of our heart. We must be receptive soil to God's Word, not hard stone.

(b) Samaria, which had rebelled, was guilty. It was true that Jerusalem had the Temple, but this was 'full of idolatry and superstition'. Nor did its mere presence among them sanctify the persons who entered it 'polluted by their iniquities'. This teaches us that we who have the Gospel purely preached to us must not glory in having God's blessings, unless we know how to profit by them. We must remember that our Lord said that Sodom and Gomorrah would be better off than we at the day of judgment. 'See then why the Prophet couples these two cities, Samaria and Jerusalem.'

(c) But was not the Prophet too hard on those who had received such blessings? Not at all. Men like to be flattered; but we must learn to humble ourselves and repent, like good King Hezekiah.

(d) We see what happens to faithful preachers who proclaim God's threatenings, for we have an example in the person of the Prophet Urijah, murdered by King Jehoiakim (Jeremiah 26. 20-23). But what happened to Jehoiakim? He was soon after carried away captive to Babylon. This shows us that the only way to forestall God's judgments is to condemn ourselves and repent.

The interpretation of the verse is the same on the two occasions, but the greater emphasis on application is obvious in the sermon, as is its slower pace, using about four thousand words to some eight hundred in the lecture. Of course, one may find lectures with more exhortation and sermons with less, but the example given fairly represents the differences between the two forms.

In this book we shall be dealing very largely, but not exclusively, with the commentaries and lectures, for I do not want to repeat what I have already written in my book on the sermons, *The Oracles of God*. Nevertheless, what we have to say about Calvin's Old Testament exposition will apply to the sermons also.

Chapter Two

The Two Testaments

1 One substance in different forms

To say the word "Bible" is to bring to mind a book
containing the writings of the Old and New Testaments, with
perhaps that third set sandwiched between called the Apo-
crypha. The mental image shows how much modern Christians take for granted not only that the two Testaments belong
together in some way, but also that to some extent, in some
way, the Old Testament has a place in Christianity. And
because one very rarely, apart from scholarly or two-volume
editions, finds an Old Testament on its own, although New
Testaments are common enough, it is too easily forgotten that
there was a time when for Christians "Holy Scripture" meant
the Old Testament without the New, which had not yet been
written, or, if written, had remained isolated and localized and
had not been accorded a place of authority alongside or above
the Old Testament. Indeed, the very title "*Old* Testament'
could only come into being when there was also a "*New*
Testament".

Even after it had become accepted that certain apostolic and
sub-apostolic writings, grouped together, ought to be called
"New Testament", the relationship between the Old and the
New remained in debate. There have been movements in the
Church (or on its fringes) that down the ages to our own day
have rejected the Old Testament as a thing annulled, outworn
and outmoded, like the sacrifice of bulls and rams. And there
have been other movements which have been more at home in
the Old than in the New.

The relationship itself is not something adventitious which

has sprung up in the course of history. It belongs to the very being of Christian faith. The claim asserted in the first verse of the New Testament is not simply one of continuity but of necessary and exclusive continuity: 'The book of the generation of Jesus Christ, the son of David, the son of Abraham'.[1] It was not simply a question of Christianity growing up in and developing out of a Jewish and therefore an Old Testament environment, so that the New Testament would be comprehensible only if read in the light of the Old, but of Christianity being the sole legitimate continuation of the Old Covenant, and therefore of the New Testament being the sole legitimate continuation of the Old. Thus a balance is seen between the Testaments, forbidding a Marcionite annulment of the Old Testament and a Judaizing annulment of the New, forbidding a swallowing up of the Old in the New and a relativizing of the New in terms of the Old.

Yet the nature of the relationship has continued debateable. The history of Biblical study from the eleventh to the sixteenth centuries shows a recurring conflict, not so much over the relationship in general as over its more precise working out and especially over the use of the Old Testament. The conflict was far from being what the nineteenth century might have called 'a mere wrangling of scholastic pedants'. We are talking about two books which were believed to possess supreme authority over men as the direct expression of the will of God. What these books taught was the absolute truth; what they commanded was unconditionally binding; what they promised beyond all that could be desired or deserved. Where a man's reach did not exceed his grasp, they might be obeyed with a stark literalness, a Kierkegaardian heroic faith that takes the breath away. In any case, acceptance or depreciating of the Old Testament manifested itself not only in personal "spirituality" or moral behaviour, but in terrifying or trivial social, cultural, legal, political, and ecclesiastical consequences, with the admission of the Mosaic judicial system into the law of a land (therefore the burning of witches – Ex. 22.18) or, at the other extreme, the denial of the physical world by medieval Manichees.

[1] Matt 1.1

The relationship was no less problematical in the sixteenth century. Indeed, the same views were carried on by groups with different names from their medieval intellectual fathers. The questions were now increased in number as the number of sects proliferated, and in particular as the spiritualists within and outside the Anabaptists ranks increased in influence and in formulation of their beliefs. Broadly speaking we may say that there were three positions – the traditional, held by the Romanists and the main line Reformers, the destructive intentions of the free-thinkers, and the multiform views of the Anabaptists. The second group, however they may have triumphed subsequently, were a minority in their own day; nevertheless Calvin saw their danger to the Church and to European society generally and bore them in mind in some commentaries as the chief enemy. Among the Anabaptists and spiritualists there was a vast range of opinions. There were those who discarded the Old Testament as annulled by the coming of Christ. And there were those like the unhappy Anabaptists of Münster who disastrously took it at last as the pattern for their way of life. But the general tendency of Anabaptists was to give the Old Testament a lower religious position than the New. And again we find Calvin's teaching on the subject directed against this view.

The relation between the Testaments is in no way peripheral to his theology. When we arrive at Book II of the *Institutio,* on redemption in Christ, the whole doctrine is summarised in the title: *On the Knowledge of God the Redeemer in Christ, first manifested to the fathers under the Law, and afterwards to us in the Gospel.* The redemption of Christ, then, was not first revealed in the incarnate Christ and therefore in the New Testament, but had already been made known to the saints of the Old Covenant.

The first five chapters of the book treat of the inescapable sinfulness of mankind, whether Old Testament man or New Testament man, and consequently of man's condemnation before God. The theme of chapter vi is that to lost man comes the invitation of the Gospel to repent, to believe in Christ and be pardoned and revived. In the first paragraph Calvin makes it plain that Old Testament sinner was saved by faith in the redeeming work of Christ no less than New Testament sinner: 'It is certain that, after the fall of the first man, no knowledge of God without the Mediator has availed for salvation' (II. vi.1).[2] And in the next paragraph: 'And so God never shewed himself propitious to the people of old, and never gave them hope of grace, apart from the Mediator' (II.vi.2).[3] And: 'the blessed and happy state of the Church always had its foundation in the person of Christ' (II.vi.2).[4] The rest of this paragraph and all the next consist of demonstrations of this statement from the Old Testament. The conclusion comes in §4: 'God wished the Jews to be so steeped in these prophecies that, to seek their freedom, they had to turn their eyes directly to Christ' (ii.vi.4).[5]

This, and not the Law, says chapter vii, is the essential message of the Old Testament. The Law was an addition, given four hundred years after God had established his Covenant with Abraham (Gal.3.17; Gen.12.1-3). It was intended, not to lead God's people away from Christ, the foundation of the Covenant, to some new way of salvation, but on the contrary to keep them looking for his coming, to kindle their desire for him, to encourage them when the time seemed long until he should come. By "Law" Calvin explains that he means the whole form or system of religion delivered by God through the hand of Moses. The whole Law – the sacrifices, ceremonies, priesthood, kingdom, and moral commands – points, in various ways, to Christ. For our present purpose, however, the larger part of chapter vii, on the purpose of the moral Law, and the whole of the very long chapter viii, an exposition of the Ten Commandments, are irrelevant.

It is the three chapters ix – xi that directly deal with our subject. Chapter ix (*Christ, although he was known to the Jews under the Law, was only exhibited in the Gospel*) is an introductory statement. The difference between the Testaments consists in the degree of clarity of revelation, in the

[2] OS 3,320[37f.]
[3] OS 3,321[31f.]
[4] OS 3,321[35ff.]
[5] OS 3,325[3ff.]

degree of intimacy of knowledge. This is hinted at in the prepositions used in both the title of this chapter and of the whole book. It was revelation *sub Lege* and *in Euangelio.* Hence also his definition of the Gospel as 'the clear manifestation of the mystery of Christ, *clara mysterii Christi manifestatio*' (II.ix.2).[6] It is not simply that the Gospel is manifestation, but that it is the clear manifestation of what in the Old Testament had been the *mystery* of Christ. Although, he goes on, it may not be denied that the term "Gospel" is to be applied also to the promises which abound in the Law, it nevertheless belongs pre-eminently 'to the proclamation of the grace manifested in Christ' (II.ix.2).[7] This is both the common signification, and, as is plain from many New Testament passages, is also what Christ and the Apostles meant by it.

At this point, however, the danger arises of appropriating the fullness and finality of Christ and his redeeming work to the Church and also to the world, so that what is true of the risen and ascended Head is true here and now of the Body. In opposition to the Anabaptist Servetus, who had done precisely this in his book *Christianismi Restitutio* (1553), Calvin insists that, although in Christ are all the blessings of eternal life, yet in their earthly life believers live still by hope and not in possession. Against Servetus' resolved eschatology Calvin sets the tension of 'in Christ we possess all that belongs to the perfection of the heavenly life and yet faith is the sight of blessings not seen – *visio bonorum quae non videntur*' (II.ix.3).[8] Christians are, therefore, so far as promise and fulfilment go, in the same experimental position as the Old Testament believers. The difference between the Testaments lies, not in the two stages of the Church, but in the clarity of Christ's revelation and therefore the assurance of the Church's knowledge: 'The distinction is to be remarked only in the nature or quality of the promises. The Gospel points out with its finger what the Law sketched under types' (II.ix.3).[9]

If this is so, runs the argument of the next paragraph, then

[6] OS 3,399[26ff.]
[7] OS 3,399[35f.]
[8] OS 3,401[16ff.]
[9] OS 3,401[19ff.]

there can be no question of the Testaments being mutually contradictory by the Law teaching one thing, salvation by works, and the Gospel another, salvation by faith. There is some truth in this opposition between Law and Gospel and it forms the basis of Paul's arguments on justification in Romans and Galatians. But it is true only to the extent that the Law commands righteousness and condemns unrighteousness. Between this and the free forgiveness offered in the Gospel is a complete contradiction. Yet this is to take the Law only as the moral code of command and condemnation. If it is considered as the whole Old Testament system of religion, containing also the promises and the expiations for sin, then the difference is only one of clarity: 'where it is a question of the whole Law, the Gospel differs from it only in respect of its clear manifestation – *dilucidae manifestationis*' (II.ix.4).[10] Nevertheless, the last word must be left with the Gospel. To the extent that it is a clear and not an obscure manifestation, it is superior to the Law: 'Yet on account of the inestimable riches of the grace which are revealed to us in Christ, there is good reason for saying that God's heavenly kingdom was set up on earth by his advent' (II.ix.4).[11]

The way is now open for Calvin to state and explain in chapter x the similarity (*similitudo*) of the two Testaments. This is the main chapter of the three, for it was more important to establish positively the relationship than to deny and demolish arguments against relationship. The relationship can be stated in one sentence which will do justice to both similarity and difference: 'The Covenant of all the fathers is no different in substance and reality ('*substantia et re ipsa*' from ours; it is simply one and the same (*unum prorsus et idem*). But the administration is different' (II.x.2).[12] In 'substance and reality' the Old Covenant is 'one and the same' with the New; but they are administered in different ways. Having used the phrase *unum et idem*, he can then go beyond similarity and talk of unity: 'in similarity, or rather, unity' (II.x.2).[13] Thus, the

[10] OS 3,402[9ff.]
[11] OS 3,402[11ff.]
[12] OS 3,404[5ff.]
[13] OS 3,404[10.]

two Covenants become one, the two Churches one, the two sets of writings one book.

He intends, he says, to make three points: First, the Jews were promised, not simply earthly blessings – the land flowing with milk and honey, a long life, children, prosperity, and so on – but 'the hope of immortality' (II.x.2).[14] Then, the Covenant did not rest on their merits but on the mercy of God. And thirdly, the Jews both 'had and knew' Christ as the Mediator through whom they were joined to God. Since, however, he has already dealt with the third in chapters vi and vii and means to deal with the second in Book III, chapter xvii, only the first is left for this chapter, with the other two summarised in a paragraph at the end.

Once again it is the extremist Anabaptists, and particularly Servetus, who provide the point of attack: 'they have no other estimate of the people of Israel than of a herd of swine fattened up by the Lord in their land, without any hope of the heavenly immortality' (II.x.1).[15] Calvin therefore sets about proving from Scripture itself that the Jews 'were adopted to the hope of immortality; and the faith of this adoption was made known to them now by oracles, now by the Law, now by the Prophets' (II.x.2).[16] They had the same promise of the Gospel, which invited them, as it does us, to lift up their minds to the hope of the future life. There was an essential unity of message – that 'sinners, apart from their own deserving, are justified by the Fatherly kindness of God' (II.x.4).[17] The Gospel declares that Christ is the Saviour of the world; but in several places the New Testament also declares that Christ and his salvation reach backwards as well as forwards. It follows, then, that Old Testament believers were justified in and by Christ, by faith in Christ, like believers under the New Covenant.

The Old Covenant had Sacraments also, and these had the same end and object as those of the New, although their sacramental form was different. His chief authority here, of course, was I Cor. 10.1-6, where it is said that the crossing of

[14] OS 3,404[16f.]
[15] OS 3,403[21ff.]
[16] OS 3,404[16ff.]
[17] OS 3,405[33f.]

the Red Sea was Baptism and that the eating of the manna and quails and the drinking of the water from the rock was a partaking of Christ. Therefore, 'The same promises of eternal and heavenly life which the Lord now condescends to give us were communicated to the Jews and also sealed with truly spiritual Sacraments' (II.x.6).[18]

Up to this point Calvin has based his arguments on the New Testament, looking back to the Old. Now he turns to the Old Testament for its own self-evidence. God's communication with men of old, according to the Old Testament, was by his Word. But God's Word was not merely communicative in the modern sense, informing, commanding, requesting, and so on, and therefore needing to be taken and acted on by the one addressed. It had always an illuminating and vivifying power, accomplishing what it meant. The word "communication" is, in its essential meaning, singularly apt in respect to the Covenant, for it means a uniting of oneself with the other. When, therefore, God spoke his Word (of course, not his "strange" Word of condemnation but his Word of promise and life) to his people, he by that act bound himself to them, them to himself, in unity. And unity with God means eternal life. 'I say that Adam, Abel, Noah, Abraham, and the rest of the fathers, cleaved to God by the illumination of this Word; so that there is no doubt at all that they had an entrance into the immortal kingdom of God. For they had a genuine participation of God which cannot be apart also from the blessing of eternal life' (II.x.7).[19] 'Let there be union with him; and it will bring eternal salvation'. (II.x.8).[20]

Moreover, although the Covenant certainly also carried the assurance that the Lord was the present God of Israel, it was not confined to the present; 'he not only testified that he was their God, but also promised that he always would be' (II.x.9).[21] This future referred both to succeeding generations in Israel, and also to themselves after death. Hence Christ's quoting of Ex.3.6 in answer to the Sadducees: 'I am the God of

[18] OS 3,407[35ff.]
[19] OS 3,408[24ff.]
[20] OS 3,409[27f.]
[21] OS 3,409[29f.]

Abraham, of Isaac, and of Jacob . . . He is not the God of the dead but of the living' (Matt. 22. 23). The promise to the fathers therefore transcended earthly blessings; their cynosure was an eternal inheritance.

But all that has so far been stated has been the Bible's understanding of the situation of the men of the Old Covenant. It is far more pertinent to ask whether they themselves knew the grace of God and looked for a city which hath foundations, whose builder and maker is God. Calvin recognizes that this is the question on which all else turns (II.x.10).[22] The next thirteen paragraphs patiently take us all through the Old Testament in an appeal to the consciousness of the many characters that 'they had a better life elsewhere and, despising this earthly life, set their minds on the heavenly' (II.x.10).[23]

The opening sentences of chapter xi are relaxed: 'What then? you will ask, Have you left no difference between the Old and the New Testaments? What about all those passages where they are contrasted as very different things?' (II.xi.1).[24] Well, yes, replies Calvin, in the tone of one who is sure of his case, there certainly are differences – four, if I remember aright; but if anyone wishes to add a fifth, I will not contradict him. But 'I say, and I propose to show, that they all belong to the mode of administration rather than to the substance' (II.xi.1).[25]

As we go through the five differences, we should remember that this is not part of the main argument. That is now behind us. Calvin's whole intention has been to establish the similarity or unity of the Old and New Covenants. The chapter on the differences should on no account be taken as a balance to that on the similarity. There could be no such balance, but either only a confirmation or a demolition of the case. He has, in fact, already warned us that chapter xi is to be read as an appendix to chapters ix and x, an appendix which looks honestly at the apparent contradictions that Scripture itself states. The sense

[22] OS 3,410[25.]
[23] OS 3,410[27.]
[24] OS 3,423[3ff.]
[25] OS 3,423[11ff.]

of the first sentence of II.x.1 (not well brought out by any of the English translations) is that the unity of the two Covenants is such an important doctrine that it must be given a chapter on its own, with an appendix dealing with the differences. Chapter xi is that appendix, which can therefore state with assurance, 'I freely accept the differences mentioned in Scripture; but they do not detract from the unity we have already established' (II.xi.1).[26]

The first difference (II.xi.1-3)[27] is that the heavenly blessing, which in the Gospel is declared plainly and directly, was set before the people under earthly blessings. Thus, Abraham was promised the land in which he was a stranger: but the land was only a figure of the reality in the promise, and the reality was God himself – 'Fear not, Abram: I am thy shield, and thy exceeding great reward' (Gen.15.1). 'Here we see that the end of Abram's reward is sited in the Lord, so that he should not seek it as the frail and evanescent reward of the elements of this world but reckon it as imperishable. The promise of the land was then added, simply as a symbol of the divine benevolence and a type of the heavenly heritage' (II.xi.2).[28]

The second difference (II.xi.4-6)[29] is a variant of the first. Under the Old Covenant the truth, the body, is absent; in its stead stands the image, the shade. The Gospel exhibits the truth and the body. Calvin calls this the most serious difference of all. If it could be shown to touch the substance of the Covenants it would constitute an actual contradiction. He therefore explains at some length that it also is a matter of the mode of dispensation and therefore does not affect the unity of substance. Underlying this difference is the significance of the "New" and the "Old", and of time past as the preparation for time present. The "New" is sited in the Cross and Resurrection of Christ. When once he had been crucified and had risen again, then what had been in force hitherto (the Covenant) became the "Old". But the Cross and Resurrection had been

[26] OS 3,423[5ff.]
[27] OS 3,423-6.
[28] OS 3,424[31ff.]
[29] OS 3,426-9.

determined from eternity. Therefore the first Covenant was never intended to be more than temporary. Yet it did not cease and disappear when the appointed time came, but was made new: 'it was not made new and eternal until Christ had consecrated and established it with his blood' (II.xi.4). [30]

This theme of the "New" and the "Old" had come to Calvin from the Epistle to the Hebrews. It was Galatians 3-4 that provided the cognate theme of preparation; the people of the Old Covenant were certainly sons and heirs of God, but as they were not yet come of age they were kept under the restraint and training of a tutor. The Law, with its commands, ceremonies, and institutions, had charge of them and ordered their lives. Their coming of age was brought to pass by the coming of Christ and consisted in their being handed over by the tutor, Law, into the care and teaching of Wisdom himself (II.xi.5). [31] No disparagement is implied by this metaphor of childhood and immaturity to the great men of faith like Abraham or Moses or the Prophets. On them was bestowed wonderful and unusual grace, whereas the people in general are intended by the metaphor. Yet even those outstanding believers still lacked something, and this lack is reflected in their writings and lives. Like all the rest, they knew Christ only in the images and figures of the Law, and were waiting for the manifestation of the fulfilment of the promises (II.xi.6). [32]

The third difference (II.xi.7-8) [33] comes from St Paul's exposition of Jer. 31.31-34 in II Cor. 3.3-6. The Lord promises to make a new Covenant with his people and to write his Law in their hearts. The New Covenant is not of the letter, but spiritual, 'for the letter killeth but the Spirit giveth life'. The Old Covenant is of the letter, literal, in that it was proclaimed without the efficacy of the Spirit, whereas the New is spiritual in that the Lord has engraven it spiritually on the hearts of believers. Consequently, the Old is death-dealing, holding all mankind under God's curse and condemnation; but the New is the instrument of life, which frees from the curse and restores

[30] OS 3,427[27ff.]
[31] OS 3,427-8.
[32] OS 3,428[18ff.]
[33] OS 3,429-31.

to God's favour. Again, the Old served to accuse and condemn the disobedient; the New is the ministry of righteousness, which reveals the justifying mercy of God. And finally, the Old, by its very nature as the image of things yet absent, was transient; the Gospel, which revealed the body itself, is firm and lasting. But, it must also be emphasized, all this must be taken relatively.

The lecture on Jer.31.31 and the commentary on II Cor.3.6 will clarify this statement, and especially the difficulty that the Old Covenant was given without the Holy Spirit. In the lecture Calvin follows the same line of argument as in Inst.II.x-xi. First he establishes the unity of the Covenants: 'God is never self-contradictory, never unlike himself. Therefore he who once made a Covenant with his elect people had not changed his purpose . . . It follows, then, that the first Covenant was inviolable. Moreover, he had already made his Covenant with Abraham, and the Law was confirmation of that Covenant . . . God has never made any other Covenant than that which he made at first with Abraham and at last established by the hand of Moses'.[34] Then he turns to the difference of form: 'Let us now see why he promises the people a new Covenant. This refers without doubt to the form, as it is called. But this form is placed, not only in the words, but first in Christ, and then in the grace of the Holy Spirit and in the whole outward way of teaching. Yet the substance remains the same. By "substance" I understand the teaching (*doctrina*), for in the Gospel God brings forward nothing but what is contained in the Law. Therefore we see that God has so spoken from the beginning that he has not since changed one syllable, with regard to the sum of the teaching'.[35] The form of the Old Covenant consisted in sacrifices and in outward teaching, which only became efficacious through the sacrifice of Christ and the regeneration of the Holy Spirit; thus it became not only a teaching according to the letter but also efficacious, not merely striking on the ear but penetrating into the heart.[36]

The comment on II Cor.3.6 further clarifies the apparent

[34] OC 38,688; CTS Jer 4,126-7.
[35] OC 38,688; CTS Jer 4,127.
[36] OC 38,689; CTS Jer 4,127.

contradiction that the Old Covenant was proclaimed 'without the working of the Spirit', and yet the believers who lived under it received spiritual profit, in fact eternal life. How could they even be believers without the Holy Spirit? For 'faith is the principal work of the Holy Spirit' (*Inst.* III.i.4).[37] Indeed, how could there be Covenant, which, according to Calvin, was union with God in Christ, when the Holy Spirit, who 'is the bond by which Christ effectually unites us to himself' (*Inst.* III.i.1),[38] is absent? The relevant clauses of the verse in II Corinthians are: 'not of the letter, but of the spirit: for the letter killeth, but the Spirit giveth life'. After rejecting Origen's understanding of it in terms of the literal and spiritual interpretation of Scripture, Calvin sets out to answer the *quaestio* 'Whether God under the Old Covenant spoke by way of merely outward voice and not also inwardly to the hearts of the godly by his Spirit?'[39] The first answer is that God did indeed speak to them by his Spirit, but not by the Law in itself as Law. Within the Law were contained the promises, and it was this good news, this affirmation of God, which was spoken by the power of the Spirit and created union with God (Covenant) and eternal life. The grace given to the men of the Old Covenant was not from Moses but from Christ – *The Law was given by Moses; but grace and truth came by Christ Jesus* (Jn 1.17). And secondly, this is not an absolute statement but a relative. That is to say, its truth stands in the relation, the comparison, between the two Covenants, not necessarily in either separately: 'even the Gospel is not always Spirit'.[40] In comparison with the Gospel, the Law is an outward teaching, not penetrating to the heart. In comparison with the Law, the Gospel teaches spiritually, as the effectual instrument of God's grace.

Out of the third comes the fourth difference (II.xi.9-10).[41] The Old is a Covenant of servitude, the New of freedom. The Law, by commanding moral righteousness and then accusing

[37] OS 4,5[14.]
[38] OS 4,5[5f.]
[39] OC 50,40; CTS Cor 2,173; CC II Cor 42.
[40] OC 50,40; CTS Cor 2,173; CC II Cor 42.
[41] OS 3,431-3.

those who transgressed, could only enslave the conscience, binding it under its authority and frightening it with its threats. It promised eternal life, but only on the impossible condition that none of its commands should be infringed in the slightest degree. The New Covenant, on the contrary, with its joyful message of free forgiveness in Jesus Christ, liberates the conscience, giving gladness in place of fear. It is true that believers under the Old Covenant knew the glad freedom of forgiveness and renewal; but they received this, not from the Law in itself and as Law, but from the Gospel promises in the Law.

Calvin now puts forward the fifth difference (II.xi.11-12),[42] which he had said, with a curious hesitancy, could be made. It is that before the Incarnation God had made his particular Covenant with the one nation, Israel; but when the Mediator was come, the middle wall of partition was broken down and the Gentiles also were received among the people of God, so that there is no longer any distinction between Jew and Gentile. This difference clearly shows the superiority of the New Covenant to the Old.

Two obvious objections remain to be dealt with. First, why should God have followed a different way in the Old Covenant from the New? Because the different times demanded different methods. 'The mode of administration', the dispensation (that is, God's dispensing or bestowing of his benefits) differs according to temporal circumstance. Thus, as in Gal. 4.1-2, the Church was a child under the Old Covenant and therefore needed treatment suitable to its age. We do not think a farmer is fickle or unstable because he fits different work into different seasons. In acting as he has done, God has remained true to himself and accommodated himself to man's changing capacity (II.xi.13).[43] Then the argument slips back into the age-old 'why?' Why did not God deal with the men before the Incarnation in the same way as with men since? Calvin gives the age-old answer that God has done everything wisely, even if we do not understand his reasons.

[42] OS 3,433-5.
[43] OS 3,435-6.

2 The shadow and the sketch

Through all the discussion in the *Institutio* of the *similitudo* and *discrimina* between the Testaments one image has dominated. I have not stressed it, because I wanted to discuss it separately and more fully. It is the image of light and shade, or rather a complex of images within the general image of light and shade. To understand Calvin's intentions here is to understand his view of the relationship between the Testaments.

In these chapters we meet seven times the word *umbra*, twice the adjective *umbratilis*, and five times the related verb *adumbratio*. There is very much more to these words than the general sense of "shadow", "shadowy", and "shaded" or "outlined" which English translators of the *Institutio* are accustomed to give them. For *umbra* Lewis and Short's Latin dictionary gives eight meanings: "shadow", "the dark part of a painting", "a ghost", "an uninvited guest", "a shady place", "a grayling", "a trace, obscure sign, imperfect copy", and "shelter". *Umbratilis* is simpler; it may mean "in retirement" or "at home", or "private". *Adumbratio* is defined as "a sketch in shadow, à la silhouette", "a sketch, outline", or "a false show". *Adumbrare* can, or course, mean "to cast a shadow on something", but it also has a technical sense: "to represent an object with the mingling of light and shade, σκιαγραφέω (therefore not of the sketch in shadow, as the first outline of a figure, but of a picture already fully sketched, and only wanting the last touches for its completion)"; but later the dictionary adds a further sense: "to represent a thing only in outline, and, consequently, imperfectly". When Calvin uses these words of the Old Covenant, which of the many meanings has he in mind?

1. Umbra

(1) John the Baptist's declaration that *no man hath seen God at any time; the only begotten, which is in the bosom of the Father, he hath declared him* (John 1.18) 'teaches us that the mysteries which were only descried obscurely *sub umbris*, have been revealed to us' (II.ix.1).[44]

(2) St Paul 'joins the body to the *umbris*' (II.ix.4).[45]

---

[44] OS 3,399[9].
[45] OS 3,401[34-5].

(3) Calvin quotes Ps. 39.7 *he who walks as an umbra*. On that verse he comments: 'By *umbra* he means that there is nothing *solidus* in man, but only an empty appearance, as they say (*inanem apparentiam*)' (II.x.15).[46]

(4) The patriarchs 'possessed something hidden which does not appear in the *umbra* of the present life' (II.x.17).[47]

(5) The Old Testament 'puts forward an *umbram* for the body' (II.xi.4).[48]

(6) Heb.10.1 'concludes, therefore, that [the Law] was in itself an *umbra* of good things to come and not the living image of the things (*vivam rerum effigiem*)' (II.xi.4).[49]

(7) 'Those who were content with present *umbris*' (II.xi.10).[50]

Umbra has no single meaning in these quotations. Twice (2 and 5) it is contrasted to "the body". Twice (1 and 4) it is related to obscurity or hiddenness. Once (6) it is contrasted to 'the living image'; and once (7) it is indeterminate. In the remaining quotation (3) I would suggest that Calvin has in mind the idea of a "shade" or "wraith", as, for example, we hear in folk-lore of the wraith of a person who is dying or in deadly peril appearing to a loved one far away.

2. *Umbratilis* is easier to settle, as bearing the sense of shadow and obscurity:

(1) In Jesus Christ God in a way 'makes himself visible, whereas his appearance had before been *obscura et umbratilis*' (II.ix.1).[51]

(2) 'the Old Covenant of the Lord, which he had delivered enwrapped in the *umbratili* and inefficacious observation of ceremonies' (II.xi.4).[52]

3. *Adumbrare*:

(1) 'The Gospel actually points with the finger to what the Law *adumbravit* under types' (II.ix.3).[53]

[46] OS 3,415[35]; Ps 39.7, OC 31,400.
[47] OS 3,417[16.]
[48] OS 3,426[12.]
[49] OS 3,426[31.]
[50] OS 3,433[3.]
[51] OS 3,399[21.]
[52] OS 3,427[24.]
[53] OS 3,401[21.]

(2) David '*adumbravit* the heavenly mysteries more obscurely than did [later Prophets]' (II.x.15).[54]

(3) 'The better to commend God's goodness, the Prophets *adumbrasse* it for the people in temporal blessings, as in outlines, so to say; but yet they painted such a portrait (*effigiem*) of it as carried their minds beyond the earth, beyond the elements of this world' (II.x.20).[55]

(4) 'He did not give them the spiritual promises naked and open, but as it were *adumbratas* in earthly things' (II.xi.2).[56]

(5) The Lord '*adumbrabat* spiritual happiness in types and symbols' (II.xi.3).[57]

Apart from the fact that the verb is used in connection with 'types', 'temporal blessings', 'earthly things', and 'types and symbols', no clear-cut meaning emerges. But we do have a clue to something more definite in the third quotation, where Calvin speaks of outlines and of painting a portrait. This clue is strengthened when we note that he refers us in the passage to Heb. 10.1. If we then take his commentary in conjunction with the *Institutio*, as he undoubtedly meant us to do, and read his exposition of Heb. 10.1, we find the metaphor fully worked out.

For the Law having a shadow of good things to come – σκιὰν τῶν μελλόντων ἀγαθῶν. His comment runs: 'He borrowed this metaphor from the art of painting. Here *umbra* is applied differently from its use in Col. 2.17, where the ancient ceremonies are called *umbrae* because they do not have within themselves the *solidam substantiam* of the things they figure. But here he says that they were like the rough lines which are the *adumbratio* [first sketch] of the living picture. For painters are accustomed *adumbrare* with charcoal what they intend to express, before they lay on the living colours with a brush. This more obscure drawing (*pictura*) the Greeks call σκιαγραφία, or, as you would say in Latin, *umbratilem*; whereas their εἰκών [image, likeness] is *expressa effigies*. Hence also *eiconicae* are called *imagines* in Latin, representing to the life men or animals or landscapes

[54] OS 3,415[30.]
[55] OS 3,424[24f.]
[56] OS 3,424[21.]
[57] OS 3,425[31.]

(*locorum faciem*). Thus the Apostle makes this distinction between
the law and the Gospel: Under the Law what is today expressed
with a masterly hand and in living and varied colours was only
adumbratum [sketched out] in rough and incomplete lines (*rudibus
et inchoatis lineis*)'.[58]

But now Calvin has given us a cross reference to Col. 2.17, a
verse he mentions also in *Inst.* II.xi.4, and we must see what that
place and its comment has to say.

Which is a shadow (σκιὰ) *of things to come, but the body is of
Christ.* Calvin here uses the metaphor in two ways. First he takes
umbra as opposed to the revealed reality. To adhere to ceremonies,
which are *umbrae*, is like contemplating a man's form from his
umbra when the man himself is present in one's sight. Christ is
now before our eyes in the Gospel; we therefore no longer need to
look at the *umbrae* of him. Here *umbra* may mean a man's shadow
cast by the light; or less probably, his wraith. He goes on,
however, to meet the objection that Christians also do not behold
Christ immediately but by means of the Christian Sacraments;
and now he turns to the other sense of *umbra* in order to
distinguish the Old Testament Sacraments from the New: 'As
painters do not express the image in their first sketch in living
colours and   εἰκονικῶς [a finished likeness], but first set out
rough and obscure lines in charcoal, so under the Law the
representation of Christ was unfinished and, as it were, a first
draft (*primae manus*), whereas in our Sacraments it is seen
expressed to the life'.[59]

The first point to be made is that Calvin seems to reserve the
painting metaphor for discussion of the ceremonies and Sacraments. We find that it occurs again, together with references to
Heb. 10.1 and Col. 2.17, when he comes to the comparison of
Old and New Testament Sacraments in *Inst.* IV.xiv.18-25. It is
used, therefore, not as a designation of the old Covenant itself but
of the form in which it was given. God did not give the Jews his
Covenant in the plain and clear portrayal of a finished painting,
where the direction and relation of lines and the variety of colours
would make the object represented at once recognizable and
understandable, but in the obscure indication of a charcoal

[58] OC 55,121; CTS Heb 221-2; CC Heb 132.
[59] OC 52,110-1; CTS Col 193; CC Col 338.

outline, black lines on plain canvas or wood, which, from its lack of detail and colour and from its unfilled-in body, is recognizable only with difficulty, and could, indeed, present the viewer with problems of ambiguity. What distinguished the finished painting from the sketch for Calvin was its colour, its detail, and its masterly workmanship.

It also appears from such quotations as 'David *adumbravit* the heavenly mysteries more obscurely than did [later Old Testament writers]' (II.x.15)[60] that Calvin saw the formation of the painting as a gradual process, with successive writers adding to its formation over the Old Testament centuries. But we must note that his usage differs from the explanation in Lewis and Short: 'not of the sketch in shadow, as the first outline of a figure, but of a picture already fully sketched, and only wanting the last touches for its completion'. For Calvin, on the contrary, the picture is only a rough sketch even at the end of the Old Testament. And when we come to the Incarnate Christ and the Gospel the metaphor breaks down and needs to be supplemented by that of the shade and the body.

But, as we said earlier, this complex of images is a part of the general image of light and shade; and it is the general image which is all-pervasive – light, clarity, brightness, shining, and so on. Above all, however, there is Christ the Sun of righteousness, who at his rising at once scatters the dark – 'Pack, clouds, away, and welcome day'. Calvin can hardly mention Christ in this context without calling him "the Sun of righteousness".

This is, he says in his lectures on Malachi, 'an extremely appropriate title if we consider how the condition of the fathers differed from ours. God has always given light to his Church; but Christ brought the full light, as also Isaiah teaches: *Jehovah shall arise upon thee, and the glory of God shall be seen in thee* (Isa. 60.1,2); for this belongs to the person of Christ alone. Then: *Behold darkness shall cover the earth*, etc.; *The Lord shall shine upon thee;* again: *There shall now be no sun by day nor moon by night; but God alone shall shine* (Isa. 60.19). Hence, all these sayings show that "Sun" is an apt name for Christ, for God the Father has shone much more clearly upon us in his person than previously by the Law and all the appendages of the Law. And this also is why

[60] OS 3,415[30].

Christ calls himself "the light of the world" – not that the fathers wandered like blind men in the dark, but that they were content with the mere dawn, or with moon and stars. We know that the teaching of the Law was so obscure that it can be called shadowy (*umbratilis*). Heaven was at length opened by the Gospel, the Sun arose and brought to view the full light of day. Hence it is Christ's proper office to illuminate'.[61]

The above passage would suggest a uniform obscurity throughout the time of the Old Covenant; but in fact Calvin envisaged a gradually increasing brightness, analogous to the increasing clarity of the portrait. Thus he will say: 'In the beginning, when the first promise of salvation was given to Adam, some faint sparks shone out. Afterwards, more was done and a greater fullness of light began to show. This more and more appeared and shed its brightness still further. And then at last all the clouds were scattered and Christ, the Sun of righteousness, fully illuminated the whole terrestrial globe' (*Inst*. II.x.20).[62] If the metaphor is stretched further, it will break. The qualification has to be made that these faint sparks and all the pre–Incarnation light were the light of Christ, the only light of the world.

The imagery of light-shadow, body-shade is used not only of Christ but also of the Holy Spirit and his work. Just as men of the Old Testament believed in Christ under the wrappings of external things, so also they received the Holy Spirit and his gifts: 'the power and grace of the Spirit was vigorous and reigned in the very truth of the shadows, and all the blessings that came from them was applied by the gift of the same Spirit for the use of believers'.[63] The Spirit was given to the saints;[64] it was by him that they were regenerate and made the children of God, for there can be no regeneration apart from the Spirit;[65] it was by him that they worshipped God acceptably.[66] Then the same qualifications that we have seen already re-appear. The Spirit is not the Spirit of the Law but of Christ; he was therefore not given by the Law as

[61] Mal 4.2. OC 44,490; CTS Mi 5,617-8.
[62] OS 3,420[7ff.]
[63] Ex 30.22ff. OC 24,446; CTS Mo 2,223.
[64] Joel 2.20. OC 42,566; CTS Mi 2,91.
[65] Jer 31.33. OC 38,690-1; CTS Jer 4,130-1.
[66] Jn 4.23. OC 47,88-9; CTS Jn 1, 161-2; CC Jn 1,100.

Law but by the New Covenant of the Gospel which was transferred to the Old Covenant in the promises. Moreover, this is a relative matter. The believers under the Old Covenant had only a weak and sparse gift of the Spirit in comparison with believers at Pentecost and thereafter. The New Testament shows the substance; that is, it shows the Spirit openly and plainly and in all his power. The Old Testament shows him under coverings and as the shade of the substance. Thus the bundle of hyssop with which the blood was sprinkled was a type of the Holy Spirit who applies to our hearts the blood shed on the Cross. The golden candelabra which gave light in the Tabernacle was a type of the Holy Spirit who illuminates the Church. So also the oil for anointing – 'It is incontrovertible, I conclude, that this oil mixed with precious perfumes was a figure of the Holy Spirit ... The Tabernacle was sprinkled with oil that the Israelites might learn that all the exercises of godliness profited nothing without the secret working of the Spirit'.[67] The Holy Spirit was therefore present and active with his people of the Old Covenant, not openly and plainly, but under these obscure figures or types, the shades of which he was the body.

We should not, of course, think of two concurrent sets of types or prophecies, finding their fulfilment in two separate entities, Jesus Christ and the Holy Spirit. The typified work of the Spirit under the Old Covenant was the same as under the Gospel – *he shall take what is mine and shall show it unto you*[68] – to reveal and bestow Christ and his work.

The last word on light-shadow may be left with the comment on Gal. 3.23, *Before faith came*. 'Faith was not yet revealed. Not that the fathers lacked light altogether, but that they had less light than we. For whereas ceremonies sketched out (*adumbrarent*) an absent Christ, he is represented to us as present. Thus, what they had in a mirror, we today have in substance. However much darkness (*obscuritas*) there might be under the Law, the fathers were not ignorant of the road they had to take. The dawn may not be as bright as noonday, but it is sufficient for making a journey, and travellers do not wait until the sun is right up. Their portion of light was like the dawn; it could keep them safe from all error and guide them to everlasting blessedness'.[69]

[67] Ex 30.22. OC 24,445-6; CTS Mo 2,223.
[68] Jn 16.15.
[69] OC 50,220; CTS Gal 107; CC Gal,66.

3 The Law the Pedagogue

The Pauline image of the Law being a schoolmaster to lead to Christ does not dominate Calvin's thinking as the other does. Nevertheless, since it is very strong, we may more briefly discuss it.

The primary concept here is positively that of preparation, negatively that of unfulfilledness and waiting. All that is learnt from the schoolmaster, however true and useful in itself, is learnt in order to go on to something more advanced. And on the other hand, there is a certain dialectic of learning and needing still to learn, of learning in itself never having an end, for every step taken in learning is a step into a wider ignorance.

In *Inst.* II.xi.2 Calvin applies the metaphor to the form of the promises made under the Old Covenant. Their form of earthly blessings corresponded to the childhood of the Church, which was not yet old enough to enter into the possession of the spiritual inheritance without its earthly wrapping. Here the emphasis is on the knowledge suitable for a child, and therefore on the unperfectedness of the child and the teaching, and the longing of the child who is told, 'When you are grown up' you will do this or that.

In the commentary on Gal. 3.24 the image is examined more closely. *So that the Law was our schoolmaster to bring us to Christ.* Calvin's interpretation was governed by the educational system that he knew. The basis for the more advanced part of the baccalaureate was (not necessarily under that name) the *trivium,* that wearisome grind of grammar, rhetoric, and dialectic – learning Latin, learning to think, learning to express your thoughts. You learn *qui, quae, quod* in order that one day in the future you will read and write Latin. You learn the rules of logic so that you may talk sense and not nonsense. You learn the tiresome rules of grammar so that you may go on to speak and write pleasingly and persuasively. All this is at the back of Calvin's mind as he says that a schoolmaster is only for one's childhood and the time will arrive when one comes of age (educationally) and then, farewell the *paidagogos*! The Law taught the elements. It taught a fixed age-group and could not go beyond that age. At that point the pupils had to be handed over to a higher education: 'in training a boy, the object is to prepare him by childish elements for greater things . . . [the purpose of the Law] was to advance its scholars only to the stage where, when the elements had been learned, they could make progress in further education'.[70] It is noteworthy that Calvin avoids saying that the elementary schoolmaster Law hands his pupils over to the higher schoolmaster Christ. Although his text is *unto Christ,* he seems to make it 'unto the teaching of the Gospel', contrasting the Law and the Gospel: 'The grammarian trains a boy and then hands him over to someone else who polishes him in the higher disciplines. Thus the Law was, as it were, the grammarian who started its pupils off and then handed them over to the theology of faith for their completion'.[71] And: 'in this way Paul compares the Church before the Incarnation to a child and since the Incarnation to a growing youth'.[72] The elementary teaching (*doctrina*), Calvin goes on, might more properly be called "training" (*disciplina*), for it consists primarily in moral awakening, making them aware of their sin and the need to seek for righteousness outside themselves, that is in Christ. What he calls the appendages of the Law, the promises, the threats, and the ceremonies, had the same purpose. 'The whole Law, in short, was nothing but a manifold variety of exercises in which the worshippers were led by the hand to Christ.'[73]

Just as Christ was the light that shone dimly for the fathers, so also he was the Teacher of his people of old. And in saying this we have moved from Gal. 3.24 with its preparation and state of suspension to a positive present blessing and training in godliness; but we are still thinking within the same metaphor of teaching and training. Chapter viii of Book IV of the *Institutio* is concerned with the authority of the Church; but in this chapter Calvin is drawn necessarily to the assertion that Jesus Christ is the Teacher, the *doctor* or *magister Ecclesiae.* The Church's authority, so runs the

[70] OC 50,220; CTS Gal 108; CC Gal,66.
[71] OC 50,220; CTS Gal 108; CC Gal,66. I take it that *fidei . . . tanquam theologiae* is a synonym for "the Faith" or "the Gospel".
[72] OC 50,220; CTS Gal 108; CC Gal,66. *Hoc modo pueris confert Iudaeos Paulus, nobis adulescentiam attribuit.*
[73] OC 50,221; CTS Gal 109; CC Gal 67.

argument, resides in the Word of God, for clearly it is God who possesses supreme authority. The Word of God (that is, Holy Scripture) therefore, as God's declaration of his will, itself has the supreme authority in the Church, authority in doctrine, government, and legislation. It is with the first of these that we are now concerned. Doctrine is a matter of teaching the truth about God (so far as it concerns man to know), about himself, and about the universe as a created entity. Teaching demands a teacher, and 'the one and only Teacher (*unicus magister*) of the Church' is Jesus Christ. 'For it is not written of any other at all, but only of him, "Hear him"' (IV. viii.1).[74] Consequently ministers of the Church may not preach or teach anything save only what they have been taught by Christ. But this is a universal truth; it applied to 'the Priests and the Prophets' as well as to the Apostles and their successors. In one way or another, they were all not only commanded to proclaim the Word of God but also what they were commanded to speak was given to them: 'none of them spoke without the Lord dictating his words' (IV.viii.3).[75]

Thus all the writers of the Old Testament as well as of the New are taught personally by Christ himself. That the writers of Scripture were inspired by the Holy Spirit is frequent enough in Calvin, and has so often been discussed that we need now only summarise the matter.

On the one hand, Calvin not only speaks of the teaching or inspiration of the Spirit but also very often of dictation by the Spirit, using the strong metaphor of an amanuensis taking down a lecture or sermon (as was done with his own). If we take this literally and by itself, like some writers, we have a mechanical or almost mechanical process, by means of which the words (and not merely the ideas) spoken by the Spirit are written down by a man. On the other hand, there are those who, while accepting that Calvin uses this language, point also to another strain in him which is inconsistent with a literal interpretation of "dictation" and "amanuensis". They draw attention to a few places where he accepts trifling contradictions between one passage and another; they show that the Latin word *dictare* was often used by Calvin as a synonym for *suggerere*, "to suggest"; and I would add (for I am

[74] OS 5,134[4f.]
[75] OS 5,135[22f.]

one of these myself) that "amanuensis" should be interpreted, not according to the dictionary definition but according to the practice with which he was familiar, not only in the work of Raguenier and the others but in that of des Gallars, where two books written by des Gallars in his own style were called "my commentaries" by Calvin and published under his name. Nevertheless, I think it is a mistake to be concerned with the How? of this matter rather than the fact itself; and the fact is that for Calvin the Bible, the whole Bible and every nook and cranny of the Bible, is the Word of God as completely as if God himself had spoken the actual words. At every point, therefore, we are confronted by God's will, God's mind, and not by human purposes and ideas. And this, on which the authority of the Bible and the Church rests in practice, is overwhelmingly more important than that he uses the techniques of literary criticism to understand the Bible.

We shall take up this subject again when we come to the Prophets. Our present thesis is that Christ is the Teacher of Prophets as well as of Apostles. We should not think of "dictation" by the Spirit without recalling that the Spirit is both the Spirit of the Father and the Spirit of the Son who is the Teacher of the Old Testament writers. 'If Christ's words are true that no-one has seen the Father except the Son and he to whom the Son wills to reveal him, then the foundation is that they who wish to arrive at the knowledge of God must always be directed by that heavenly Wisdom [that is, the Son of God]. For how would they themselves have understood or spoken the mysteries of God unless they had been taught by him to whom alone the secrets of the Father are open? Therefore the saints (*sancti homines*) of the past knew God in no other way than in his Son, as one seen in a mirror. When I say this, I mean that God always revealed himself in no other way than through his Son, that is, his unique Wisdom, Light, and Truth. From this fountain Adam, Noah, Abraham, Isaac, Jacob, and the others drew all the heavenly doctrine they had. From him also all the Prophets drew what they themselves published as heavenly oracles' (IV.viii.5).[76]

But Christ did not teach them all in the same way. The first stage came with the Patriarchs, to whom the Wisdom of God

[76] OS 5,137[3ff].

(Christ) used "secret revelations" – a vague expression, meaning perhaps that we do not know and ought not to try to discover. To the secret revelations were joined visible signs, like the trees in Eden or the rainbow after the Flood. The next step was an oral transmission; the Patriarchs handed on to their successors what they themselves had received. 'Can we think that man was so placed on the earth as to be ignorant of the origin of himself and of the things he enjoyed? No sane man doubts that Adam was well instructed about them all. Was he afterwards dumb? Were the holy Patriarchs so ungrateful as to suppress in silence such necessary teaching? Did Noah, warned by God's memorable judgment, neglect to transmit it to posterity? Abraham is expressly honoured with this title, that he was the teacher and master of his family'.[77] But this again was not a purely human transmission, for 'the children and grandchildren knew, by the inward suggestion of God (*Deo intus dictante*), that what they were hearing was not of the earth but from heaven' (*Inst*. IV.viii.5).[78] The third stage came when at the Exodus and the giving of the Law God re-formed his Church. After the Law had been given it was committed to writing and was henceforth to control the practice and teaching of the priests. Thus we have the Pentateuch accounted for. Finally came the Prophets, 'through whom God published new oracles – yet not so new but that they flowed from the Law and had reference to it (*Inst*. IV.viii.6).[79] In regard to doctrine the Prophets were only interpreters or expounders of the Law. Their sole original contribution consisted of predictions of the future.

On the actual recording of the prophecies Calvin gives a fuller account in more than one place. We may hear it from an unpublished sermon on Isaiah: 'We must note carefully what is put here, that, when the Prophets had proclaimed what had been ordained to them by God, they made, so to say, a summary, and it is from these that we have the prophecies. For Isaiah did not write down word for word everything that he had declared with his voice. It would have made it far too long to have assembled all the sermons and make books of them. But Isaiah collected the

[77] OC 23,6–8; CTS Gen 1,58-9.
[78] OS 5,137[22f.]
[79] OS 5,138[2ff.]

summaries. And this is how the other prophecies were made. When they had preached a sermon treating some subject at length, they made a short resumé of its statements and put that on the gate of the Temple or in some raised place where people came to read. And when the people had read it, those who had not heard the sermon, or even those who had heard it, to be the better confirmed, came there to see what had been said'.[80] A corollary of this is that the Biblical book was not necessarily written by the Prophet whose name it bears; for 'there were scribes who collected the summaries and made from them the books now extant . . . this book we have now in our hands was not written by Jeremiah himself, but it contains collected summaries afterwards formed into one book'.[81] And so we have the whole Old Testament written, for the Psalms are included with the Prophets (although their manner of composition was different) and the histories were added at the same time, 'the composition of the Prophets, but dictated by the Holy Spirit' (*Inst.* IV.viii.6).[82]

These secret revelations, oral traditions, and writings were all, through the Spirit, the teaching of the Son, the Wisdom of God, before his Incarnation. But when he had been manifested in the flesh and had declared all that the human mind can comprehend about the heavenly Father, the Apostles and their successors had to allow him alone to be their Teacher. Yet even so, this does not mean that the Apostles were to confine themselves to the teaching of Jesus while he was with them on earth. They were to confine themselves to the teaching of Jesus, certainly, but that teaching embraced also all the Old Testament. Calvin goes further and puts the Apostles on the same level with the Prophets in this respect: 'nothing else was permitted to the Apostles than was formerly permitted to the Prophets; that is, that they should expound the old Scripture and show that the things delivered there are fulfilled in Christ. Yet they were not to do that apart from the Lord; that is, by the Spirit of Christ ruling and in a certain way dictating their words' (*Inst.* IV.viii.8).[83]

The place of the Old Testament in the Christian Church is

[80] *Ms. Sermons sur Esaie 30-42*, Class-mark Ms.fr.18. fo.13^v-14^r.
[81] Jer 45.1ff. OC 39,277; CTS Jer 4,565.
[82] OS 5,138$^{11ff.}$
[83] OS 5,140$^{1ff.}$

therefore established as one of equality. It is very common in Calvin to meet the trio of writings as the supreme authority, the Law, the Prophets, and the Gospel: 'Therefore let this be a steadfast principle: No other Word of God is to be held or given a place in the Church than what is contained first in the Law and the Prophets and then in the Apostolic writings; nor is there to be any proper way of teaching in the Church except from the prescript and according to the criterion of his Word' (*Inst.* IV.viii.8).[84]

4 Principles of interpretation

We must now go on to ask how Calvin's understanding of the relationship between the two Testaments affected his exposition of the Old. Did he, living after the Sun of righteousness had risen, look back on the Old Testament from the vantage point of the Gospel and expound his texts in the light of the incarnation, death and resurrection of Christ? Had he done this, he would have had the comfort of many precedents, from New Testament days into his own. The Gospel writers certainly believed that the Old Testament not only could but even must be understood as proclaiming Jesus Christ, and that to interpret it apart from him would be to misinterpret it. The early Church, in contrast to groups like the Marcionites, held the same belief. But by the third century and in the academic milieu of Alexandria, the question had been reformulated and consequently the answer, although it could coincide with the former answer, was also reformulated. Instead of asking directly after Jesus Christ ('who is the Christ?' 'who is Jesus?' 'a suffering Christ?' 'a victorious Christ?' and so on) and receiving the equally direct answers recorded in the New Testament, Clement of Alexandria and then Origen, asked the questions that Greek commentators had asked about their classical poets and that Hebrew commentators had asked about the Old Testament. How are we to understand those actions of the gods which are unworthy of divinity? How shall we read those passages where the saints of old behaved badly? Were there not inconsistencies, even irreconcileabilities, between one passage and another? Were not some stories downright absurd? The way in which the Alexandrians answered their questions was itself

84 OS 5,139[29ff].

borrowed from the Greeks and Hebrews; it was to say that behind what the text said literally there lay hid a corresponding meaning on another level, a spiritual or mystical meaning. This was a most ingenious solution. By it anything absurd could be made reasonable, anything immoral moral, anything mundanely ordinary heavenly and uplifting. The Old Testament and its *dramatis personae* could be upgraded to the level of spirituality achieved by any succeeding century. With few exceptions Christian Biblical expositors made use of the method and it became schematized in the Middle Ages into the well-known "four senses", by which a passage could be interpreted literally and historically, or interpreted in reference to God's dealing with the individual soul (tropological or moral), or his dealing with the Church (allegorical), or in reference to eternal things in heaven (anagogical).

In the sixteenth century, the "four senses" came into disfavour among the Reformers and some humanists. It may be that the Reformers' dislike was based more on theological, the humanists' on literary grounds. It may also be that this is a problem which should be investigated in individuals rather than in amorphous groups. So far as Calvin is concerned, it must be said at once that it is misleading to think of his expositions in the category of the four senses, for these are, at least in their usual form, irrelevant to his interpretation. It is true that he will use the terminology – *sensus literalis, allegoria,* and *anagogē* – that he expresses occasionally a preference for the literal sense, and and that he frequently voices impatient criticism of allegory. But he is not using the words with their classic "four-sense" meaning. His attacks on "allegory" are not directed against the *sensus allegoricus*, but against an over-elaborated use of allegory in its general sense of extended metaphor as well as against an allegorical interpretation imposed arbitrarily on a passage. While he can define allegory calmly in terms of literary criticism: 'This whole speech is metaphorical; in fact properly speaking, it is an allegory, for allegory is nothing but extended metaphor (*continua metaphora*),'[85] he more often treats it as a hermeneutic aberration and sets it in opposition to simple truth and edification. As example we may take the instructions for constructing and furnishing the Tabernacle.

[85] Dan 4.10ff. OC 40,657; CTS Dan 1,257.

These had been a happy hunting ground for allegorists, but Calvin preferred practical explanations: 'I now come to the details, and here readers must not look for subtleties from me to tickle their ears. For it is best to keep within the bounds of what is edifying. It would be childish to heap up all the details (on which many philosophize), for it was not at all God's purpose to include a mystery in each hook and loop. Even if every part contained its mystical sense (*mystico sensu*) – which no sane man would admit – it is still better to confess ignorance than play parlour guessing games (*frivolis divinationibus ludere*). A good master to teach us sobriety is the author of the Epistle to the Hebrews. Although he sets out to show an analogy between the shadows of the Law and the truth revealed in Christ, he only touches on the chief points, and that sparingly. By this moderate procedure he holds us back from over-much enquiry and deep speculations.'[86] On Gen. 49.1ff: 'Interpreters have seen that this prophecy was noble and magnificent, and thought it needed further adornment with some new mysteries. So it was that, in struggling to drag out profound allegories, they departed from the genuine sense of the words and by their own inventions corrupted everything that was intended for the solid edification of the godly. But if the literal sense is not to become base in our eyes as not containing sufficiently profound speculations, we must observe the purpose of the Holy Spirit'.[87] And he goes on to interpret the passage in a literal sense, by a 'simple treatment'(*simplex tractatio*), to show that what it says is very well worth knowing. Yet more impressively on Dan. 10.5-6: 'I have left the allegory aside here, as in the whole verse. I know that allegories are plausible; but when we reverently ponder what the Holy Spirit teaches, those speculations vanish away which pleased us much at first sight. I am not taken in these snares, and I would wish everyone to be persuaded that the best thing is to treat Scripture soberly and not bring subtle and very alien meanings to it. The sense will, as I said, flow of its own accord when the thing itself is pondered better'.[88]

The definitive point in these quotations is not the obvious one of sobriety and moderation being opposed to guessing games and

[86] Ex 26.1ff. OC 24,415; CTS Mo 2,172-3.
[87] Gen 49.1ff. OC 23,590; CTS Gen 2,439.
[88] OC 41,199; CTS Dan 2,242.

speculations, but the use of the word 'analogy' in the first, with the fleeting reminder that we are in the context of *umbra-veritas*, the use of 'genuine sense', 'literal sense', and 'the purpose of the Holy Spirit', in the second, and the use of 'the Holy Spirit teaches', 'alien meanings', and 'The sense will flow of its own accord', in the third. The literal sense is that "dictated" by God himself; give the literal sense a chance, learn from it what God intended in general, and then it will all come together and of its own accord make excellent sense.

This does not mean that Calvin disregarded the use of words or events as signs and symbols and *suppositiones* or substitutes. We find him on occasions accepting an "allegorical" interpretation, so long as it is kept simple: 'I rather like the allegory which Ambrose introduced on this passage'.[89] 'Some may like the thought that chewing the cud is a symbol of internal purity and the cloven hoof of external, and this is perhaps the probable meaning (*sententia*). I mention this distinction which came to my mind, so that, although I myself do not delight in clever speculations, the reader may choose it or not as he will'.[90] Indeed, this latter quotation is part of a much longer one which we shall come to later in this chapter.

To make this movement from the literal sense to another, Calvin uses *anagogē*, by which he understands, not the *anagogē* of the "four senses", but a transference or application of a Biblical person or event to some theological truth. *Anagogē* is not merely a comparison that happens to arise in the expositor's mind, but an application that is demanded by the letter of the text. 'And now we have to cross over (*transitum facere*) from the serpent to the author of evil himself; and this is not only a comparison but a true literal *anagogē*'.[91] Sometimes his use of the word comes close to *analogia* or similiarity, as in: 'We must hold that between us and the Israelites there is anagogē, or similiarity'[92]; but this does not alter its general use. The important element is that, if the Old Testament is allowed to stand in its own right and not be dissolved into time-less spirituality or even into Christianity, it is

[89] Gen 27.27 OC 23,378; CTS Gen 2,91.
[90] Lev 11.4. OC 24,349; CTS Mo 2,64.
[91] Gen 3.15. OC 23,70; CTS Gen 1,168.
[92] Ex 6.7. OC 24,80; CTS Mo 1,130.

inevitable that in the first instance it will have to be treated on its own; therefore, a certain gap will have to be bridged, a transference made. The bridge, the act of transference or application, is *anagogē*.

The following quotation shows Calvin criticizing an interpretation for the grounds on which it was advanced and then accepting that same interpretation if it were reached by *anagogē*. The passage in question is Dan. 8.24–25, which he treats at great length. By 'the rough goat' the Prophet means Antiochus, a fact which Calvin proves from an historical survey of Greece and the Middle East after Alexander. He becomes quite angry at the suggestion that Antichrist is intended: 'To twist so violently to Antichrist what any boy can see was spoken of Antiochus, where is it going to lead, except to the whole of Scripture losing its authority? . . . I desire the sacred oracles to be treated so reverently that no-one will introduce arbitrary variety but that all will hold to what is certain. I would prefer people to aim at adapting this prophecy to the present use of the Church and to transfer by *anagogē* (*per anagogen traducere*) to Antichrist what is here spoken of Antiochus. We know that whatever happened to the olden Church relates also to us, because we have come into the fulness of time . . . But, as I have already said, it seems frivolous to me to look for allegories. Let us be content with transferring (*transferamus*) to ourselves what happened to the olden people'.[93] A direct identification of the 'rough goat' with Antichrist is therefore a violent distortion of the passage; the indirect identification by *anagogē* is legitimate and proper. He goes on to expound the passage on these lines and concludes that 'this is a useful *anagogē* and does not twist the simple sense of Scripture'.[94]

The actual use of the word *anagogē* occurs fairly often in these expositions, but the method is so common that, under the form of the application of the passage, we may meet it several times a page. By using this method of interpretation Calvin is being faithful to his view of the relationship between the two Testaments: the substance of the Testaments is one and the same; only they differ in form. Were the substance not one and the same, it would be impossible to make the transference by *anagogē*;

93 OC 41,121; CTS Dan 2,129.
94 OC 41,122; CTS Dan 2,131.

we could only compare and contrast. If the form were the same, there would be no need for a transference. The form is, not the text of the passage, but what the passage means according to its literal sense. *Anagogē* is demanded by the difference, justified by the unity. If we express the relationship in terms of the two metaphors, shadow-body and childhood-adulthood, then it is easy to see that *anagogē* is, so to say, the hyphen separating and connecting each.

It will not be improper to ask, as a last word on *anagogē*, whether this is not the *sensus spiritualis*, *sensus mysticus*, under another name, so that what Calvin was doing was admitting the spiritual sense in such a way as to safeguard the historicity of the text – the historicity which was as good as dissolved by arbitrary spiritualising. In the following passage on Gen. 15.11 it is hard to see much difference between his comments and "allegory": *And the fowls came down upon the carcases, and Abram drove them away.* Calvin's whole comment is an application without reference to the history: 'Although the sacrifice had been dedicated to God, it was not immune from the attack and violence of the birds. For after believers have been received into the care of God they are not so covered by his hand as to cease to be assailed on every side. Satan and the world do not give up molesting them. Therefore, that the sacrifice we have once offered to God may remain pure and unharmed and not be violated, attacks against it must be driven away, but this will be with trouble and striving.'[95]

From *anagogē* we move to types and figures. The history of the Jews was not only a preparation for the coming of Christ; it was also a deliberate pre-enactment of him and his work. Certain persons and institutions were types or figures or images (he uses the words interchangeably). But when we say that they were types of Christ, this is a generalization for the whole new Covenant in Christ. Some things were types of Christ himself, some of the Holy Spirit of Christ, some of the Gospel, which can never be separated from Christ, some of the Church, which, as the Body, can never be separated from the Head. A type is not for Calvin an accidental resemblance between the two Covenants, but something deliberately set up by God's providence to pre-enact the Incarnate Christ, and thus to stand for Christ and

[95] OC 23,217; CTS Gen 1,414.

stand for him effectually. This does not mean that the historical entity had no reality of its own. The types were real people or events with their own history. The institutions were no less actual than all other human institutions. But the primary – not the secondary but the primary – meaning of those people's lives and of the events and institutions is that they were types, figures, images of the Christ to come, of the Spirit, of the Gospel, of the Church, of the new Covenant. He expressly says, 'David. was created king, not so much for his own sake, as to be the image of the Redeemer'.[96]

There can be no question of a commentator having the right to invent types arbitrarily. All he can do is to recognize types that have been already set up by God and thus recorded as such in Holy Scripture. Here we may work either from the Old to the New Testament, or from the New to the Old. Inasmuch as Christ is the end, or goal, of the Law, it follows that the Law must lead to Christ. Hence the Law, that is, the religious system, with its priesthood and ceremonies, its sacred kingship settled on David and his line, and the prophetic office which interpreted the whole system, is to be understood of Christ, not merely preparatively, for this would not do justice to the unity of substance, but both preparatively and also effectually. Or one can work backwards from Christ. The New Testament bears witness to him as the High Priest of his people and the sacrifice for his people, as the King sprung from David's line, and as the Prophet. Hence the Old Testament religious system was, so to say, a reflection of his light, so that all the power and efficacy it had were borrowed from him. More, they corresponded to him as the image on a coin corresponds to the pattern of the die that stamps it. They were types or images or anti-types of the primal pattern, Jesus Christ.

As we should expect, Calvin is cautious in his typology. Israel is the Church; Moses the Prophet corresponds to Christ; the Passover and the Pascal Lamb are types of the Lord's Supper; the seven-branched candlestick and the pure olive-oil for the lamp are figures of the Holy Spirit; the Tabernacle is the type of the Church. Beyond these broad relations and their explanations lie the over-elaborated likenesses which he called "allegories". Thus some interpretations of Ex. 26, with its precise details on the fabric

[96] Ps 2.1ff. OC 31,43; CTS Ps 1,11; CP 1,32.

and making of the Tabernacle (vv. 14 & 23, *And thou shalt make a covering for the tent of rams' skins dyed red, and a covering above of badgers' skins . . . And two boards shalt thou make for the corners of the tabernacle*) provoke him to satire: 'Many may be pleased by the allegory that the two bases meant the Old and New Testament, or the two natures of Christ, because believers rest on these two separate supports. With no less probability we might say that the two bases stood for the two Tables, either because godliness has the promises of the present and the future life, or because we must resist on both sides the temptations which assail us on the right or the left, or because faith must not limp or turn to the right or the left. There is no end to such nonsense. They allegorically expound the covering of the Tabernacle by rams' skins as the Church being protected by the blood of Christ, who is the spotless lamb. But I ask, what do badgers' skins, which were added, mean? Soberness is more profitable'.[97] Calvin's own treatment of the passage is restrained and practical.

The next verse to be expounded is v. 31, *And thou shalt make a veil*. Here his manner abruptly changes. After an initial statement that the veil taught the Israelites reverence before God's majesty, he explains it as 'the obscurity of the shadows of the Law (*legalium umbrarum obscuritas*)',[98] which taught the Jews to look forward to the revelation of the Messiah. He therefore takes us into the New Testament, to *the veil of the Temple was rent in twain*,[99] *the veil was taken away*,[100] and to *he spoke of the Temple of his body*,[101] ending on the note that although the Temple and the veil no longer exist, this still contains a truth for us, teaching us that the very revelation of God in the flesh 'is a hidden and incomprehensible mystery', as I Timothy 3.16 says (*great is the mystery of godliness*).

Very occasionally, however, he himself will pursue typology into allegory. Lev.11.2ff. (*These are the animals which ye shall eat among all the animals which are on the earth: whatsoever parteth the hoof and is cloven-footed, and cheweth the cud, among the animals, that shall ye eat*) gives rise to these comments: 'although, I am afraid, there

[97] OC 24,416–7; CTS Mo 2,175.
[98] OC 24,417; CTS Mo 2,175–6.
[99] Matt 27.51.
[100] II Cor 3.16.
[101] Jn 2.21.

is little solidity in allegories, I neither attack nor reject one that has been handed down from the early writers, that by parting the hoof is meant wisdom (*prudentia*) in understanding (*diiudicandos* – "distinguishing") the mysteries of Scripture and by chewing the cud, serious meditation on the heavenly teaching. I do not like their subtlety when they add that those rightly distinguish who know how to elicit the mystical sense from the literal ... I embrace a simpler view, that there is no dividing [*fissuram* i.e. "parting" – the hoof] in anyone who favours the mind of the flesh; for only the spiritual man judges all things, as St Paul says (I Cor. 2.15). The chewing of the cud belongs to preparing and distributing digestively the spiritual food; for many gulp down the Scripture without any profit . . . Therefore under the first clause is condemned brute-like stupor, under the second the ambition and levity of the inquisitive'.[102] This play on the idea of parting or dividing or distinguishing reads more like one of Miss Beryl Smalley's commentators from the earlier Middle Ages than the man who has said 'Soberness is more profitable'. But, as I say, such departures from his norm are very rare.

Even when he is drawing out and explaining a type, he usually continues to expound the passage in its Old Testament context, whereas a parallel passage in the New Testament will be treated with theological openness. We may illustrate this by comparing I Cor. 10.1–4 with the relevant passages in the Pentateuch on the pillar of cloud, the passing through the Red Sea, the eating of manna, and drinking of water from the rock.

In his commentary on I Cor. 10, Calvin is led by the context to insist on the parallels between the Israelites and the Christian Church: 'They were given the same benefits that we enjoy today. There was then the same Church of God as is today among us. They had the same Sacraments, which were testimonies to them of God's grace'.[103] 'The same Sacraments?' Yes, for they had Baptism and the Holy Supper, but under different forms from those that we know. 'He treats first of Baptism and teaches that the cloud which protected the Israelites from the hot sun in the desert and also guided their course, and the crossing of the sea, were equivalent to Baptism for them. In the manna and the water

102 OC 24,347; CTS Mo 2,61-2.
103 OC 49,451; CTS Cor 1,312; CC I Cor 200.

flowing from the rock he says there was a Sacrament corresponding to the Holy Supper'.[104] But these in themselves were all
purely earthly benefits. Why did Paul call them Sacraments?
Because God's main purpose did not lie in the bestowal of earthly
benefits but in declaring by means of them that he was Israel's
God. In this declaration is included eternal salvation. For when
God makes himself one with his people and his people one with
himself, they are blessed with eternal life. Hence, these events and
ordinances were Sacraments and corresponded to Baptism and
the Lord's Supper.

What is more, these Sacraments were efficacious to them just
as they are to us. The only difference is one of degree, that our
Sacraments are clearer in meaning and fuller in content. But the
efficacy was the same, in that the Sacraments brought them
Christ, just as they do to us. But how could the Israelites be
partakers of the Body and Blood of Christ when he had not yet
taken flesh? Calvin replies, not with reasoning but simply with a
firm statement: 'The flesh which did not yet exist was
nevertheless food for them. And this is no empty and clever
sophistry. Their salvation depended on the benefit of his death
and resurrection, and therefore on the Body and Blood of Christ.
Therefore they had to receive the Body and Blood of Christ that
they might share in the benefit of redemption. And this receiving
was the secret work of the Holy Spirit, who so worked that the
flesh of Christ, although not yet created, should be efficacious for
them'.[105] Their mode of "eating" Christ was different from ours
and we now have a fuller measure of revelation.

This is the full and direct theological discussion in I
Corinthians of the cloud, the passage of the Red Sea, the manna,
and the water from the rock. Now let us see how he deals with
these Sacraments in their original setting in the Pentateuch.

The pillar of cloud and fire is indeed treated sacramentally in
Ex. 13.21[106]. God had redeeemed his people; now he was their
constant leader and guide. He could have guided them and
protected them from the sun in some other way, but he chose to
be with them visibly, that is, in these visible forms. And this is a

[104] OC 49,451-2; CTS Cor 1,313; CC I Cor 200-1.
[105] OC 49,455; CTS Cor 1,319-20; CC I Cor 205.
[106] OC 24,145f.; CTS Mo 1,236f.

sacramental manner of speaking – here Calvin explains the relation of the sign and the thing signified in the Sacrament. The cloud and the fire were not God but were symbols by means of which God was present. And when we are talking of the presence of God, it is the presence of Christ, for God led the Israelites 'by the hand of his only-begotten Son'.[107] What was true for them is true for us now; God extends the same blessing and guidance to us as to them, but without the visible symbol, which was only temporary.

The crossing of the Red Sea (Ex.14.19ff.)[108], however, is treated almost purely as history. It is true that Calvin makes clear at the beginning that the Angel, 'the leader of the people, was God's only-begotten Son, who afterwards was manifested in the flesh,'[109] and he refers to I Cor.10.4. But after this, in Ex.14 or in the Song of Moses, Ex.15,[110] nothing at all about the typical meaning of the events, nothing of Baptism.

Ex.16[111] contains the account of the providing of manna. Here again Calvin's main point of interest is the explanation of the story. What had the children of Israel been living on before this? Some say this and some say that. My own opinion is that they had not yet been in the really barren desert and had lived on fruits and herbs. But now they are in the desert and are hungry. Instead of praying to God, as they should have done, they become seditious and quarrel with Moses. The result is that 'God fed this wretched people with the heavenly bread',[112] using the phrase of Psalm 78.24. St Paul calls it 'spiritual meat', 'because it was a type of the flesh of Christ which feeds our souls unto the hope of everlasting life'.[113] But Calvin at once added 'But the Prophet [Moses] does not mention that mystery'. Therefore Calvin also, following the mind of his author, did not mention it again but confined himself to a reconstruction and explanation of the narrative, discussing what manna was, what the word was derived from, and so on. At

[107] OC 24,145; CTS Mo 1,236.
[108] OC 24,153f.; CTS Mo 1,248ff.
[109] OC 24,153; CTS Mo 1,248.
[110] OC 24,157ff.; CTS Mo 1,255ff.
[111] OC 24,165ff.; CTS Mo 1,268ff.
[112] OC 24,166; CTS Mo 1,270.
[113] OC 24,166; CTS Mo 1,270.

one point, on Paul's application of sharing the manna to almsgiving (II Cor. 8.14), he was led away from the narrative into a defence of private possession as against the 'mutual communication of property', and, on the other side, of the equitable distribution of wealth and food. The typological exposition has taken up ten lines out of four hundred and seventy in the edition I use.

Ex. 17.1-7[114] tells the story of Moses striking the rock with his rod to give the people water. We need not recite all the details, but again the emphasis is the same, a full explanation of the narrative with only one mention of St Paul's typological use of it: 'God set out a wonderful example of his goodness in it, that he not only gave them drink for the refreshing of their bodies but also deemed their souls worthy of spiritual drink, for Paul testified that the rock was Christ, and therefore he compared the water which flowed from it to the cup of the Holy Supper'.[115] The main message both here and in the story of the manna is the goodness and constancy of the Lord and the perversity and ingratitude of the people.

The difference between Calvin's treatment of the same subject in the two Testaments is plain and is to be attributed to the fact that he binds and confines himself to the conditions of the respective authors and their subjects. This is another way of saying that he faithfully observes the context. At its simplest, observance of the context means that any sentence or shorter unit must be understood according to the sense of the passage in which it occurs and any passage according to the sense of the whole document. But it goes further than this. The document itself must be understood in its own context. The Pentateuch and Daniel have to be interpreted according to their very different historical contexts. The fact that, for Calvin, both were equally the Word of God, equally inspired by the same Holy Spirit, makes no difference in this respect. For it is evident that he did not see inspiration or even dictation as destroying the individual writer's characteristics and style, far less as creating a timeless teaching in an impossible historical vacuum.

[114] OC 24,175ff.; CTS Mo 1,285ff.
[115] OC 24,178; CTS Mo 1,289-90.

Respect for the context does not impair the unity of Scripture. On the contrary, the unity is enhanced and made more visible; for the context of any single book is the rest of the Holy Scripture. No book can be interpreted as if it stood outside the Bible. That certain books belong together historically is demonstrably true – the Synoptic Gospels, for example, or the books of Samuel, Kings and Chronicles. But that I Corinthians and Ruth form a unity and are part of a larger unity rests on the belief that each is the word of God and witnesses in its own way to the Word made flesh. In its widest sense context means the whole of Scripture.

But there is another aspect of context which is decisive for the understanding of Calvin's Old Testament work. It lies in his statement on the task of the commentator. Almost his only duty, he says in the dedicatory preface to Romans, is to lay bare the mind of the author.[116] The expression *mens authoris* seems to occur less often in the Old Testament expositions than in the New. In its place comes the near synonym *consilium*, "purpose". For example, 'We must note the Prophet's *consilium*, which interpreters have strayed from'.[117] And it is common for him to sum up discussion of a verse with 'We now see the *consilium* of the Prophet'. The application of this principle of concentrating on the mind or purpose of the author to the Old Testament writers leads to Calvin's sober, apparently indirect manner of interpretation. All the Old Testament writers lived in the obscurity and shadow which was to be dispersed only after their deaths by the rising of the Sun of righteousness. They lived by faith and hope, not by sight and possession. The commentator who would faithfully lay bare their minds and purpose must accept their limitations and conditions, even to the extent of making these his own for the time being. Calvin therefore takes the men of the Old Covenant as they were, men of the twilight, men who lived under and taught a figurative religion, obscure and incomplete; yet men who looked forward with unconquerable hope to a mysterious reality. By taking them as they were, his exposition in turn was conditioned and limited by their conditions and limitations.

[116] Ep. ad Rom. p. 1 see *Calvin's NT Commentaries*, pp. 54ff.
[117] Jer 7.4. OC 37,673; CTS Jer 1,364.

Calvin knew that the Mediator had come. But if he had put into the minds of the Old Testament authors all that he himself knew from the New Testament and fifteen hundred years of New Testament exposition, he could not have been a faithful interpreter of *their* minds and intentions.

Chapter Three

The Exposition of History

1 The Church in its childhood

Our task in this chapter is to investigate Calvin's treatment of Old Testament history. We shall want to see how he handles narrative and character and, that which makes the Old Testament unique, the Divine history which gives meaning and direction to the human history. But we must first mark out our way; and this is not at all easy to do in such a way as to be faithful to Calvin. Could we, for example, model the chapter, or parts of it, on the image which we discussed in Chapter 2, shadow-body? Should we be able, perhaps, to see the history unfolding and the "shadow" gradually giving place to the "body" or the "light"? If we tried to do this, we should soon find our exposition becoming forced and artificial. There is more to be said for the image of childhood, for here Calvin made a definite historical division. The period before the Incarnation 'was the *Ecclesiae pueritia*, the childhood of the Church: but now, from the time of Christ's advent, it has grown up and in a sense arrived at manhood'.[1]

The Old Testament is the book that recounts and describes the childhood and growing up of the Church. But more precisely, since this was no sailing a calm sea in halcyon days, it recounts and describes the way in which God preserved his Church in the midst of disasters and persecutions. It is this theme that runs through all Calvin's exposition of the Old Testament. The concept of Covenant is vital, certainly, and we could well have made this our starting point and guiding line, if it were not that the period before the Covenant with Abraham would have been left on its own, Calvin not treating the creation in terms of covenant.

[1] Gal 4.1 OC 50,225; CTS Gal 115; CC Gal 71.

83

Moreover, important as the Covenant is in Calvin's expositions of Old Testament history and in his theology generally, he did not make it into a basic and all-embracing doctrine, as did seventeenth century Calvinist scholasticism with its *Summa Doctrinae de Foedere et Testamentis Dei* (Cocceius) or *Oeconomia Foederum* (Witsius) and the rest. There is, for example, no chapter in the *Institutio* devoted to the doctrine, and the word *foedus* itself does not occur in any chapter heading, although we have *testamenti* in II. x and xi as synonyms for it. Apart from Gen. 9.8ff., Calvin keeps the concept of covenant for the Covenant with Abraham and his descendants, and therefore for the calling into being of the Church. The Covenant with 'Noah and his seed' was made with all living creatures of whom Noah was the representative; first, with Noah and his immediate family, secondly, with all Noah's descendants to the end of time, and thirdly it embraced all the non-human living creatures.[2]

But the Covenant we have to consider is that made with Abraham, first in Gen. 12.1ff., where Calvin stresses God's love and the intimacy of the Covenant relationship: 'Here God's wonderful kindness is shown, that he makes a familiar pact with Abram, as men do with their associates and equals. For it is a solemn covenant-formula between kings and others to promise to have the same enemies and friends. It was indeed an inestimable pledge of a rare love that God should so abase himself, and that for our sake'.[3] On this passage Calvin does not explicitly speak of the birth of the Church, but, following his text and linking it with Gal. 3.17, understands from it that 'the Covenant of salvation which God made with Abram is only steadfast and firm in Christ. I therefore interpret the present passage as meaning that God promised to his servant Abram a promise which should afterwards flow and stream to all peoples'.[4]

The exposition of the renewal of the Covenant in Gen. 17.1ff., however, after saying that it was two-sided ('The first part was the testimony of gratuitous love, with the promise of life joined to it. The second was an exhortation to cultivate sincere

[2] OC 23,147-8; CTS Gen 1,297.
[3] OC 23,177; CTS Gen 1,347-8.
[4] OC 23,178; CTS Gen 1,349.

righteousness'),[5] goes on in v. 7 to distinguish between the different stages of adoption to Covenant relationship. In one sense, all the physical descendants of Abraham are included in the adoption. In another, only the elect, that is, 'the children of promise' (Rom. 9.8), are adopted. 'In the beginning, before the Covenant, the state of the whole world was one and the same. But when it was said, "I will be God to thee and to thy seed after thee", the Church was divided off from the rest of the nations, just as at the creation of the world light emerged out of darkness. So the people of Israel was received into their own fold as the flock of God, and the rest of the nations wandered about in mountains and woods and deserts like wild animals'.[6] Israel as a whole was therefore the Church of God, the promise was made to all the people indiscriminately. But Calvin distinguishes at this point between the promise offered and the promise believed and received, between external and inward grace, and therefore makes a distinction within Israel between faith and unbelief, the true and the illegitimate sons.

This, in its turn, brings us to adoption and rejection, in fact, to God's choice and election of his true Church, the invisible Israel, so to say, within the visible Israel. These are "the remnant" spoken of by the Prophets. The Covenant in this sense was not made with all the physical descendants of Abraham but, as a Covenant of grace, only with those whom God had eternally chosen. The rest, whether descendants of Abraham or Gentiles, were deservedly cast off and rejected, having no part among God's people and denied the hope of everlasting life. The human race was kept in being for the sake of the Church: 'The whole span of the history in Genesis points towards mankind being preserved by God but in such a way that he may show his peculiar care for the Church'.[7] Nevertheless, after all mankind apart from the Church (Noah and his family) had perished in the Flood, the Covenant which God made with his people contained a blessing and a promise of Divine preservation to all men: 'It was not therefore a private Covenant made with a single family, but one

[5] OC 23,235; CTS Gen 1,444.
[6] OC 23,237; CTS Gen 1,448.
[7] OC 23,11-2; CTS Gen 1,64.

common to all people, and which will flourish in all ages to the end of the world'.[8]

This is the theme that runs through the *Argumenta* of *Genesis*, the *Mosaic*, and *Joshua* and the beginning of the *Homilia* on I Samuel. The early part of that in *Genesis* treats of the believer's knowledge of God in creation; but this is only the beginning, for the story soon turns to man's sin, that 'he fell by his own fault' and so was deprived of the blessings he had been given. But God had compassion on him and restored him 'through the benefit of Christ'.[9] At once the Church enters, for God's purpose was 'that there should always be an assembly on earth which was adopted in the hope of the heavenly life, and might worship God in this confidence'.[10] Later he says: 'From this point [i.e. man's restoration after the Fall] Moses not only narrates continuously the unique providence of God in governing and guarding the Church, but also commends to us the true worship of God, teaches wherein man's salvation lies, and exhorts us, from the example of the fathers, to steadfast perseverence in bearing the cross. Whoever, then, wishes to profit from this book, let him turn his mind to these main topics (*capita*) . . . Therefore, the perpetual succession of the Church has flowed from this fountain, that the holy fathers, one after another, embracing by faith the offered promise, were gathered into the family of God, to have a common life in Christ'.[11] The rest of this *Argumentum* follows the same line of thought, as also does the Dedication.

The *Argumentum* to the *Mosaic* tells us that there is a twofold use to be made of it; on the one hand a message of encouragement and hope, 'for the deliverance of the ancient people is a bright mirror of God's incomparable power and boundless mercy in raising up and as it were begetting the Church'.[12] On the other hand, terrible warnings; and we must apply to the deceivers of our own day what happened to the hypocrites among the Jews. Although this is all that he says on this head, it is the guiding line in his exposition of the narrative in the commentary.

[8] Gen 9.8. OC 23,148; CTS Gen 1,297.
[9] OC 23,11-2; CTS Gen 1,64.
[10] OC 23,11-2; CTS Gen 1,64.
[11] OC 23,11-2; CTS Gen 1,65.
[12] OC 24,5-6; CTS Mo 1,xv.

The *Argumentum* to *Joshua* dwells on the weakness and disillusionment of the people when they at last reached and entered the promised land. 'The Covenant of God seemed to be obscured in a sort of eclipse'.[13] But 'the failure reminded the children of God to look forward to a more excellent state, in which God's grace would be clearer, nay, would prove stronger than everything in its path and shine at its brightest. Hence by being raised up to Christ they learned that the perfect felicity of the Church depends on its Head'.[14] It was, however, going to be a long time before 'the state of the Church was properly settled, when in the person of David the image (*effigies*) of the Mediator in whom the perfect felicity of the Church rests, was set before the eyes of the people'.[15]

The first sermon on I Samuel (the set extant only in Latin) summarizes the history from Exodus to I Samuel. It is true, Calvin says, that God daily shows his beneficence to all men, but 'in a special way towards his Church, which is the house of God'.[16] After the Exodus and the settlement in Canaan God raised up, 'in most difficult times', judges to care for the people and maintain peace until at last Saul was elected king. Calvin is following Paul's sermon at Antioch in Pisidia, (Acts 13.14ff.) that God first chose Abraham and his seed, then gave the people judges until the time of Samuel, when Saul was chosen and afterwards replaced by David – 'the kingdom was kept in the family of David until the promised Redeemer should come, our Lord Jesus Christ',[17] who was given when the people returned from captivity. (This particular idea will be considered more thoroughly in the chapter on the Prophets).

Because the birth, growth, and preservation of the Church is the constant theme of Calvin's expositions of Old Testament history, the doctrines of predestination and providence, and particularly the latter, have a large part to play. Predestination, in that the Church is composed of those whom God has chosen to be his people. The eternity of the choice, the number of the elect, and

---

[13] OC 25,423-4; CTS Josh xxii.
[14] OC 25,423-4; CTS Josh xxii.
[15] OC 25,423-6; CTS Josh xxii.
[16] OC 29,241.
[17] OC 29,242.

the hidden will of God are not to the fore, at least in the expositions of narrative. Whereas a verse like Mal. 1.2-3 (*Was not Esau Jacob's brother? says the Lord; and I loved Jacob, and Esau I hated*) will provide a whole lecture asserting the doctrine of predestination uncompromisingly,[18] a different line will be taken on the accounts of the promise to Abraham or the birth of Esau and Jacob. God's covenant with Abraham's seed (Gen. 17.7) does not refer to the elect in the sense of the faithful of whatever race but to the physical descendants of Abraham, for whom Christ came as a minister, according to St Paul in Rom. 15.8. Calvin stressed the word "naturally". 'Nothing is more certain than that God made his Covenant with the children of Abraham – those who would be born of him naturally'.[19] He proceeds, as we have seen, to distinguish between stages of adoption and so moves on to prove his point from the New Testament: 'If Paul deprives the Gentiles of God and eternal life on the ground of being strangers to the Covenant, it follows that all the Israelites were the household of the Church and sons of God and heirs of eternal life . . . In Gal. 2.15 and elsewhere Paul calls them saints naturally, because God willed that his grace should continue towards the whole seed without cessation (*continua serie*). In this sense even the unbelieving Jews are called children of the heavenly kingdom by Christ (Matt. 8.12)'.[20]

Calvin certainly seems to be going very far. What of Rom. 9.8? – *They which are the children of the flesh, these are not the children of God: but the children of the promise are counted for the seed.* We must distinguish between the verbal promise which was common to all and the inward calling of the Holy Spirit. Many hear the verbal promise (the outward word of preaching) without believing it. 'Here, then, a twofold order of sons in the Church emerges. Since the whole body of the people is gathered together into God's fold by one and the same voice, all without exception are in these respects regarded as children, and the name of "Church" belongs to them all in common. But in God's secret sanctuary [i.e. the unrevealed will of God] only they are reckoned sons of God in

[18] OC 44,401-9; CTS Mi 5,471-82.
[19] OC 23,237; CTS Gen 1,447-8.
[20] OC 23,237; CTS Gen 1,448.

whom the promise is confirmed by faith'.[21] It is noteworthy, however, that at this point Calvin does not ask the question as to why it is that some believe the external call and some do not (the question which formed the starting-point in predestination for both Augustine and himself) and kept firmly to the pragmatic distinction of faith and unbelief. 'Although the difference flows from the fountain of free election, from which faith also springs, yet, since the counsel of God is in itself hidden from us, we distinguish the true from the illegitimate children by the marks of faith and unbelief'.[22]

The same argument runs through the exposition of Gen. 25.23: *Then the Lord said unto her, Two nations are in thy womb, and two peoples shall be separated from thy belly, and people shall be stronger than people, and the elder shall serve the younger.* It looks as if the promise "to thy seed" embraced the whole race originally. But here we find a distinction made within Abraham's family, so that of twins one child was chosen, the other rejected. Isaac and Rebekah were taught by the Lord's words 'that the Covenant of salvation would not be common to the two peoples but would be kept only to the posterity of Jacob . . . God divides the seed of Jacob [*read* Isaac] . . . and adopts the one part and rejects the other; the one part obtains the name and right of "Church", the rest are reckoned as foreigners; with one part resides the blessing, of which the other is deprived'.[23] Here also Calvin puts away discussion of predestination and distinguishes between adoption, at least as used in the present context, and election. 'When an entire people is under discussion, it is not the secret election confirmed to a few, but the common adoption which extends as widely as the external preaching of the Word which is denoted . . . God therefore chose the whole seed of Jacob without exception, as Scripture testifies in many places; for he has conferred on all alike the same testimonies of his grace, that is, in the Word and Sacraments. But another and peculiar election has always flourished, which was contained in a certain and limited number of men, in order that in the common destruction, God

[21] OC 23,238; CTS Gen 1,449.
[22] OC 23,238; CTS Gen 1,449.
[23] OC 23,349; CTS Gen 2,44.

might save whom he would'.[24] The reason why God chose
Abraham and his seed and then, rejecting Esau, chose Jacob and
his seed, was that he 'might have a Church, separated from the
rest of the world.'[25]

Old Testament history, as seen in Calvin's expositions, is
therefore the story of the children of Israel, adopted to be the
Church and so separated from all other peoples, on the one hand
persecuted and afflicted but yet preserved by the hand of God, and
on the other hand at conflict within themselves, in that a remnant
is faithful while the majority are "hypocrites" – by which is meant
in the present context those who were members of the Church
outwardly but not at heart. Even when Calvin's exposition of
narrative is at its most matter of fact, the preservation and
well–being of the Church must always be presupposed.

If in this sense predestination is prominent, even more
pervasive is the doctrine of providence, the activity of God in the
world. By the laws of creation that he has set up and continually
maintains, or apart from those laws, by means or immediately, in
secret ways or openly, God is continually and continuously active
in his world, both for the welfare of his creation and especially for
the safety of the Church. It is for the preservation of the Church
that Joseph is sold into Egypt, pestered by Potiphar's wife, put
into prison for over two years (but 'the Lord went to prison with
him, to uphold him with his strength');[26] in all this we can see 'the
winding course of Divine providence'.[27] And so through all the
long history, empires grow up and are destroyed, the Israelite and
Jewish monarchs pursue this or that policy which results in this or
that state of affairs; but nothing happens by chance, nothing by
simple cause and effect, all is the incredibly complex working of
God's secret providence on behalf of the Church.

2 Narrative

It has been necessary to emphasize the central point of Calvin's
understanding of the Old Testament history precisely because it is
so often, in the exposition of the narrative, left unsaid, He believes

[24] OC 23,350; CTS Gen 2,45.
[25] OC 23,351; CTS Gen 2,47.
[26] OC 23,510; CTS Gen 2,305.
[27] OC 23,518; CTS Gen 2,318.

that all the actions, words, and thoughts of men are determined by God in order to bring his will to pass; but in the main he treats narrative as if it were purely an account of man's self-moving activities.

And indeed, we find Calvin in his element here. There seems to be nothing he enjoyed more than re-constructing from the document the course of events, filling in the missing connections in a narrative, investigating the springs of character, working out motives of behaviour, relating Biblical history to what he knew of ancient history in general, understanding the past by his experience of the present and from his reading.

Few expressions meet us so often as "probable" and "we may conjecture"; for Calvin is well aware that the detailed exposition of an ancient document in a foreign tongue rests to a large degree on choosing the most likely of possible interpretations. Thus he will supply a reason for a baldly stated action in Gen. 19.27: *And Abraham rose up early in the morning to the place where he stood before Jehovah.* Abraham comes to a place where he can see what God has done to the cities of the plain. Does this suggest that Abraham doubted the truth of what God had told him and wanted to verify it by his own senses? No; rather he was seeking confirmation, as an eye-witness, of what he already believed. Besides this, he must have been in deep anxiety all night about the safety of Lot. 'Whether he was re-assured we do not know. I rather incline to the conjecture that he was anxious about him. And it is possible that, halting between hope and fear, he went forward to meet him, to see whether he was delivered or not'.[28]

In Exod. 12.37 we are told that *the children of Israel journeyed from Rameses to Succoth,* which suggests that the whole people lived in that city. Here Calvin admits a sociological probability but prefers a theological and contextual explanation: 'It is probable that they were more widely dispersed, since that region could not have held so great a multitude, especially as the Egyptians lived there too. Yet the memory of the promise was still alive and from it some hope of redemption always remained among them. So it would not be surprising if they preferred to be kept within narrow bounds at great inconvenience rather than to

[28] OC 23,279-80; CTS Gen 1,515ff.

look for somewhere else to live and so separate from the body. That this was the proper abode of the nation appears also from what has gone before'.[29]

In Josh. 3.6, all that Joshua said to the priests was, *Take the ark of the covenant, and go over before the people.* But Calvin cannot accept that the Priests, ignorant of what was toward, were suddenly given the apparently absurd command to walk through a deep river. 'It is probable that the Priests were told why God wished the ark to go first, that they might be the more ready to execute the command. For the whole people is at once told of the division of the waters. As the prefects had already declared in the camp that the people were to follow the Ark of the Covenant, the Priests could not possibly be ignorant of the office they were to perform'.[30]

Gen. 25.1 says that Abraham (Sarah's death having been recorded in Gen. 23.2) took a new wife and had other children by her: 'It seems quite absurd', says Calvin, 'that Abraham, who was said to be dead in his body thirty-eight years before the death of Sarah, should take another wife after her death. Such an act was certainly unworthy of his gravity . . . Therefore Abraham acted foolishly, if, as a widower, he married again in the decrepitude of old age. Further, it contradicts Paul's statement that in his hundredth year he was impotent and sterile, if he should beget many sons forty years later'.[31] Some suppose that Keturah and Hagar were the same woman; but the context refutes this conjecture. 'Others conjecture that he took a second wife while Sarah was still alive. This, although deserving grave censure, is not unbelievable. We know it is common for men to be made bold by excessive license; so that when Abraham had once transgressed the law of marriage, he perhaps did not, after the quarrel over Hagar, cease from practising polygamy. It is also probable that his mind had been wounded by the divorce from Hagar which Sarah had forced on him. It was, of course, infamous in this holy patriarch, or at the least improper.

[29] OC 24,139; CTS Mo 1,227.
[30] OC 25,448; CTS Josh 60.
[31] OC 23,342-3; CTS Gen 2,32-3.

Nevertheless, no other of all the conjectures seems to me more probable'.[32]

The literary criticism into which Calvin is led by this story brings us to another aspect of his treatment of narrative. 'If we accept this conjecture, then the story is put in the wrong (*alieno*) place'.[33] We encounter this criticism in practically all his Old Testament expositions. That he does not make it a reason for blaming the writers and that he does not work it into his doctrine of the Word as Scripture, is because he views it, or professes to view it, as a deliberate rhetorical device: 'It is Moses' habit often to place earlier events in a different order . . . the fact itself shows ὕστερον πρότερον in this history'.[34] (Thomas Tymme, the first English translator of *Genesis*, rendered ὕστερον πρότερον as 'that is, a setting of the cart before the horse'). This excuse occurs often enough in the expositions; but it is hard to see just what artistic advantage Calvin thought Moses was deriving from adopting a device that needed such constant correction.

In *Genesis* Calvin kept the Biblical order of the text and was content merely to indicate within his exposition places that Moses had put out of chronological order. But the *Mosaic* is a different matter. There he not only drastically re-arranged the last four books of the Pentateuch but also printed the text according to his re-arrangement. In the chapter on the Law we shall see how he ordered the doctrinal and moral material to make what he called a harmony. Apart from that, however, he re-arranged the historical matter on the basis of chronological probability.

He was aware that he would incur the criticism that he was tampering with Holy Scripture and trying to improve on Moses, indeed, 'altering the order which the Holy Spirit himself has prescribed to us'.[35] He exculpates himself and explains his method in a preface. 'There cannot be any doubt that what was dictated to Moses was excellent in itself, and perfectly adapted for the instruction of the people. But what he delivered in four books it has been my endeavour so to gather together and arrange that it could seem, *prima facie* and before the matter was fully

[32] OC 23,343; CTS Gen 2,33.
[33] OC 23,343; CTS Gen 2,33.
[34] OC 23,343; CTS Gen 2,33.
[35] OC 24,5-6; CTS Mo 1,xiv.

considered, that I was trying to improve it, which would be an act of audacity close to sacrilege . . . But I have had no other intention by this arranging than to help unpractised readers to acquaint themselves profitably with the writings of Moses more easily and conveniently'.[36] He goes on to say that although the books consist of the two principal parts of narrative and doctrine, Moses himself 'does not observe this distinction, not even relating the history in a continuous form and delivering the doctrine unconnectedly, as opportunity occurred'.[37]

Following this plan, Calvin's re-arrangement is both radical and a masterpiece of organization or systematization. He makes Ex. 1-20. v. 21 a continuous narrative by omitting the three sets of Passover regulations (Ex. 12.1-20; 12.43-49; 13.1-16) and the Ten Commandments (Ex. 20.1-17). Deut. 1.9-18 is included as the parallel to Ex. 18.13-27, and Deut. 5.22-31 as the parallel to Ex. 20.18-21. This forms the first part of his commentary. The second part consists of the Law itself with the regulations on the priesthood, the sacrifices, and the ceremonies arranged systematically under the heading of each of the Commandments.

When he has completed his exposition of the Law, he takes up in the third part the thread of the history where he left it and follows it through to the end of the Pentateuch. But whereas he had left the historical order of Exod. 1-20 intact, he now moves backwards and forwards to construct a convincing narrative as follows:[38]

E 31.1-11	making of the Tabernacle
E 35.20-39.43	making of the Tabernacle
E 24.1-18	blessing the Tabernacle
E 31.18-32.6	Tables of testimony
E 32.7-34.10	worship of golden calf – Tabernacle outside the camp – God reveals himself to Moses – renewal of Tables of testimony
E 34.27-35 = D 9.7-21 + D 9.25-29 + D 10.1-5, 10-11	second giving of the Law

[36] OC 24,5-6; CTS Mo 1,xiv-xv.
[37] OC 24,5-6; CTS Mo 1,xv.
[38] E = Exodus; L = Leviticus; and so on. An equals sign (=) indicates a parallel passage. A plus sign (+) indicates that the passages are taken together, either in a harmony or consecutively.

E 40.1-35 + N 9.15-16	setting up of Tabernacle
E 7.1-89 + L 8.4-36	offerings of princes – consecration of Aaron and his sons
L 9.1-24	Aaron's sacrifice and blessing
N 8.20-22	purification of Levites
L 10.1-7	Nadab and Abihu offer strange fire
L 10.12-20	Sin of Eleazar and Ithamar
N 1.1-54 + D 10.8-9	census of people
N 2.1-4.3	connected narrative
N 4.21-23	service of Gershonites
N 4.29-30	sons of Merari
N 4.34-49	service of Kohathites
N 10.11-28	the journey to Paran
D 1.6-8	the command to continue
N 9.17-23 +	journeying
E 40.36-38	
N 10.29-36	departure of Hobab – the cloud
N 11.1-14.45	connected narrative
+ D 1.34-36, 39-46	
+ 9.22-24	
N 13.1-25 =	
D 1.19-25/N 14.1-9	
= D 1.26-33	
L 24.10-14	stonings
+ N 15.32-36	
N 16.1-17.13	connected narrative
N 20.14-22 = D 1.37-38	king of Edom
+ D 2.2-8	
N 20.23-29	Aaron's death
= N 33.38-39	
+ D 10.6-7	
N 21.1-27.11	connected narrative
N 21.1-3 = N 33.40/	
N 21.10-20	
= D 2.9-23/	
N 21.21-32	
= D 2.24-37/	
N 21.33-35 =	
D 3.1-11/N 25.10-18	
= D 4.3-4	
N 36.1-13	inheritance of daughters
N 31.1-34.29	connected narrative
N 32.28-42 =	
D 3.12-20, 4.41-43	
D 31.1-8 +	calling of Joshua
N 27.15-23	
= D 3.21-29, 4.21-22	
D 31.14-34.12	connected narrative
D 32.44-52 = N 27.12-14	

Calvin usually explains at each point the reason for his ordering of the material. His general plan is 'to follow the course (*contextum*) of the history until the end of Deuteronomy, where the death of Moses himself is related'.[39] Deuteronomy is not, until near the end, taken as the frame of the narrative; first it is Exod. 31–40 and then Numbers. But neither of these is followed through in its canonical order. When he skips from Ex. 31.11 to Ex. 35.20, he says: 'No-one need be put off by the change in narrative order. It is plain from innumerable places that Moses did not always keep to the chronological order. In this passage he seems to connect the people's fall with the previous commands about the construction of the Tabernacle and the rest of the worship of God. But I have shown by strong arguments that the people fell into idolatry before the Tabernacle was built. Therefore, Moses now supplies what he had earlier omitted. And in my care for simplicity (*facilitati*) I have kept to the thread of the history'.[40] Inversion of the narrative by Moses is the common reason, but occasionally (e.g. Lev. 24.10–14 + Num. 15.32–36) narratives are coupled because of their common theme. Leaving aside the passages arranged for the sake of systematization, it is clear that Calvin could not accept the historical order as given in the Canon but was unwilling to ascribe error to the author and was unaware of the possibility of much later redaction. He therefore took *hysteron-proteron* as his way out.

When we come to consider his treatment of factual matters, we find that he accepts every fact as true. What is recorded may need explanation, it may even need a certain moulding into what was acceptable to the sixteenth century mind, but of its factuality there could be no question. And indeed, improbability causes him no problems. He even goes out of his way to emphasize the improbability of some stories. We might say that the more improbable a story is, the better he is pleased. For Calvin's world was one in which God himself was present and active continuously, a world in which, although men had wills and could use them, God's will was done, a world in which God

---

[39] Ex 31.1. OC 25,57; CTS Mo 3,290.
[40] OC 25,60; CTS Mo 3,294.

continuously and continually did miracles, the ordinary miracles of the created order or the extraordinary miracles transcending the created order. Improbabilities therefore point to miracles.

Nowhere does this appear more strongly than in the exposition of the passages on Noah's Ark (Gen. 6). After saying characteristically that 'there is no reason why we should anxiously labour about its structure',[41] he at once proceeds to do just that, if with the proviso that it is 'so far as our edification is concerned'.[42] What kind of wood was it made of? Cedar-wood, fir, or pine? How many storeys had it? Five or three? Were there many windows, or, if only one, whereabouts was it? All these questions are considered in terms of commonsense and probability and in the context of the conjectures of earlier commentaries. The next point, the size of the Ark, he regards as more difficult to determine, partly because 'I do not know the length of a cubit at that time'.[43] He disagrees with Origen and Augustine who make Moses employ sophisticated geometry, whereas 'we know that Moses everywhere spoke in a homely style (crassa Minerva), so that the common people could grasp it'. This leads him on to a highly important statement of his understanding of the whole story: 'for me it is enough that God (whom I acknowledge without controversy to have been the primary builder of the Ark) knew what things the place was capable of holding . . . If you exclude God's extraordinary power from this story, you are saying that it relates only fables'.[45] And a little after: 'I say that this entire narrative of Moses, unless it were full of miracles, would be cold and empty and ridiculous'. And therefore, as the story unfolds, he brings out all the difficulties: the enormous number of trees needed; the work of felling them and cutting them into planks; the carting; the provisions for humans and animals over almost a year; how the various wild animals were first to be caught, then tamed, and then taught to live peaceably with one

[41] OC 23,122; CTS Gen 1,255.
[42] OC 23,122; CTS Gen 1,256.
[43] OC 23,123; CTS Gen 1,257.
[44] OC 23,123; CTS Gen 1,256.
[45] OC 23,123; CTS Gen 1,257.
[46] OC 23,123; CTS Gen 1,257.

another; how the humans were going even to survive for three days shut up in a box – 'the smell of dung alone' he says, 'would have stifled all the living creatures in the Ark'. [47] But all these problems would be looked after by God. He is able to appeal to Gen. 7.16 for direct confirmation: *And the Lord shut him in*. It must have been a big door, because it had to admit an elephant. How could such a door have been made watertight, especially considering the force and pressure of water envisaged in the Flood? Moses, therefore, 'to cut off any occasion for the vain speculations which our inquisitiveness suggests, declares in a word that the Ark was made watertight from the deluge, not by human workmanship, but by divine miracle'. [48] In what this miracle consisted he does not attempt to say. In some hidden manner it all came to pass as it is recounted.

Calvin is aware that the Biblical writers could be accused of using the device of *Deus ex machina*, that device frowned on by Aristotle in *Poetics* XV. When Abraham's hand is raised to slay Isaac, the Angel of Jehovah called unto him from heaven: 'When things get desperate in their fables, poets make a *Deux ex machina* suddenly appear. It is possible that by this sort of fiction Satan has tried to obscure the wonderful and amazing interventions (*occursus*) of God in helping and rescuing his people unexpectedly. All peoples ought to know and acclaim this story; but by Satan's cunning the truth of God is not only adulterated and turned into a lie but also treated as a fable and a great joke. No, it is for us to consider attentively how wonderfully and at the critical moment God both recalls Isaac from death to life and restores to Abraham his son as it were from the very grave'. [49]

Besides the recourse to miracle, Calvin also, as is well-known, explained difficulties by calling them "accommodations". This is a concept that he uses in more than one context. In the *Institutio* he compares God's condescension in encountering man in a form and a manner that man can grasp to a woman using baby-talk to her infant. God, otherwise unknowable, accommodates himself

[47] OC 23,125-6; CTS Gen 1,261.
[48] OC 23,133; CTS Gen 1,272.
[49] Gen 22.11. OC 23,317; CTS Gen 1,569.

to man's capacity. In much the same way, Moses, a learned man, accommodates his knowledge to the primitive people for whom he wrote. By this method a primitive world-view is easily assimilated to the more sophisticated outlook of the sixteenth century. Calvin treats the creation story of Gen. 1, for example, as a factually true but, so to say, simplified version for this uncivilized people. "Accommodation" is first used under v.5: *And it was evening, and it was morning, the first day*. This can mean 'either that this was the evening and morning of the first day or that the first day consisted of the evening and the morning'.[50] The sense is the same whichever we choose. Moses is beginning the day 'with the evening according to the custom of his nation, and . . . he was accommodating his language to the received custom'.[51] The second use of the concept, but not the word, occurs in the same verse. The world was not made in a moment but over six days, 'for the purpose of accommodating (*temperaret*) [God's] works to the capacity of men'.[52] The concept, again without the word, appears under v.6: *Let there be a firmament* (extensio) *in the midst of the waters*. This should not be treated allegorically or applied to angels, for 'nothing is treated of here but the visible form of the world'.[53] It is written in order that all men may understand the works of God; the created order is the book of the unlearned. 'Whence I conclude that the waters here meant what the primitive and unlearned may perceive'.[54] The idea of simplicity is brought up again under v.14: *Let them* [the sun and moon] *be for signs*. 'It must be remembered that Moses does not speak with scientific acuteness of hidden mysteries but relates things which are everywhere observed even by the primitive and which are in common use'.[55] Under the next verse also (*Let them be for lights*) he says that we are here concerned with theology and not with philosophy (that is, the natural sciences) in general or astronomy in particular. The opening sentence sums up Calvin's theological principle: 'it is not here scientifically discussed how

[50] OC 23,17; CTS Gen 1,77.
[51] OC 23,17; CTS Gen 1,78.
[52] OC 23,18; CTS Gen 1,78.
[53] OC 23,18; CTS Gen 1,79.
[54] OC 23,18; CTS Gen 1,80.
[55] OC 23,21; CTS Gen 1,84.

large the sun is in the heavens and how large or small the moon, but how much light comes to us from them'.[56] Moses is not to be blamed for not speaking more exactly, 'for, as became a theologian, he had more thought of us than of the stars'.[57] The exposition of v. 16 (*The greater light to rule the day and the lesser light to rule the night*) goes further than usual in admitting, if not an actual error, at any rate a defect in the account: 'Moses makes two great lights, but astronomers have proved conclusively that the star Saturn which, on account of its great distance, seems the least of all, is larger than the moon. The difference is that Moses wrote in a popular way what all the unlearned and unlettered understand by common sense, but astronomers investigate with great labour whatever the genius of the human mind can grasp'.[58] Calvin is here saying that Gen. 1.16 interpreted literally is scientifically incorrect. How far he thought that Moses accommodated the account of creation in those verses where the concept is not mentioned must remain an open question.

Accommodation is used also to explain anthropomorphisms. Gen. 2.8 says, *And the Lord planted a garden.* 'Moses thus accommodates himself by a simple and crude style to the common capacity'.[59] It will also account for obscurity in such matters as geographical description. After a full discussion of the geography and topography of the Garden of Eden, Calvin says: 'Moses, in my judgment, accommodated his topography to the capacity of his age'.[60] (This does not stop him from going on at length and even including a map of the whole area). And again, accommodation will account for the incredible, as in the serpent speaking in Gen. 3: 'We have elsewhere said that Moses, in a simple and crude style, accommodates what he delivers to the popular capacity – and with good reason, for he not only had to teach the ignorant masses, but the Church was in the age of childhood, and it was unable to grasp any higher teaching. There is, then, nothing absurd if they who were at that time, as we know and confess, infants, so to say, were fed with milk. Or, if another

[56] OC 23,21; CTS Gen 1,85.
[57] OC 23,22; CTS Gen 1,85-6.
[58] OC 23,22; CTS Gen 1,86.
[59] OC 23,36; CTS Gen 1,113.
[60] OC 23,40; CTS Gen 1,119.

comparison is more acceptable, Moses is not to be blamed if he thinks over the office of schoolmaster laid upon him by the Lord and persists in the childish rudiments'.[61] Once again, however, there is no question of doubting the truth of the account of the serpent speaking. 'When Satan, by God's permission, procured the serpent as a fit organ for himself, he formed words also by its tongue, which God permitted . . . If men decide that whatever is unusual must be fabulous, God would be allowed to work no miracle'.[62]

We have earlier spoken of Calvin's view of Old Testament history as a whole, that it is the history of the Church, elect, preserved in the midst of persecution and distress, awaiting the advent of its Head. We come now to the treatment of individual stories, and in particular to their significance and purpose. Here we have to distinguish between story and story. Where the one may be expounded in a matter-of-fact way, without reference to theological considerations, another will show openly its place in the course of Church history or put forward some developed doctrine. It is the former which is the most common way of exposition; the other will appear usually only when the history concerns a type of Christ or his Church or Gospel, or where the passage is so interpreted in a New Testament citation, or, of course, where a story itself contains theological teaching.

The plain, historical exposition will usually serve as a basis to convey moral or religious exhortation, or to carry a warning, or provide an example to imitate. It is astonishing how much of Calvin's Old Testament exposition consists of moral application. Those who know only the theology of the *Institutio* would often not believe they were reading the same man. Let us look at some examples.

Ex. 8.5: *And the Lord said unto Moses, Go unto Pharaoh, and say unto him, Thus saith the Lord, Let my people go* – continuing with the threat of the plague of frogs. God had a right to demand this of Pharaoh, says Calvin, and in refusing, Pharaoh showed himself cruel to the people and a despiser of God. Therefore God added threats to enforce his demand. Two points should be noticed about the plague of frogs. First, the Nile and the marshes of Egypt

[61] OC 23,53; CTS Gen 1,141.
[62] OC 23,56; CTS Gen 1,145.

were full of frogs and it was only by God's restraining hand that they had not invaded the cities before. Secondly, it not only punished the Egyptians but also made them a laughing stock. Thus far the explanation. Now the lesson. 'But let us learn from this story that there are many deaths mixed in with our life and that our life is only lengthened because God restrains the evils which everywhere beset us. And again . . . all creatures are ready to execute his judgements and therefore we must ascribe it to his kindness and long-suffering that the ungodly do not perish at every moment. Finally, if we are ever galled by ignominy or disgrace, let us remember that this happens designedly, that the shame may bring down our pride'.[63]

Gen. 29.4ff. *My brethren*, said Jacob to the shepherds at the well, *whence be ye*? And then they told him that Rachel, the daughter of Laban, was coming with her father's sheep, and Jacob helped her water the flock. *And Jacob kissed Rachel, and lifted up his voice, and wept*. What strikes, and indeed shocks, Calvin is the unceremonious meeting without introductions. 'The great innocence of that age appears in this meeting . . . Jacob saluted unknown men as brethren, undoubtedly according to received custom. Frugality is also apparent, in that Rachel sometimes looks after the flock; for, since Laban had many servants, how did it happen that he employed his own daughter in a low and sordid service except that it was thought disgraceful to educate children in idleness, softness, and delicacy? Nowadays, on the contrary, ambition, pride, and softness have made manners effeminate, and domestic work is so despised that most people think it a disgrace to do it. It was from the same innocence of manners that Jacob dared to kiss his cousin. For in a chaste and modest life there was much greater liberty. In our times, impurity and ungovernable lusts are the reason why not only kisses are suspect but even looks are feared . . . That ancient simplicity ought to make us groan with grief at the horrible thought of the vile corruption into which the world has fallen and lest its contagion should infect us and our homes'.[64] Then comes ὕστερον πρότερον, to remove the impropriety of the kiss: 'But Moses had inverted the order; for

---

[63] OC 24,97; CTS Mo 1,159.
[64] OC 23,400; CTS Gen 2,127-8.

Jacob did not kiss Rachel till he had informed her that he was her cousin'.[65] Had Calvin been able to read *War and Peace*, he would have learned '*Cousinage – dangereux voisinage*'.

Ex. 16.19ff: *And Moses said to them, Let no man leave any of it till the morning*. Calvin has already expounded the theological significance of manna; at this point he turns to the lesson to be drawn: 'Now, although the case of the manna and the ordinary bread by which we are nourished is not altogether similar, yet the *anagogē* holds to a certain extent. For it is lawful to keep our corn and wine stored in granaries and cellars; yet all should still ask their daily bread from God. But this will only happen if the rich do not greedily swallow up all they can lay their hands on, if they do not avariciously scrape together here and there, if they do not gorge themselves on the hunger of the poor, if they do not suppress God's blessing so far as they can; in a word, if they do not immoderately accumulate huge possessions but are liberal out of their present abundance, are not over-anxious about the future, and are not troubled that, if it has to be so, their wealth should diminish; nay, if they are ready to endure poverty and do not glory in their abundance but rest on the fatherly goodness of God'.[66]

Another favourite device is from an event or character to draw a general maxim.

Ex. 6.9: *And Moses spoke thus to the children of Israel; but they did not hearken to Moses for anguish of spirit*. 'Moses relates that their minds were shut against the announcement of the coming grace that he had made. The afflicted often close their ears like this and so shut the door on God's promises. What a monstrous thing! It is not surprising that those who are full and drunken with prosperity should reject God's grace; but it is against nature that the sorrow which ought to make those overwhelmed with troubles feel famished should be an obstacle to their receiving the comfort that God freely offers them. But it is too common for people, the more they are afflicted, to harden themselves against letting God help them'.[67]

Ex.15.26: *I am the Lord that healeth thee*. This was said because

[65] OC 23,400; CTS Gen 2,128.
[66] OC 24,172-3; CTS Mo 1,281.
[67] OC 24,81; CTS Mo 1,132.

the Israelites were not immune from the diseases that had attacked the Egyptians. But they did not suffer from them because God was their healer. 'And truly, whatsoever diseases affect mankind, we may see in them, as so many mirrors, our own miseries and know that there is no health in us except in so far as God spares us'.[68]

Character-study plays a large part in Calvin's expositions of narrative. What the characters were like within themselves, why they acted in this or that way, what their aims and hopes were, how experience affected them, how the inter-action of characters produced such a result. His understanding was determined not simply by a study of character in Scripture but rather by his own experience of people and by his reading – and in particular his reading of classical history and ethics; a close examination of his character studies would probably reveal that he was much indebted to Erasmus' *Adagia* and the ethical treatises of Aristotle and Plutarch.

It is in the explanation of details in a story that he looks for motives or motivation. Thus Gen. 25.28 tells us that *Isaac loved Esau . . . but Rebekah loved Jacob.* One would think there was little to add to this simple statement, but Calvin wants to know why there was this difference of affection. On one level, he says, Isaac was blameworthy because, although it was natural enough that he should prefer his first-born, God had already declared that the birthright should be Jacob's. On the other hand, Rebekah's love of Jacob was suspect. Did she love him out of obedience to God's declaration, or was it from a natural opposition to her husband? 'For we usually see the favouritism of parents so divided that if the wife sees one of the sons loved by her husband, she inclines by a contrary jealousy more to the other'.[69]

Or Gen. 24.10: *And the servant took ten camels* – that is, Abraham's servant, going to seek a wife for Isaac. Ten camels seems an excessive number, but it was, says Calvin, to make a display of Abraham's wealth and thus to act as a bait to possible wives. 'For even a simple girl would not lightly submit to being carried off to a distant land without the promise of being supplied

[68] OC 24,164; CTS Mo 1,266.
[69] OC 23,353; CTS Gen 2,50.

with life's comforts. Exile is bad enough, without poverty on top of it'.[70]

Or the more sophisticated study of Nebuchadnezzar in Daniel 1-5, of which the beginning in Dan.1.3-4 is a fair sample: '*And the king commanded Ashpenaz, the master of the eunuchs, that he should bring certain of the children of Israel, and of the king's seed, and of the princes. Children in whom was no blemish, but well-favoured, and skilful in all wisdom, and understanding learning, and clear in expressing knowledge, and in whom there was strength, that they might stand in the king's palace to be taught the writing* (literatura) *and the language of the Chaldeans*'. Now, why did the king do this? Partly to show that they were captives, in his power, possibly also to use them as hostages, to keep the Jews submissive. Partly, however, he viewed them, when they had been brainwashed, as future infiltrators of Babylonian culture and religion among the Jews. For this purpose he wanted youths who were well-born and had outstanding talents, so that they might easily take a place of authority among the Jews. What the king aims at seems highflown for boys – 'that they should be accomplished in prudence, knowledge, and experience. But we know that kings have no moderation in their demands'. What he wanted, however, was to Babylonize them. So he sets to work to undermine their opposition and their scruples by feeding them well, and at his own table – 'we know that, if there is any cunning in the world, you will find it reigning in king's palaces'.[71]

Another character that Calvin finds more than usually interesting is Laban: 'He was as suspicious as he was covetous – dishonest men usually measure others by their own standard; and this is why they are always distrustful and anxious':[72] 'he was a cunning old fox. He kept silence, but his face betrayed his malice':[73] 'the mean-ness of Laban was like an insatiable whirlpool'.[74] He will trace Laban's changes of mood in Gen. 31.22ff. Laban had intended to keep Jacob captive all his life 'like a

---

[70] OC 23,333; CTS Gen 2,16.
[71] OC 40,536–40; CTS Dan 1,89-93.
[72] OC 23,417; CTS Gen 2,155.
[73] OC 23,422; CTS Gen 2,163.
[74] OC 23,425; CTS Gen 2,167.

slave bound to the soil or sentenced to the mines';[75] but Jacob fled
by stealth and got a three-days start, in which time Laban's rage
('he was like a savage wild beast, breathing nothing but
slaughter')[76] was cooled and restrained by the Lord. When,
therefore, he caught up with Jacob 'he did not dare to threaten
harshly, but laid aside his ferocity and descended to insincere and
hypocritical charm'.[77] But then he changed again and accused
Jacob of theft. When he was satisfied on this head (wrongly, as it
happens, and Rachel, who was the real thief, 'deserves manifold
censure')[78] he 'begins to speak [v. 43] very differently . . . he
buries all strife, and slips into placid and friendly conversation
. . . He now speaks like a very fair man'.[79] And this is an
indication that he was not completely beyond hope, for he, like all
men, had a certain knowledge of truth: 'there yet remains a
knowledge of truth engraven in the minds of men, which, being
stirred up, emits sparks, unless wickedness is in complete
control'.[80] And so Laban departs from the scene a very different
character: 'not only was Laban's fury quietened, but he had put on
fatherly affection, as if changed into a new man'[81] – not a new man
in the Pauline sense, perhaps, (for the next verse puts him firmly
in his place: 'A trait of personality is here to be noticed, that
Laban, who had lapsed from godliness and was a man of
dishonest and wicked ways, yet retained the custom of
blessing')[82] but at least relatively new.

Just as the events contain lessons to be applied to Calvin's
readers or hearers, so the characters serve as examples to follow or
shun.

Gen. 12.8: *And Abram removed from thence.* Abram was
compelled to move because he found the inhabitants unfriendly:
'but if Abram bore his continual wanderings patiently, our

[75] OC 23,426-7; CTS Gen 2,171.
[76] OC 23,427; CTS Gen 2,171.
[77] OC 23,427; CTS Gen 2,172.
[78] OC 23,429; CTS Gen 2,175.
[79] OC 23,431; CTS Gen 2,177-8.
[80] OC 23,431; CTS Gen 2,178.
[81] OC 23,434; CTS Gen 2,182.
[82] OC 23,434; CTS Gen 2,182.

hard-to-please ways are quite inexcusable, when we grumble against God if he does not allow us a quiet nest'.[83]

Gen. 19.15: *And when dawn arose, the angels hastened Lot* – that is, to leave Sodom immediately. Why was he lingering? Perhaps because he was worried about going into exile, leaving his house and furniture, and finding himself in some desert place with nothing but what he stood up in. 'In his person the Spirit of God sets before us a mirror of our own slowness, so that we may shake off sloth and learn to gird ourselves for prompt obedience as soon as the heavenly voice sounds in our ears'.[84]

Dan.3.19-20 recounts the story of Shadrach, Meshach, and Abed-nego being cast into the burning fiery furnace. 'This story is told to us, not merely to make us praise and admire the courage of these three saints, but to set before us their constancy as an example to be imitated'.[85]

But we could go on quoting example after example; there must be hundreds, perhaps thousands, in the Old Testament expositions. Of course, not everyone or everything ought to be imitated. Calvin makes a firm distinction between following good examples and imitating or aping (a favourite expression) anything that takes our fancy: 'it is not always right to imitate the things related in Scripture. Whatever the Lord commands in general is to be reckoned an inflexible rule; but to rely on particular examples is not only dangerous but downright foolish and absurd'.[86] Therefore he can 'thank the Lord that this barbarity [of slavery] has been abolished'.[87] But the slaughters by Joshua's army of whole populations put Calvin into a difficult position. As a man he is shocked, recognizing that this was 'detestable savagery, surpassing anything that books tell us of savage and almost brutish tribes'.[88] But the Scripture says that these slaughters were commanded by God; therefore 'we must embrace with reverence as proceeding from God what would

[83] OC 23,182; CTS Gen 1,356.
[84] OC 23,274; CTS Gen 1,506.
[85] OC 40,635; CTS Dan 1,226.
[86] OC 23,335; CTS Gen 2,21.
[87] OC 23,227; CTS Gen 1,431.
[88] OC 25,505; CTS Josh 163.

otherwise horrify us'.[89] Joshua was blameless, for he was obeying God's command. But this is not to be taken as a precedent for commanders: 'each must prudently consider what his calling demands, lest, by giving the rein to his zeal in imitation of Joshua, he should be judged cruel and bloody rather than a strict minister of God'.[90]

3 Two expositions

Hitherto in this chapter we have looked almost exclusively at isolated passages. We will now take two longer examples of Calvin's method of treating narrative. Both stories are expounded on their own Old Testament level, without overt dependence on the New. We see Calvin analysing the account in the way we have explained, filling in the details, searching into causes and motives, applying events and characters to his own day as lessons and examples.

Gen. 47.1-7:[91] *And Joseph came and told Pharaoh, and said, My father and my brothers, and their flocks and herds, and all that they have, have come out of the land of Canaan; and behold, they are in the land of Goshen. And he took five men from the extremes of his brothers and presented them before Pharaoh. Then Pharaoh said to his brothers, What is your occupation? And they said to Pharaoh, Thy servants are shepherds, both we and our fathers. And they said to Pharaoh, We have come that we might be in this land as aliens. For thy servants have no pasture for their flocks, because there is a severe famine in the land of Canaan. Now therefore we ask that thy servants may live in the land of Goshen. And Pharaoh spoke to Joseph, saying, Thy father and thy brothers have come to thee. The land of Egypt is before thee; make thy father and thy brothers live in the best of the land, let them live in the land of Goshen. And if thou knowest that there are any strong men among them make them overseers over my cattle.*

(I paraphrase Calvin's exposition).

Joseph's roundabout way of asking the land of Goshen for his people sprang not from cunning but from modesty. Pharaoh saw

[89] OC 25,505; CTS Josh 163.
[90] OC 25,509; CTS Josh 170-1.
[91] OC 23,565-8; CTS Gen 2,398-404.

at once what he wanted and gladly granted it. Hence we gather that he gave it deliberately and not in ignorance of the situation.

That Joseph had already told his father and most of his brothers to stay in Goshen is easily excused. They could not bring their cattle with them when they came to salute the king and they could not leave their cattle behind unattended. Jacob and the brothers are merely staying there until a fixed place has been settled for them.

That Joseph brought five men from the extremes of his brothers is usually taken to mean that he brought the five shortest ones before the king, out of a fear that the taller ones might be pressed into the army. But the Hebrew word for extremity means both the first and the last. I therefore think it means "oldest and youngest", so that the king should get an idea of their general age.

The confession of the brothers that they were shepherds was a terrible disgrace to Joseph, who had been advanced to such heights in Egypt; for the name of shepherds was shameful and hateful there. Why did not Joseph advise them to say that they were farm workers, or engaged in some other honest trade? After all, they must have learnt something about other agricultural crafts in the course of their shepherding, and they could surely have branched out on a new life in a new country, especially with the backing of the king. In fact, if they had been so inclined, they could have had jobs in the court itself. But Joseph deliberately lets them make the confession because he was not much worried about earthly contempt. Moreover, if the Israelites had lived in splendour among the Egyptians, they would have lost their identity. As it was, their mean and lowly way of life formed a barrier separating them from the Egyptians. And even if this thought was not in their minds, the Lord was governing their tongues in what they said in order to prevent them from mixing and 'to keep the body of the Church pure and distinct'.[92] This passage also teaches us that it is better to have a remote corner in the courts of the Lord than to dwell inside palaces but outside the Church. So we must not think it a bad bargain to purchase unity with the children of God at the expense of being despised by the world. But on the other hand it would be quite silly to try to get

[92] OC 23,566; CTS Gen 2,400.

ourselves hated by the world, as if we could not serve God without persecution.

God's purpose in this was to keep the sons of Jacob in abasement until he should restore them to the land of Canaan. They kept themselves blameless for their promised liberation and did not deny that they were herdsmen. We, in our turn, must not be swayed by desire of empty glory; for the Lord shows that the only way of salvation is when we are forced into our proper order in life. Let us willingly be ignoble on earth 'so that one day the Angels may receive us into the society of their heavenly glory'.[93] This also serves as an example for those who have menial jobs. There is no need for them to be ashamed. It should be more than enough for them that their way of life is honest and pleasing to God.

Some shame lay also in what they go on to say, that they had been forced by the famine to come to live as aliens. But this redounds to the glory of God, who brought them to Egypt in poverty and lowliness, but led them out again three hundred years later as a great people.

Pharaoh's reply in vv.5-6 is unexpected. He had, in effect, offered them citizenship in Egypt, and they had said they would prefer to live as aliens. Kings do not like their favours to be spurned; therefore his mild reaction must be ascribed to God's grace. It would be plausible, but incorrect, to put their rejection of his offer down to humility, that they were not worthy of so great an honour. What they were really doing was safe-guarding their liberty. Sophocles said that anyone who entered a tyrant's court laid down his liberty at the door. The sons of Jacob came to an agreement with the king while they were still on the threshold. Therefore when, later, they were refused permission to leave and were oppressed, this was not only cruelty but also breaking an agreement.

Isaiah seems to contradict this last point when he says: *My people went down at first to Egypt to sojourn there, and the Assyrian oppressed them for nothing* (52.4) – for this makes it sound as if Pharaoh had some excuse for his oppressions. But he is speaking comparatively: If the Egyptians had no excuse then, the

[93] OC 23,567; CTS Gen 2,401.

Babylonians have less than none now. So it was a wicked violation of the law of hospitality. The lesson for believers now is that they must train themselves in patience. (Presumably he is referring to Christians under persecution).

The point of v.6 is not only to narrate that Jacob was received courteously but also to show Joseph's integrity. He gave his people only what the king wished. He had great power and he was bound to use it strictly and honestly. I wish that noblemen today showed the same spirit. They seem to think that the only value of power is giving them greater license to sin. But Joseph used only half of the king's permission. He settled his people in Goshen, but without making them keepers of the king's cattle. They would, in any case, have become objects of envy and so it would have proved a snare.

Gen. 32.24-32:[94] *And Jacob remained alone; and there wrestled a man with him until the dawn arose. And he saw that he did not prevail against him, and he touched the hollow of his thigh, and the hollow of Jacob's thigh was out of joint as he wrestled with him. Then he said, Let me go, for the dawn is arising. He replied to him, I will not let thee go, except thou bless me. And he said to him, What is thy name? And he said, Jacob. Then he said, Thy name shall be called no more Jacob, but Israel; for thou hast been a prince with God, and with men thou shalt prevail. And Jacob asked him, and said, Tell me, I pray, thy name. And he said, Why dost thou ask after my name? And he blessed him there. Therefore Jacob called the name of that place, Peniel: for I have seen God face to face, and my soul has escaped. And as he passed over Penuel, the sun rose upon him, and he limped upon his thigh. Therefore the children of Israel eat not of the sinew which shrank, which is upon the hollow of the thigh, unto this day; because he touched the hollow of Jacob's thigh in the sinew which shrank.*

The purpose of this vision was in the first place to teach Jacob that he had many severe conflicts before him and that he would be victorious. But it was also to show all God's people, by means of the example of Jacob, that they also would undergo many temptations and trials and that they must submit to them.

[94] OC 23,442-7; CTS Gen 2,195-203.

Therefore 'all God's servants are like wrestlers in this world'.[95]

The antagonist against whom Jacob was fighting was neither Satan nor a man. He was God. The same thing is true with all believers. All afflictions are from God who, by means of them, tests and tries our faith – 'he comes into the arena as the opponent to test out our strength'.[96] [Calvin is interpreting the story in terms of one of his favourite metaphors – Christians are like wrestlers in a Greek or Roman arena.]

But it seems absurd that any mortal man could be able to resist the All-mighty. If in our afflictions God attacks us, we must surely be destroyed. But there is a strange paradox here. We fight against God with his power and using the weapons which he gives us. So that God may be said both to fight against us and on our side. He both attacks us and defends us. But he gives us more strength to resist him than he uses to attack us – ' we may truly say that he fights against us with his left hand but for us with his right hand.'[97] This sounds illogical and absurd, yet we know it to be true in practice.

The story begins by calling the opponent 'a man' but later terms him "God". This way of speaking is quite common in the Bible; the Holy Spirit, for example, is called 'the dove'. But the significance of it is that God was breaking Jacob in gently, like a raw recruit or like a young ox not yet put to the plough. Jacob is being taught that the whole of his life would be a struggle – and this is the lesson that the story teaches us as well.

In v. 25 the Antagonist saw that he did not prevail against him. Moses puts this anthropomorphically, for obviously God would not beg for mercy from a man. But when God descends to us, he takes to himself human properties. [Calvin is not here alluding to the Incarnation, but to any coming of God in Scripture.] Jacob has therefore emerged victorious in the encounter, but at a cost, for he is wounded. This vision took place during the night; but the wound was permanent, so that every day its effect would show that it had not all been an empty dream. The wound and the lameness was not only for Jacob, but for believers of every age: 'This sign is shown to all the godly of how they will emerge as

[95] OC 23,442; CTS Gen 2,195.
[96] OC 23,442; CTS Gen 2,195.
[97] OC 23,442; CTS Gen 2,196.

victors in temptations and trials – only with injuries and wounds'.[98]

Nevertheless, in v.26 God acknowledges that Jacob has won and asks to be let go, because he is not Jacob's equal. What a victory! A mere man has overcome the Almighty. And this contains a lesson for us as well, that the way for us to wrestle is to persevere and never grow weary until the Lord himself gives way.

Jacob then says, *I will not let thee go except thou bless me*. This means that the one who has been victorious asks a blessing of the one he has overcome. The superior asks a blessing of the lesser. This is precisely the opposite of the nature of blessing. Jacob knew that he had to do with God, with the Lord to whom he was only a servant, in spite of his victory in the contest. [Calvin does not develop this point, but I take him to mean that God remains the Lord even when he gives himself to man to be known.] There is a further lesson here for us, that we should look for God to bless us even when he is assailing us in some affliction. Better for the children of God to be half destroyed and then blessed by God rather than never to meet with him at all.

There comes the interchange of names, or rather, the bestowal of the new name on Jacob and the refusal of the Name from God. Calvin explains the meaning of the word Israel and states a preference for the Vulgate translation: 'If thou hast been strong against God, how much more shalt thou prevail against men!'[99]

Tell me thy name, prays Jacob. Why should he ask that, when he already seems to know that it is God with whom he has wrestled? The solution is easy: 'Although Jacob recognized God he was not satisfied with an obscure and lowly knowledge, but wanted to ascend higher. It is not surprising that the holy man broke out in this prayer, for God had revealed himself to him under many wrappings (*involucris*), so that his knowledge was not yet familiar and clear. And it is certain that all the saints under the Law burned with this sort of desire'.[100] But God did not grant the request. Why? Calvin's answer is central for our study: 'because the time of full revelation was not yet mature. For the patriarchs in the

---

[98] OC 23,444; CTS Gen 2,198.
[99] OC 23,445; CTS Gen 2,200.
[100] OC 23,445; CTS 2,200-1.

beginning had to walk in the dim light of the dawn, and the Lord gradually revealed himself to them, until at last Christ, the Sun of righteousness, arose, in whom shone forth perfect brightness'.[101] And again the application that God has drawn still nearer to us and how terrible is our ingratitude if we do not run to meet him with a burning desire for such great grace.

Jacob is repulsed because he goes beyond the limits set for his age. We have greater measure of illumination than he; how much worse is our curiosity if we try to go beyond it.

Jacob has seen God and yet has been kept from death. In many places of Scripture we are told of the terrifying and death-dealing sight of God. Any encounter with God would be mortal unless God himself protected us. Believers feel themselves to be like smoke vanishing away when God reveals himself to them. And if we think that God is not present with us, we do as we like and live an imaginary life.

If, as we have said, Jacob had only a slight taste of God's glory, how could he claim to have seen God face to face and praise him for it? The answer is that he had certainly seen God in a wonderful way, but in comparison with the Gospel and even with the Law [Calvin is thinking of Moses seeing the glory of God – Ex.33.18-23], it is only 'sparks or obscure beams'.[102] But, if he praised God for such a revelation of himself, what should not we do, 'before whose eyes Christ, the living image of God, is set in the mirror of the Gospel? Let us therefore learn to open our eyes and not be blind at midday'.[103]

The lameness of Jacob is put as a spectacle for all ages, to teach believers that none is such a tough fighter as not to carry some wound or other out of the spiritual combat. It was not superstition that led the Jews to refrain from eating that part of the thigh in which Jacob was wounded. It happened in the childhood of the Church, when God was keeping believers under tutorship. But since Christ has come, we are free from such restrictions. Yet we should remember the thing itself in which the Lord trained his people under an outward ceremony.

Calvin's exposition of this story is a microcosm of his

[101] OC 23,445-6; CTS Gen 2,201.
[102] OC 23,446; CTS Gen 2,202.
[103] OC 23,447; CTS Gen 2,202.

treatment of Genesis. It is all here – the genuineness of the revelation, its obscurity as belonging to the time before the Mediator appeared, the reconstruction of narrative and character, the continual generalizing of it as a message for his own generation, and above all, the whole story treated on its Old Testament level – the name of Christ is mentioned only the three times that I have brought it out: for Jacob there was no Jesus Christ, and therefore there was none for his expositor while he kept to Jacob.

4 Oracles, visions, and Angels

The story of wrestling Jacob has reminded us that Old Testament history is not the history of man without God but the history of the Church in its childhood. We need to be reminded of this fact because, as we have seen, Calvin often takes it for granted and seems to be relating man's earthly history. But the history of the Church is the history of God with man, and this history has many facets. In the first place it means that God meets and communicates with men. In expounding passages in which God addresses men by word, Calvin is reticent on how God speaks and how man hears the supernatural speech. Thus Gen.4.6: *And Jehovah said to Cain*. 'How God spoke, Moses does not say.. Either a vision was sett before him or he heard an oracle from heaven or he was warned by a secret inspiration. He felt himself hemmed in under the divine judgment'.[104] But, the interpretation of certain 'good men' that it means that Adam spoke as 'the prophet and interpreter of God' is inadmissable. Their motive is good, in wanting to safeguard 'the external ministry of the word' (that is, Scripture and preaching) against the anti-Word spiritualizing of Anabaptists; but this is foreign to the meaning of Genesis. 'From the beginning the Word of God was published in oracles'; before the heavenly doctrine was written down and published, God often revealed his will in extra-ordinary ways'.[106] The word "vision" we shall soon consider more fully, but "oracle" may here need a word of explanation. Calvin does not confine "oracle" to

---

[104] OC 23,87; CTS Gen 1,198.
[105] OC 23,87; CTS Gen 1,198.
[106] OC 23,88; CTS Gen 1,199.

speech but uses it also of visions, as when he calls Jacob's dream at Bethel 'a wonderful oracle'. But when it refers to speech, it will mean a direct speaking by God, a speaking without a prophet or interpreter. (Of course, it goes without saying that this is the "voice" of the Son of God).

The important thing, then, is not how God speaks, but the fact of his speaking and what he speaks and for what purpose. Most important of all is that God speaking to man means his presence with him, whether for judgment and blessing (e.g. Adam and Eve; Jacob at the brook Jabbok) or for judgment alone (e.g. the serpent; Cain). In confirmation of the word that he spoke God gave also symbols of his presence.(We note that Calvin commonly, but not always, used "signs" to denote absence, "symbols" to denote presence). Thus in Gen.3.8 *they heard the voice of Jehovah God walking though the garden at* [literally] *the breeze of the day*; for Calvin prefers to keep the sense of wind or breeze in the word *ruach*. And the breeze was a symbol: 'I do not doubt that a remarkable symbol of God's presence was in that breeze . . . Therefore Moses, by referring to the wind in this place, meant (in my judgment) that an unusual and remarkable symbol of the divine presence was shown'.[107] Similarly the pillar of cloud and pillar of fire going before the children of Israel were symbols that 'God would always be the leader and guardian (*dux et praeses*) of the people he had redeemed'.[108] This is 'a sacramental mode of speaking, by which God transfers his name to the visible figures'.[109] It is not as if God's essence were somehow attached to them or his infinity confined within them; but at the same time, 'the manifestation (*exhibitio*) of the thing signified is truly joined with [the signs of his presence]'.[110] All such signs or symbols are treated as Sacraments and therefore are always yoked with the Word as the effectual confirmation or seal of its truth. The rainbow in Gen.9.12-15, already in existence as a natural phenomenon, was taken into service by God to be a *symbolum* added to the promise contained in the Covenant. It is therefore added or joined to the Word; and 'it is wrong to separate signs

[107] OC 23,65; CTS Gen 1,161.
[108] Ex 13.21. OC 24,145; CTS Mo 1,236.
[109] OC 24,145; CTS Mo 1,236.
[110] OC 24,145; CTS Mo 1,236.

from the Word';[111] 'if the Sacrament is torn from the Word, it ceases to be what it is called'.[112] To keep its power and nature a Sacrament must be a vocal sign (*vocale signum*).

These symbols or signs were always natural in themselves, a breeze, a rainbow, a tree, a bush on fire. From them we move to another means of revelation, not supernatural but not possessing an independent existence outside the person's experience. "Vision" (*visio*) is used by Calvin in this context not as the act of seeing but as the thing seen. It bears more than one meaning, however. In the one sense it will always refer to God's self-revelation, whether by some natural symbol or by a mental conception, or by an angel, or by the assumption of humanity. The burning bush (Ex.3.1-6), Jacob's dream at Bethel (Gen.28.10-15), the angel appearing to Hagar (Gen.16.7-14), and "the captain of the Lord's host" appearing to Joshua (Josh.5.13-15) are all severally examples of this sort of vision. In the second sense the word is used as almost a synonym for "parable" and occurs frequently in the expositions on the Prophets. We may conveniently leave this meaning until the relevant chapter.

Visions, then, are self-revelations of God presented to other senses than the hearing, but particularly to the sight. Calvin's doctrine of the knowledge of God has sometimes been presented as if it consisted exclusively of hearing God's Word. Were it true, he could consistently have no place for the Sacraments. As it is, we find that he gives due weight to the Biblical strain of light and seeing; and this is what we are concerned with here. Nevertheless, it cannot be over-emphasized that the concept of light-seeing does not stand on its own but is always bound to Word-hearing in the same way that the Sacraments are bound to the Word. Although it was 'one of the two ordinary modes in which the Lord used to manifest himself to his Prophets',[113] this was in confirmation and strengthening of the Word, or rather, for the Word needs no strengthening, of man's weak and vacillating faith in the Word. 'This vision . . . was a preparation, so that [Isaac] should listen the more carefully to God and realise that it was with God that he had to do. Because the voice on its own has less force, God appeared,

[111] OC 23,148; CTS Gen 1,298.
[112] OC 23,149; CTS Gen 1,298.
[113] OC 23,207; CTS Gen 1,399.

in order to gain trust and reverence for his Word. In fact, visions were like symbols of the divine presence, so that the holy patriarchs should not doubt that it was God who was to speak to them'.[114] Commonly visions are distinguished from oracles as showing from speaking, but, if distinguished, never separated. "First Moses says that the Lord appeared to [Abram], so that we may know that the oracle was not only given by a secret revelation but that a vision was added to it at the same time. Nor was the vision silent (muta), but it had a conjoined word, to help Abram's faith'.[115]

Visions are, in fact, appearances of God (sometimes translated by Calvin as Dominus apparuit, sometimes as Dominus visus est). The naturalness of the means in no way diminishes the reality of the divine presence. Jacob's dream was a genuine dream, but in it the Lord genuinely appeared to him and spoke to him. The Lord was not a figment of his sleeping mind.

A special form of vision was by the agency of Angels. This was not, however, a merely representative appearance of God, as if he sent an Angel to be his ambassador and did not himself appear. For in all the stories of the appearance of an Angel, Calvin identifies the Angel, or the leading Angel if there are more than one, with Christ. Gen.32.22-32 seems to be an exception; but the man who wrestled with Jacob is not called an Angel in the Scriptural account. When, however, Calvin lectured on Hos.12.4. (and in his strength he had power with God, and he had power with the Angel and prevailed), he expounds it directly of Christ. The passage is so relevant to our purpose that we must stray into the Prophets and quote it. Taking the following verse (And Jehovah the God of hosts, Jehovah is his memorial), he says: 'Here the Prophet plainly expresses the essential Name of God, so testifying that he who was the eternal and only God was at the same time an Angel. Now, it may be asked how God could be both the Eternal and yet also an Angel. This comes so frequently in the Scriptures that we ought to be familiar with it: whenever God appeared by his Angels, the Name of Jehovah is given to them – not to all the Angels indiscriminately, but only to the leading Angel, through whom God revealed himself. This, as I

[114] OC 23,364-5; CTS Gen 2,69.
[115] OC 23,234; CTS Gen 1,442.

have said, ought to be well-known to us. It therefore follows that that Angel was truly God, and God in essence. But this cannot properly belong to God unless there is a certain distinction of Persons [in him]. Therefore, there must be in God a certain Person to whom the name and title of Angel belongs. For if we take the Name of God without distinction and confusedly, representing it as his essence, it will be absurd that he should be both God and Angel. But when we distinguish the Persons in God, the absurdity vanishes. Why? Because Christ, the eternal Wisdom of God, put on the person of Mediator even before he put on our flesh. He was therefore Mediator then, and as Mediator, also the Angel. Yet he who is now God manifest in the flesh, was also Jehovah . . . Christ, since he was God, was also Mediator, and in that he was Mediator was deservedly and aptly called God's Angel or messenger (*nuntius*), because he voluntarily interposed between the Father and men'.[116]

We return to the historical books, and the appearances of Angels there. In every instance the Angel is Christ in a human form. What is the relationship of these appearances to the Incarnation? 'I willingly accept what the old writers teach, that when Christ appeared in those early times in the form of a man, it was the prelude of the mystery which was revealed when God was manifested in the flesh. But we must beware of imagining that Christ then was incarnate (*induisse carnem*); for we do not read that God sent his Son in the flesh before the fulness of times; and again, so far as he is man, he must be the Son of David. But we read in Ezekiel that it was only the similitude of a man. Whether it was a material (*substantiale*) body or only an outward shape (*forma*), it is useless to dispute subtly and harmful to wrangle over'.[117] These appearances, then, in human form were related to the Incarnation as the *praeludium* (a late, non-classical Latin word) to the play. This is a nice concept, for it both relates and also distinguishes it as a part of the play, but while it is spoken, the play has not yet begun. The all-important fact is that Christ appeared and was seen. To go beyond this is to become *argutius*, over-subtle.

Thus the three who came to Abraham (Gen.18.1ff.) were to all

[116] OC 42,455; CTS Mi 1,420-1.
[117] OC 25,464; CTS Josh 88.

appearances men. They looked like men, they spoke like men, they ate like men. But 'God, who created the whole world out of nothing and is daily a wonderful workman in forming his creatures, gave them temporary bodies in which they could fulfil their allotted office'.[118] After their mission had been fulfilled, 'God had created bodies for temporary use, and now at once reduces them to nothingness'.[119] They were, in fact, and were recognized as, Angels; and of these one was their leader, Christ: '[Abraham] saluted one particularly, probably because he excelled the other two. For we know that Angels usually appeared with their Head, Christ. Thus, in these three Angels Moses indicates the Leader of the legation'.[120] The association of the three with the Trinity is, however, 'frivolous and open to ridicule and calumny'.[121]

Similarly the Angel at the burning bush (Ex.3.2) 'not only calls himself Jehovah but claims for himself the glory of eternal and unique Divinity'[122] – that is, in vv. 6 and 14. He is therefore Christ, the Mediator: 'the ancient doctors of the Church rightly felt that the eternal Son of God was so called in respect of his person of Mediator. Granted he only truly undertook it at his Incarnation, yet he performed the figure of it from the beginning'.[123]

Although every appearance of God by an Angel was in the person of Christ, yet Calvin does not treat every appearance of Angels as an appearance of Christ. For example in Jacob's dream at Bethel, it is the ladder which is a figure of Christ: 'It is Christ alone who joins heaven and earth; he alone is the Mediator, who extends from heaven right down to earth; he is the one through whom the fulness of all the heavenly blessings flows down to us and through whom we on our side mount up to God . . . Therefore, if we say that the ladder is an image (*effigiem*) of Christ,

[118] OC 23,252; CTS Gen 1,472.

[119] OC 23,252; CTS Gen 1,472. Cf. Sermon on II Sam 24.16: 'By nature, the Angels are spirits and consequently invisible; but God forms a body for them when he pleases. He also gives us spiritual sight to see what by nature is hidden from us'. (SC 1,754).

[120] OC 23,251; CTS Gen 1,470.

[121] OC 23,251; CTS Gen 1,470.

[122] OC 24,35; CTS Mo 1,61.

[123] OC 24,35; CTS Mo 1,61.

the interpretation will not be forced. For the similitude of a ladder very well fits the Mediator, through whom, by the ministry of Angels, righteousness and life, and all the graces of the Holy Spirit gradually descend to us'.[124] The Angels are in the vision as the ministers of Christ.

[124] OC 23,391; CTS Gen 2,113.

Chapter Four

The Law

We have seen already that Calvin re-arranged the narrative of the *Mosaic*, and I suggested that his reason was to correct unconvincing relations of time. The doctrinal parts of the four books were reconstructed even more thoroughly; but now his purpose was different. He saw a unity in them, centred on the Law, and the Law itself centred on the Decalogue. The Decalogue itself comprehends all the parts and every aspect of man's behaviour towards God and his own fellows (cf. *Inst.*II.viii.11); there is therefore no precept, whether theological, moral, or ceremonial, which does not come under one of the Ten Commandments. But this unity and relevance is obscured for "the unpractised reader" who may not have "sufficient understanding" to perceive the significance of the many scattered commands and prohibitions and to relate them to their centre in one or other of the Ten Commandments. The dissipation implies no blame on Moses or the Holy Spirit; the Biblical order is that 'which the Holy Spirit himself has directed (*praescripsit*) for us. There is no doubt that what was dictated (*dictatum*) to Moses was excellent and entirely perfect in every sort of usefulness'.[1] Moses 'delivered the doctrine unconnectedly, as opportunity allowed'.[2] Whether Calvin's apologia is itself convincing is another matter; we are now concerned only with the fact that he did re-arrange the teaching by grouping commands and prohibitions and penalties under their particular commandment. In this way he was able to make the *Mosaic* easily comprehensible, for it must be allowed that his reconstruction achieved its end, even if a few passages seem to have been forced into place or could (as he acknowledges more than once) have been ranged under a different commandment.

[1] OC 24,5–6; CTS Mo 1,xiv.
[2] OC 24,5–6; CTS Mo 1,xv.

In this present chapter we will describe Calvin's arrangement in fairly general terms but treat two commandments, one from the first Table and one from the second, in detail to serve as examples. Besides the moral and ceremonial Law there is a body of doctrine which stands in a different category and cannot be properly assigned to any of the commandments. This material Calvin divides into three groups – *Preface to the Law* and, after he has completed the exposition of the Law, *The Summary of the Law*, and *Sanctions of the Law*, *Containing Promises and Threatenings*.

Preface to the Law

(1) Ex.20.1-2, repeated Deut.5.1-6,4.20.

God comes before the people in all his greatness to establish his authority and claim their obedience. But he comes, not only as the God and Creator of all men, whom all are bound to obey, but in particular as the God of Israel; 'for it was necessary that the people should be not only frightened by God's majesty, but also sweetly charmed, so that the Law might be more precious than gold or silver and sweeter than honey (Ps.119.72,103). For it would not be enough for men to be forced by servile fear to bear its yoke unless they were also attracted by its sweetness and bore it willingly'.[3] God therefore reminds them of what he has done for them and what their redemption from the land of Egypt, the house of bondage, signifies; that it was 'the sure pledge of their adoption'[4] to be his people, a testimony that they had not been elected in vain. It followed that they did not belong to themselves but to God, who had purchased them.

Although Deut.5.1-6, 4.20 is a repetition, it brings out some things more clearly and looks at them rather differently. The Law is not 'empty speculations, which it is sufficient to understand intellectually and discuss',[5] but it is the rule for shaping our life to his teaching, *regula formandae vitae in sua doctrina*, and for this reason demands serious *meditatio*. Here *meditatio* bears the double meaning of pondering over and exercising oneself in. He now

[3] OC 24,209-10; CTS Mo 1,339.
[4] OC 24,210; CTS Mo 1,339.
[5] OC 24,210; CTS Mo 1,340.

overtly connects the Law with the Covenant, though without
discussing their relationship. For God to take this people into
covenant fellowship was a unique blessing, a wonderful privilege;
in the Covenant they had been united with God. This blessing and
privilege was true also of the Law; therefore they ought to
embrace it with all their heart. Moreover, God had given more to
them than to their fathers. Hence, 'they have no excuse at all if
they do not show their gratitude by giving up themselves
completely to God and with sincere affection reciprocally
worship Him whom they have experienced to be such a bountiful
Father'.[6] Deut. 4.20 again says that they belong entirely to God
because he had purchased them. 'Whence it follows that they are
under his authority and rule; for it would be wicked and
detestable ingratitude to shake off the yoke of their Redeemer'.[7]

The tone of the exposition has now been set. The Law will be
considered as a blessing, a free gift from the loving, gracious
Father who has chosen this people to share his own life, who
freely accepts the condition of the Covenant that he shall share
their life, being present with them, blessing them in this world
and the next, protecting them in all their affliction; and now
graciously demanding that they shall consciously, inwardly and
outwardly, take up their condition of the Covenant and inwardly
and outwardly conform to the character of the God who has
chosen them. The two key-words are grace and gratitude, which
show their unity more clearly in Latin than in English – *gratia*,
"grace"; *gratias ago* "I am grateful". Throughout the exposition
the word "gratitude" goes on sounding, gratitude for the free and
undeserved goodness of God, gratitude as the motive force for
obedience to the declared will of God. And negatively, the
hideousness of ingratitude, which is the spring of disobedience.

(2) Lev. 19.36–37; 20.8; 22.31–33; Deut. 4.1–2; 5.32–33; 13.18.
In this cluster of verses some new ideas are added and former ones
confirmed. Of the new, the first is the maintaining the purity of
the Law. It is to be kept free from all adulterations, all
corruptions; it is to be followed just as it was given, without any
mingling of their own ideas: 'all the fabrications that men think up

[6] OC 24,210; CTS Mo 1,340.
[7] OC 24,211; CTS Mo 1,342.

are so many profanations of God's Name'.[8] Morover, the Law is
sufficient in itself and needs no additives. Again, it would not be
truly kept if it were kept entirely yet with something extraneous
added to it: 'he enjoins them to be content with its pure teaching
(*simplici doctrina*). Indeed, it is only semi–obedience for men to
accept as right and just all that God has commanded, if they do not
soberly refrain from importing any other thing into it';[9] 'they
honour the Law that allow nothing foreign to its genuine sense'.[10]
To add to the Law means in effect to try to be 'more righteous
than it teaches them to be'.[11] Thirdly, Moses urges the people to
be teachable, willing to listen, ready to learn; 'for the beginning of
good and right living is to know what pleases God'.[12] And finally,
'the rule of godly living must be sought from the mouth of God.
He adds that he is to be obeyed, not partially but entirely'.[13]

(3)   Deut.4.5–14 returns to the willing observance of the Law.
The people must keep it "readily", for 'nothing is better or more
to be desired for them'.[14] God is not glorified if the Law is kept by
compulsion; only a ready mind and willing obedience give him
honour. Moreover, taking up the point that the keeping of the
Law is for their welfare, Calvin calls this relationship of the people
with their Lawgiver and Teacher (*magister*) 'Israel's greatest
distinction'.[15] This "rule of living" was like a stage on which the
Jews would act out their nobility before the nations of the world.

(4)   Deut.4.32–40. This passage not only praises the miracles
God did when he gave the Law and appeals to their own
testimony – 'seven hundred thousand witnesses to whom God's
glory had clearly and certainly appeared'[16] – but goes on to stress
that God had delivered his people from Egypt simply out of love
and not for any dignity or worth of their own: 'by the word

[8] OC 24,213; CTS Mo 1,344.
[9] OC 24,214; CTS Mo 1,345.
[10] OC 24,213; CTS Mo 1,345.
[11] OC 24,214; CTS Mo 1,345.
[12] OC 24,213; CTS Mo 1,344.
[13] OC 24,214; CTS Mo 1,345–6.
[14] OC 24,215; CTS Mo 1,347.
[15] OC 24,215; CTS Mo 1,347.
[16] OC 24,218; CTS Mo 1,351.

"love" is expressed the favour which flows from sheer generosity, so as to exclude all worthiness in the person'.[17]

(5)   Deut.7.6–8; 10.14–17. Calvin continues with the theme of "gratuitous love" and "the greatness of God's grace". The purpose of God's choice of this people was that 'he might gain for himself a people holy and pure from all pollutions',[18] a people "peculiar" not only in the secondary sense of "separated" but, according to the Hebrew word (סְגֻלָּה), "special" – 'some take it for "treasure" or some precious and desirable thing . . . certainly it appears from many passages that gold, silver, pearls, and the like are designated by this word. But essentially it is agreed that this title is given to the elect people because God delights himself in them'.[19] And his love was entirely free: 'there was no other reason for God's choice of them than his sheer love of them'.[20] His love for them was not some new thing, for he had loved their fathers, adopting Abraham, Isaac, and Jacob as his own. Now he was 'handing down his Covenant from the fathers to the children, to show that he is faithful and true to his promises'.[21] And again, grace and gratitude: 'he urges upon them the grace by which, as we have seen, the people were bound to God. For this was the most effectual way to move them to subject themselves to their Redeemer; to whom, he tells them, they owed themselves and all they had'.[22] Therefore, 'the Israelites could never be sufficiently grateful to God, who had dealt so generously with them, apart from any merit of their own'.[23]

Such love demands reciprocal love, 'for nothing could be more base than not to show their gratitude by godly and righteous living'.[24] But man, even Jewish man, the chosen man, is a sinner; he has no desire or inclination to obey God. And so another theme is introduced – the need for the denial or renunciation of self, *abnegatio sui*, the circumcision of the heart; that is, the subduing and correcting "carnal affections" ("carnal", of course, refers to

[17]   OC 24,219; CTS Mo 1,353.
[18]   OC 24,220; CTS Mo 1,355.
[19]   OC 24,220; CTS Mo 1,355.
[20]   OC 24,221; CTS Mo 1,356.
[21]   OC 24,221; CTS Mo 1,356.
[22]   OC 24,221; CTS Mo 1,357.
[23]   OC 24,221; CTS Mo 1,356.
[24]   OC 24,222; CTS Mo 1,358.

the soul as well as to the body); for 'to circumcise the heart is equivalent to cleansing it from depraved desires'.[25] This mention of circumcision, however, is also a reminder of the rite itself, the initiation 'into the worship of God and true godliness',[26] the sign of repentance. Here Calvin is keeping to the sense of *metanoia,* and so equates repentance with newness of life. The heart of the matter is that 'because God had chosen them to be his people and by an external symbol had devoted them to himself so that they should cultivate holiness, they ought sincerely and really to prove themselves different from heathen nations, circumcised spiritually no less than in the flesh'.[27]

As nearly all the leading ideas have now been stated, the rest of the *Preface* can be gone through more quickly.

(6) Deut.27.9-10.

(7) Deut.26.16-19. God requires not only a ready and a willing, but also a sincere obedience, 'for nothing displeases God more than hypocrisy'.[28] The people are exhorted to serve God with all their heart; this is an object for them always to aim at, even if the weakness of their flesh prevents them from attaining it.

(8) Deut.6.20-25. 'The one thing that Moses urges in these verses is that the people shall testify their gratitude by obeying the Law and that the same religion shall descend to their posterity'.[29]

(9) Num.15.37-41; repeated Deut.6.6-9; repeated again Deut.11.18-20; Ex.23.13. God's purpose in commanding the use of phylacteries was that the Jews should meditate on the Law continually. Such things were *aides mémoires.* They ought not to be necessary; but people are forgetful and lazy. Therefore God gave them these "crude elements" to keep their memory of the Law awake, and not only to remind them but also to prick and penetrate their minds. These devices are not, however, to be taken as a substitute for genuine *meditatio Legis.*

(10) Deut.27.1-4,8.

(11) Deut.31.10-13. The Levites were to be both the guardians and also the interpreters of the Law. Also, for the sake

---

[25] OC 24,222; CTS Mo 1,358.
[26] OC 24,222; CTS Mo 1,358.
[27] OC 24,222; CTS Mo 1,358.
[28] OC 24,224; CTS Mo 1,360.
[29] OC 24,224-5; CTS Mo 1,362.

of reminding the people, the Law was to be re-promulgated every
seven years, 'lest this practice [of daily teaching by the Levites]
should become obsolete, as much by the aversion of the people as
by the laziness of the Priests'.[30] That this command was not
obeyed is shown by the story of the discovery of the Law in
Josiah's reign.

(12)   Deut.6.10-12. The tone now changes into a series of
warnings and threatenings; but this is only the shadow side of
what has gone before. Instead of the gratitude that God's kindness
deserves, the danger emerges that Israel will be ungrateful. The
first threat is the perversion of the blessing; the promised
prosperity becomes a reality and is accepted without thankful-
ness.

(13)   Deut.9.1-6. And yet this very day Israel is to pass over
Jordan and enter into possession of the land promised. 'This
ought to have been a most powerful incentive to stir up the people
and ravish them to the worship and love of God'.[31] Conversely,
'it would be too disgraceful if they whom God had anticipated
with his grace' (*sua gratia praevenit*), should not, so to say, come to
meet him by willingly submitting to his lordship'.[32]

(14)   Deut.10.21-22; 11.1-7. This momentary cloud obscur-
ing the sun clears away and Calvin returns to the theme that
Israel's well-being and blessedness is to devote themselves to the
service of the God who had been so good to them in adopting
them to be his people. Hence they should show their gratitude by
obedience and reverently embrace his Law. 'Although he could
have commanded the people in an authoritarian and menacing
way, he preferred to lead them to obedience gently, by setting
before them the sweetness of his grace. In sum, he exhorts them
that, because they are actuated by God's love, they should love
him in return. Meanwhile, we should note that free affection is
the foundation or head (*principium vel caput*) of duly observing the
Law, for what is wrung out by force or servile fear cannot please
God'.[33]

(15)   Deut.8.1-9.

[30] OC 24,231; CTS Mo 1,371.
[31] OC 24,233; CTS Mo 1,376.
[32] OC 24,234; CTS Mo 1,376.
[33] OC 24,237; CTS Mo 1,381.

(16)   Deut.29.2-9.

(17)   Deut.8.7-10; repeated Deut.11.10-12; 6.1-3; 6.17-18.

(18)   Deut.8.11-18.

(19)   Ex.23.20-23, 25-31. In these verses God promises that 'he will be their leader by the hand of an Angel'.[34] The Angel does not mean Joshua, as many Jewish commentators have thought, nor simply "a common Angel", 'but the Chief (*principem*) of all Angels, because he has always been also the Head of the Church'.[35] But this presence of God is not only a blessing and encouragement, a means of winning their voluntary obedience, but also a warning that God would take vengeance on their transgressions.

(20)   Deut.29.29; 30.11-14. An ambiguous passage, says Calvin, which has been interpreted in various ways. He himself takes it as a comparison between the revealed teaching in the Law and 'the hidden and incomprehensible counsel of God, concerning which it is not lawful to enquire'.[36] In this context the reference is general and not in particular to predestination, which is not mentioned. It is simply an expression of Calvin's theological premise that men must be satisfied with God's revelation in itself and in its mode and not try either to know more about God than he has revealed or to by-pass the mode of revelation. In the Law God has both made known to his people so much of his mind as was necessary for them to know and has also interpreted his meaning. The relevance of the Law for Christians, he says, is more fully discussed in *Inst*.II.xi. Here he only says that 'the rule of godly and righteous living still keeps its force today, although we are released from the yoke of bondage and from the curse'.[37] The ceremonies have been cancelled by Christ's advent in such a way as to show that, although they were shadows, they were not empty shadows.

The companion passage (Deut.30.11ff.) treats of the *facilitas* of the Law; not easiness of observance, but clarity and straightforwardness. It has no labyrinthine windings (*ambages*) or enigmas in it to keep us uncertain and worried; 'but he teaches

[34] OC 24,251; CTS Mo 1,402.

[35] OC 24,251; CTS Mo 1,403.

[36] OC 24,256; CTS Mo 1, 410-1.

[37] OC 24,256; CTS Mo 1,411-2.

familiarly and on the elementary level of the people whatever was necessary'.[38] And again: 'Moses denies that the Law is obscure and needs immoderate hard work to be understood. God there speaks explicitly and distinctly, and requires only that they shall be diligent'.[39] But, as he says a little later, it is one thing to understand and quite another to perform.

(21) Lev.27.34; Deut.1.1-5; Deut.4.44-49; Deut.29.1. The Law consists of the Ten Commandments, together with the *sententiae*, the determinations and interpretations, appended to them 'to explain the mind of God more clearly'.[40] The *sententiae*, no less than the Commandments, are from God himself. 'For God not only proclaimed those Ten Words, but also interpreted what he had briefly condensed there'.[41] The Law was given first at Sinai and then renewed when two and a half of the tribes had taken possession of their part of the promised land.

So much for the *Preface*. We go on now to the Commandments themselves, treating the first and the eighth more fully, and the others in a skeleton form. We follow Calvin's own headings, which are more precise in the French edition than in the Latin.

The First Commandment

1. Ex.20.3; repeated Deut.5.7.

At the very beginning Calvin changes the negative 'Thou shalt not have alien gods over against [*e regione = coram facie*] me' into the positive 'God commands that he alone is to be worshipped, and requires a worship free from all superstition'.[42] God is to be glorified, but God alone; he will have no associates, no pseudo-gods brought and stood up in front of him; 'they only are to be accounted legitimate worshippers of God that bid adieu to all fabricated commands and cleave to him alone'.[43] In this commandment the reference is to inward worship and not the actual making of idols, which is covered by the second com-

---

[38] OC 24,257; CTS Mo 1,412.
[39] OC 24,257; CTS Mo 1,412.
[40] OC 24,259; CTS Mo 1,416.
[41] OC 24,259; CTS Mo 1,416.
[42] OC 24,261; CTS Mo 2,419.
[43] OC 24,262; CTS Mo 1,419.

mandment. There are many forms of inward idolatry. God requires the affections of the heart and spiritual worship. He is rightly worshipped only if he is worshipped in his own integrity, without any adulterations added by men. This is indeed the difference between true religion and superstition; the former keeps to and reflects God's self-revelation in his Word, the latter invents its own god and offers worship to it.

2. Passages Relating to the Exposition of this Commandment.
(1) Deut.6.4; 6.13; 10.20; 6.16.

That God is one refers not only to his incomprehensible essence but also to his revealed and known power and glory. He bears not only the title of majesty, Jehovah, but is also "thy God", the God of Israel. The people, on their side, must keep steadfastly to the knowledge of him. Deut.6.4 was used by the Church fathers in refutation of Arianism; and they were right to do so, for 'since Christ is everywhere called God, he is without doubt the same Jehovah who declares himself the only God'.[44]

Our hearts must be fixed on God alone. This means, first, that we must fear, or reverence, him; then from fear-reverence comes worship, which is testimony to godliness. The fear of which we speak is not an extorted and servile slavishness but a ready and willing obedience 'which leads his true worshippers'[45] beyond fear of God's majesty. They are called to no less than a one-ness, a *coniunctio*, with him, so that they are firmly fastened to him as if with an adhesive (*agglutinati*).

The chief head of godliness is to render to God what belongs to him and not to take from him anything of the right which he claims as his own. But God is rightly worshipped only when he is accorded his own attributes and virtues. Hence godliness cannot be separated from faith, for God cannot be accorded his own *virtutes* unless man enjoys his goodness and power by looking to him in prayer; and this is faith. Moreover, if God is accorded his own *virtutes*, man will patiently submit to his rule.

(2) Lev.19.1-2.

First, the people are to estimate worship according to the nature of God and not according to their imaginations. Secondly,

[44] OC 24,263; CTS Mo 1,420.
[45] OC 24,263; CTS Mo 1,421.

they must apply themselves to purity; that is, they must slough off the *affectūs carnis*, the φρόνημα σαρκὸς of Rom.8.7, and form themselves to the imitation of God. For they had been adopted as God's people in order that they should bear his image, as children are like their father. It would be madness for any to claim that he was as holy as God, but the very least can aspire to [imitate] the example of God. The main point of the ceremonies was to exercise the people in holiness.

(3)   Deut.6.14–15.

The Jews are not to turn aside from the simplicity of the worship of God, whatever bad examples of superstition they may see around them. For God is jealous; that is, he will permit no rivals to himself or allow the worship due to him to be paid to another. Moreover, he is among them – a fact that is a source of fear and shame if they transgress.

(4)   Deut.18.9–14.

They are to beware of catching superstition from the infection of the Canaanites. The passage shows that to have other gods means to introduce alien elements into the worship of God (*profanas mixturas involvere cum Dei cultu*).[46] Therefore they should eschew all human inventions. But the passage is especially directed against various forms of sorcery. Sorcery comes from a good root: the desire to know and to be sure is universally innate, and the belief that certainty of knowledge can be gained only from God is quite right. But the devil has perverted this good desire, so that men on the one hand seek to know more than is lawful and on the other use illicit means of knowing. The best principle of knowing (*optima sciendi ratio*) is, however, sobriety, being willing to know no more than is expedient for man to know. There is an insatiable curiosity in men; they want, like Adam, to be as gods and know all things. Calvin continues with a review of various forms of magic and sorcery in Biblical and classical times and ends by repeating that the command to be perfect (*integer*) means that they should abstain from all admixtures in their religion, that they should be spiritually chaste. Therefore they must keep themselves separate from the heathen nations and thus from their corruptions.

[46] OC 24,266; CTS Mo 1,424.

(5)   Deut. 18.15–18.

Continuing the previous section, prophecy is here placed as the contrast to sorcery. The Jews are not to imagine that they are worse off than the Gentiles, who have so many ways of applying to so many gods for the knowledge they require, whereas they themselves have but one, the Word of God. For God had not only revealed himself (and therefore, by implication, all wisdom), but, 'although God did not openly descend from heaven, yet he would make clearly known to them, so far as was expedient, his certain will'.[47] And this he would do through the Prophets. God promises that he will not fail to send Prophets to declare his Word. Verse 18, *I will raise to them a Prophet . . .*, is to be applied to all the Prophets and not to Christ alone, otherwise it would mean that they must wait two thousand years until the Incarnation for a Prophet. Yet Peter's use of this verse in Acts 3.22 was apt, for it meant that if the Jews rejected Christ they were at the same time rejecting prophecy as a whole. As it was, prophecy continued in force, with some interruptions in practice, until the preaching of the Gospel, when 'the course of prophetic teaching was completed'.[48] The consequence of the present passage is that the people must submit to and accept the teaching of the Prophets whom God would set over his Church.

(6)   Deut. 13.1–4; 18.21–22.

What of false prophets, however? 'The faith of the godly must not only be fortified and surrounded on the outside by the bastions of the Word, lest any foreign corruption should find a way in, but it must be strengthened on the inside with the defences of the same Word, lest new ideas creep furtively in and vitiate the purity of the teaching'.[49] The teaching of God in the Law and through the Prophets has certainty, for religion ought not to be ambiguous. Therefore the people should not waver in their loyalty to that teaching; the Law was given, not only to separate them from the heathen, but also to keep them in the pure and sound faith. God had married them to himself and now commands them to shut their ears to the impostors, 'Satan's pimps whose job is to violate that sacred and special marriage

[47] OC 24,271; CTS Mo 1,433.
[48] OC 24,272; CTS Mo 1,435.
[49] OC 24,274–5; CTS Mo 1,439.

bond by which God wills to be united with his people'.[50] False prophets are a way by which God tests and proves his Church; he does not learn anything that he did not know before, but he lays bare the faith or unbelief that had been hidden. But this seems a most dangerous trial, by which a Church could be destroyed. In fact, God is simply tearing away the mask from treacherous deceit. 'The testing harms none but those whose ungodliness was previously hidden but is now convicted and condemned . . . Whoever loves God with a pure heart is armed with the invincible power of the Heavenly Spirit against being taken in the snares of falsehoods'.[51] The faithful may be temporarily misled, but they will not permanently fall away from the truth.

(7)   Lev.18.21; 19.26,31; Deut.12.29-32.

A repetition of the former section on sorcery.

3 Ceremonial Appendices of the First Commandment

I *The Institution of the Pesah (Passover)*
(1) Ex.12.1-20.

In some respects this belongs to the Fourth Commandment, in the category of the Sabbath and feast days. The reason why it is considered here is because it is a symbol of redemption. In this rite the people made the profession that they were bound to God their Redeemer or Liberator and at the same time in a sense dedicated themselves to his rule. God's purpose in instituting this ceremony was that 'he might hold the people completely bound to himself alone'[52] and that they might learn 'never to turn away from him by whose kindness and power they had been redeemed'.[53] In other words, it taught them that they must have no other gods beside or before him. The Passover was like a mirror or a picture, in which God 'represented his grace to their eyes';[54] and it was therefore an annual act of remembrance and thanksgiving.

[50] OC 24,275; CTS Mo 1,440.
[51] OC 24,279; CTS Mo 1,446.
[52] OC 24,285; CTS Mo 1,456.
[53] OC 24,285; CTS Mo 1,456.
[54] OC 24,285; CTS Mo 1,456.

To define the Passover, Calvin first looks at the etymology. Of the two words used in vv. 12 & 13, פֶּסַח and עָבַר , the former refers to the Israelites, that God would not pass through (*transitus*) them but pass or spring over (*transilitio*) them, but the latter means that he would go through the Egyptians with his wrath: 'my vengeance shall tear its way through your enemies and attack them on every hand, but I will pass over you and leave you untouched'.[55] Therefore the yearly celebration of this rite was instituted as a *symbolum*, a *monumentum* of God's grace, a yearly *memoria* of their liberation. The first Passover was celebrated in the very midst of the event itself, as a pledge (*pignus*) to strengthen their frightened minds. 'But the annual repetition was a sacrifice of thanksgiving, by which their posterity were reminded that they were the dependants in God's possession (*proprios Dei clientes*) by right of redemption'.[56] So far the Passover has been considered in reference to the earthly event of liberation from Egypt; it looks above this, however, for by this earthly event 'he wished to lead his people right on to the inheritance of the heavenly life'.[57] Therefore the Passover, no less than circumcision, is *spiritualis gratiae symbolum*, a symbol of spiritual grace. As such, it is the Old Testament analogue (*analogia et similitudo*) to the Holy Supper, 'for it contains the same promises which Christ seals to us today and teaches that God is propitious to his own only by expiation through blood'.[58] Therefore it was the *symbolum* of future as well as of past redemption.

So much for the definition of the nature of the Passover. Calvin now comes to individual points of exposition. The Exodus was the birth-day of Israel, the day on which he was re-born, the day on which he rose from the dead after his long burial in Egypt. After this little group of deep insights, it is something of bathos when he discusses at some length in what month they were freed from Egypt.

On v.3 the *quaestio* is raised, 'why, when only one Lamb was offered in sacrifice for the reconciliation of the Church and when God was appeased by the blood of Christ alone, were they com-

[55] OC 24,286; CTS Mo 1,457.
[56] OC 24,286; CTS Mo 1,457.
[57] OC 24,286; CTS Mo 1,457.
[58] OC 24,286; CTS Mo 1,458.

manded to kill a lamb in each house, as if their sacrifices were individual and separate?'[59] *Sed facilis est solutio.* Although they were all protected by the same blood and were all united by engaging in the same rite, God wished every individual household to be reminded by its own private application of the rite and to feel more personally (*propius*) that the grace was given to them. We are in a similar situation today with Baptism. The rite itself is common to all, but the baptizing is individual and personal.

The lamb was to be without blemish, (*summa perfectio* – at the height of perfection). This was to remind the people that the expiation had to be something quite beyond man's attainment: 'to propitiate God, a price more excellent was required than could be found in the whole human race'.[60] But then, if it could not be found in man, how in a sheep? Therefore, 'in that visible soundness of a lamb or a kid was shown the heavenly perfection and purity of Christ'.[61]

The sprinkling of the door-posts and lintel with blood was a *signum* to teach them that 'the sacrifice would profit none but those who were immersed (*tincti*) and sealed in his blood. The sprinkling was equivalent to each one of them wearing the mark of Christ's blood on his forehead. The shedding of his blood has not liberated all, but only the faithful, who sanctify themselves by it'.[62]

Why did the lamb have to be roasted rather than cooked in some other way? This should not be made an allegory. The reason probably was that roasting on a spit was the quickest method. It is therefore an indication of their haste, just as were the unleavened bread, the bitter herbs, and eating clothed, ready for travel. But we have already seen that this Sacrament looked both backward and forward; it reminded the people of what God had done and it promised what he would do in the future. At the advent of Christ "this spiritual mystery" was revealed more clearly – and Calvin refers to St Paul's interpretation of the leaven in I Cor.5.7-8. We must both cleanse ourselves of sin and

[59] OC 24,287; CTS Mo 1,459.
[60] OC 24,288; CTS Mo 1,460.
[61] OC 24,288; CTS Mo 1,460.
[62] OC 24,288; CTS Mo 1,460.

hasten forward, as pilgrims on earth, not hindered by the sweetness of pleasures.

The Passover is called an ordinance for ever, but its perpetuity is limited by the renovation of the Church; the context shows he is referring to the Incarnation. As with circumcision, the ceremonial use of the Passover was abolished by Christ's advent, but abolished in such a way that the substance of the Passover not only continued in force but was only then given its true solidity. Only the form (here equivalent to "accidents") was destroyed; the *substantia* was established.

(2)   Ex.12.24-27, 43-49.

The practice and the meaning of the Passover are to be taught to each succeeding generation. There is always the need for the Sacraments to be accompanied by teaching; it is the soul of the Sacraments (*anima sacramentorum*). Conversely, the children to whom it is taught must be teachable. This also means that only children who were old enough to understand could partake in the Passover meal. By analogy the same is true of the Holy Supper.

Verses 43ff. are similarly related to the Lord's Supper. The promise had been given only to Abraham and his seed. It was therefore useless for aliens. Circumcision was like a hedge, marking off the Israelites from the rest of the world. Only the circumcised were to partake of the Passover. By analogy of the Holy Supper with the Passover, the same discipline must prevail today; that is to say, 'none who is polluted or unclean may intrude into the Holy Supper; the faithful only are to be received, after they have engaged themselves to Christ [Fr.: affirmed their faith and Christianity]'.[63]

Verse 46 is, of course, the source of the well-known event in St John's account of the crucifixion. In its Passover context Calvin professes himself uncertain of the meaning, but, after glancing at and rejecting one interpretation, thinks that it might have been a sign of haste in their eating the Meal. On the fact that it was a type of Christ there was no uncertainty. 'What God commanded about the lamb, he wished to be fulfilled openly in his only-begotten Son, in order that, the truth corresponding to its type, the substance to its shadow (*umbra*), he might show that

[63] OC 24,292; CTS Mo 1,467.

God was reconciled to his people only by the blood of Christ'.[64] That, by 'the wonderful providence of God', the soldiers refrained from breaking the legs of Jesus, proved that he was the true Passover.[65]

(3)   Ex.13.3–10.

Largely a repetition of the previous instructions on eating unleavened bread; but now intended as exhortation.

(4)   Deut.16.3–4; Ex.23.18; 34.25.

Another repetition on unleavened bread; but now intended to remind them of their affliction.

(5)   Num,9.1–14.

It was a sign of the people's ingratitude that they needed to be reminded of the Passover within a year of its institution. What would happen after fifty years?

Verses 6ff. are narrative, but they are treated in this context as an example from life of a difficulty in the enforcement of the Passover regulations.

II *Another Appendix: On the Consecrating of the Firstborn.*

Ex.13.1–2, 11–16; 22.29–30; 34.19–20; Lev.27.26; Deut.15.19–20.

This set of regulations belongs to the First Commandment because it concerns the Covenant relationship of the children of Israel to God. Here, too, God asserts his possession of the whole people by claiming a right over a part of the people, and that part Calvin hints at by calling them the *genus Abrahae*, the heirs in the next generation. It is intended as a perpetual reminder that God separated and passed over them, when the first-born of the Egyptians were slain, so that they should always remember their redemption and in gratitude sanctify not only their own first-born and the first-born of their beasts, but all that they were and possessed.

III *Another Appendix: On the Payment of Tribute.*

Ex.30.11–16.

Economics is a subject that always stirs Calvin's interest. His

---

[64]   OC 24,292; CTS Mo 1,467.
[65]   OC 24,292; CTS Mo 1,468.

relatively short note on this passage is no exception. The matter
is dealt with under the First Commandment because tribute is
paid by a *tributarius* to an over-lord (Calvin is probably thinking
of it in terms of the Roman system) who has a right to demand
the tax. Thus the demand for the tribute by God was an assertion of his right as the Lord, and the people's payment of the
tribute was an acquiescence in this assertion. The tribute-
payment was a *symbolum* 'to witness that they lived under the
rule of him who had redeemed them'.[66] But there was a difference between this tribute and the customary state taxes, in
that this was a willing payment (*voluntarium munus*). Only so
would it truly express their gratitude.

Another aspect has to be considered. This people had been
Pharaoh's slaves, bound to him by the rights of servitude. They
therefore had no right of themselves to leave Egypt. Only the
fact that God had liberated them prevented them from being
runaway slaves whose duty would have been, when they came
to their senses, to return to Egypt and servitude. But, by paying
tribute, they signified that they had been liberated by God
himself and were now his servants (with the implication that
even Pharaoh must recognize that God had the higher claim).

Calvin then goes on, with the assistance of Budé's book, *De
Asse*, to calculate how much each paid in terms of sixteenth
century French money.

IV *Another Appendix: On the Vow of the Nazarites.*

Num.6.1-21.
The payment of tribute was a general devoting of themselves
to God by all the people. This was a special, stricter vow by
particular individuals whose title of Nazarite indicated their separation from the rest of the people or their excellence. 'They
were ornaments of the Church; in them God willed a special
splendour of his glory to shine'.[67] But such vows stood under
two conditions. The first was that they were temporary; at the
end of a stated term the Nazarite became just one of the people
again. The second was, according to Amos 2.11, that God alone

[66] OC 24,301; CTS Mo 1,482.
[67] OC 24,304; CTS Mo 1,486.

could authorize the taking of any vow; for a man to take it of his own will and without command from God would be a rash intrusion. Although the Nazarites were separated from "the common people", their life nevertheless was of value to all; they were *Ecclesiae lumina*, they were the *antesignani*, the soldiers who preceded the standards of the legions, 'to show the way to others', 'they shone among the people of God like precious jewels, and, although few imitated them, they were like standard-bearers and leaders, who kindled in the masses a desire to serve and worship God'.[68]

Samson was different from the generality of Nazarites in that he was a life-long Nazarite. In this he was a type of Christ. Indeed, 'all that is taught here [i.e. Num. 6] should be referred to the unique fount of sanctity; it is as if the image of Christ were set before the Jews in a mirror. For the nearer anyone under the Law drew to God, the more Christ shined in him. We know that the whole legal priesthood was nothing other than his image (*effigies*); and the same is true of the Nazarites, who were adorned by purity and abstinence with a remarkable privilege'.[69]

Calvin then expounds the details – abstinence from wine, long hair, and avoiding contact with dead bodies. The whole of his exposition of the passage is coloured by opposition to late medieval monasticism. At the end he comes back to 'the law of the Nazarites'. The offering to be made at the close of a Nazarite's term was twofold; it was a thanksgiving, and it was an offering for sin: 'In this we can see that however readily and strenuously men strive to offer themselves wholly to God they never attain to perfection or reach what they desire. They would always be liable to God's judgment did he not pardon their faults'.[70]

V *Another Appendix: On the Offering of First Fruits.*

Deut.26.1-11; Num.15.17-21; Ex.22.29; 23.19; 34.26.

The first fruits stood in the same category as the tribute-payment, to show that the people and all that they possessed belonged to God. But whereas the tribute was a *symbolum* of their

[68] OC 24,304; CTS Mo 1,487.
[69] OC 24,304; CTS Mo 1,487.
[70] OC 24,307; CTS Mo 1,491-2.

manumission from slavery, the offering of the first fruits bore
witness to the terms under which they held the land. God himself
owned the land as, so to say, an investment (*vectigalem Deo terram
esse*). The Jews were merely tenants under God, and this their
offering of the first fruits testified. It was therefore an annual
reminder of this fact; but more, it was a reminder of their
adoption to be the children of God, so that God gave them this
good land to live in and feed them, not as he did the Gentiles,
without distinction, but as children.

VI *Another Appendix: On the Purification of Women after Childbirth.*

Lev.12.1-8.

The purpose of this cleansing was twofold; it reminded the
Jews that their nature was corrupt and it showed them the remedy
for their corruption. The woman was unclean because all the
children of Adam are sinners and therefore corrupt in nature; the
corrupt child infects, so to say, the mother: 'the woman not only
contracts uncleanness from the child in her womb but also is again
defiled in giving it birth'.[71] The common interpretation that she is
unclean because she and her husband had sexual intercourse from
lust and not from a desire to have a child is a stupid idea (*crassus
error*) and nothing to do with the present context, although it is
true that coitus *per se*, without consideration of having children
(*absque sobolis respectu*) is obscene and shameful.

But objection: does not this rite cast a slur on marriage itself?
No, the fact that the marrage bed (he is referring obliquely to
Heb.13.4) is undefiled should be ascribed to God's indulgence.
He sanctifies marriage with a holiness which 'covers what could
otherwise be imputed as guilt and washes the very stains of our
nature'.[72] This does not mean that the children are free from sin;
the children of unbelievers remain under the guilt and the curse,
and those of believers 'are freed from the common destruction by
supernatural grace and special adoption'.[73]

The plural pronoun in Luke 2.22 (*And when the days of* their
purification) leads Calvin to infer that, although the fact was

[71] OC 24,312; CTS Mo 1,499.
[72] OC 24,312; CTS Mo 1,500.
[73] OC 24,312; CTS Mo 1,500.

omitted by Moses, the child as well as the mother had to be purified; hence the purifying of both Mary and Jesus. Jesus, although he was already completely pure, nay, purity itself, represented all mankind (*sustinuit in se personam generis humani*)[74] and therefore subjected himself to this Law. By doing so, he abolished the ancient ceremony of purification; its essential significance of purifying resides in himself.

It may be asked 'why the time of cleansing is double for a girl child'.[75] The reason is not medical but religious. Some think ('I do not know whether this is sound')[76] that girls are more sinful (*vitiositas*) than boys and therefore infect their mothers worse. Others think, with perhaps more probability, that it is because Eve sinned first and led Adam into sin. But it seems to me that the reason is to be found in circumcision, that the punishment for sin was lightened in regard to boys because of their circumcision, a special mark of grace which girls could not have, although 'God by this symbol consecrated both sexes to himself'.[77]

VII *Another Appendix: On the Confining of Lepers.*

(i)   Deut.24.8-9; Num.5.1-3; Lev.13.1-59.

These regulations are not to be spiritualised into intricate allegories, nor are they to be taken as mere rules of hygiene. Num.5.2 gives the reason: 'by this external rite and ceremony he was training (*exercuisse*) the people in the desire and practice of purity'.[78] None could worship God while they were still defiled, for their uncleanness would infect what was otherwise holy; therefore they should not be allowed in the camp, which was God's habitation.

Calvin goes on to discuss the general nature of the disease; but on details 'I confess I am not a physician, able to argue about the finer points; and I deliberately refrain from a precise inquisition because I am sure that the particular form of the disease mentioned here was wide-spread among the Israelites but is

---

[74] OC 24,313; CTS Mo 1,500-1.
[75] OC 24,313; CTS Mo 1,501.
[76] OC 24,313; CTS Mo 1,501.
[77] OC 24,314; CTS Mo 1,501.
[78] OC 24,318; CTS Mo 2,12.

unknown to us today'.[79] It was certainly not true, and Josephus conclusively proves it, that all the descendants of Abraham had the scurvy and were driven out by the Egyptians from fear of infection.

That the Priests, and not the physicians, were given the task of examining and diagnosing the suspected disease is evidence that the regulations were religious and not hygienic. He goes on to deny the application of this task of the priesthood to the *sacrifici Papales*, the Papist sacrificers, who, with the advice of physicians, adjudge cases of physical leprosy. Far less can it be made an allegory of confession and absolution, at least in the form currently practised by the Romanists. Nevertheless we must still hold the *analogia* between ourselves and the Jews (note that, having denied an identity (univocal) in the relation, Calvin now asserts, consistently with his whole theological approach, an analogical relation). The similarity in the analogy lies in the defilement of sin, represented under the Old Covenant by certain physical "uncleannesses", and the cleansing of the defilement by God; the dissimilarity lies in the difference between the figure or type, and the reality, Christ and his salvation. By analogy, therefore, we learn 'that we are not to tolerate or cherish among us any uncleanness, for it corrupts the purity of the worship and service of God'.[80] The correspondence to this ceremony of casting out is excommunication. Following the caution to be observed by the Jewish Priests, the "judge" must neither pardon too lightly nor forget to be fair; especially he is not to judge in a hurry.

Calvin professes himself ignorant of the meaning of a leprous house or leprous cloths, but comments in general that God 'has surrounded the human race with putrefaction, so that, wherever we look, our eyes may behold the punishment for sin'.[81]

(ii) *On the Purifying of Lepers.*

Lev.14.1-57.

The purification ceremony was "an expiatory rite" consisting of two parts, cleansing (*ablutio*) and thanksgiving. It was intended as an enacted lesson 'to teach the Israelites that God is to be

[79] OC 24,319; CTS Mo 2,13.
[80] OC 24,320; CTS Mo 2,16.
[81] OC 24,321; CTS Mo 2,18.

worshipped immaculately and purely (*caste pureque*) and to keep themselves far from pollutions, so that his religion might not be desecrated'.[82] Having said thus much in general, Calvin at once takes up again the application already made in the last section. The re-admission of the leper after he had been cleansed was a sort of reconciliation after excommunication. The way this is done is a pattern for us. The office of cleansing (*munus purgandi*) was laid on the Priest. Nevertheless, he was forbidden to cleanse any save those who were already clean. The significance of this is twofold: on the one hand, God alone effects the healing of the leper; and on the other, he sets up a system of discipline in his Church. 'It is for God alone to forgive sins. What, then, is left for man, except to testify and proclaim the divinely given grace? Therefore the minister of God can only absolve him whom God has already absolved'.[83] As with the other ceremonies of the Law, the rite itself ceased at the coming of Christ but the expiation (which is his) is still in force. Moreover, the rite itself has a counterpart in excommunication and re-admission to the Church: 'He who has once been cast out by public authority from the holy congregation may not be admitted again before profession of penitence and a new life'.[84] The Priests of the Old Covenant held the office of purifying, not only as types of Christ (*gestabant Christi personam*), but also on account of their ministry, and this ministry we have in common with them.

He goes on to consider the details of the rite, emphasizing the image of new life. The rite of the two birds, one of which was dipped in the blood of the other and then released, shows that 'cleansing from leprosy is a certain image (*species*) of resurrection';[85] those who were cleansed and restored to the Church were 'born again. For they were regarded as dead whom leprosy had banished from the holy congregation'.[86] As for all the details of the rite, 'I am undecided about the reason for them, and I would not like readers to be over-inquisitive'.[87]

[82] OC 24,324-5; CTS Mo 2,24.
[83] OC 24,325; CTS Mo 2,25.
[84] OC 24,325; CTS Mo 2,25.
[85] OC 24,325; CTS Mo 2,26.
[86] OC 24,326; CTS Mo 2,26.
[87] OC 24,326; CTS Mo 2,26.

VIII *On Pollutions occurring from Issues.*

Lev.15.1-33.

This kind of defilement could be considered under the Seventh Commandment, but it is, on closer view, part of the regulations on purity and not simply a law on chastity. Calvin proceeds with exegesis of the details, summing up the significance of the ceremonies: 'the rule must always be held that whatever proceeds from unclean man is corrupt (*vitiosus*); none can rightly offer himself or his own to God save he that is pure and sound in soul and flesh'.[88] (The last rather surprising phrase, "soul and flesh", is in fact a reference to II Cor.7.1, which Calvin quotes as the New Testament interpretation of the rite). That washing with water is enjoined leads directly to Christ: 'whenever there is mention of water, the place in John should at once come to mind, that Christ came with water and blood, to cleanse and expiate uncleanness'.[89]

IX *On other defects which exclude men from the Tabernacle.*

Deut.23.1-2.

The purpose of these exclusions is 'that the Church of God should not be defiled by shameful blemishes and so religion lose respect',[90] and to show the seed of Abraham by a *symbolum* the excellence of their dignity. Calvin concludes that these "unhappy men", those with faulty sexual organs and the illegitimate, were not altogether shut out from hope of salvation but only humbled by a temporal punishment.

X *Another Appendix: On the General Purification of the People.*

Num.19.1-22.

This passage is expounded Christologically. The purpose of the rite is first to stir the people to a realization of their impurity and then to show them that the expiation had to be sought from outside themselves, that is, from the sacrifice and the sprinkling. Having said that he will leave clever speculations on the meaning of the details to those who enjoy such things, Calvin flirts for

[88] OC 24,329; CTS Mo 2,31-2.
[89] OC 24,329-30; CTS Mo 2,32. I Jn 5.6.
[90] OC 24,330; CTS Mo 2,34.

several lines with the significance of the red-ness of the heifer before he can come to his main point, the application of the rite to Christians. The offering was to be made by the whole people because (and he drops into the first person), for us to partake of the ablution, we must each 'offer Christ',[91] and offer him daily. This is not the Papists' daily slaying and sacrificing Christ in the Mass, but 'the oblation of faith and prayers by which alone we apply the power and fruit of Christ's death to ourselves'.[92]

The people made the offering, but mediately, by the hand of the Priest. In the same way today, we appease God by presenting Christ before his face; but it is necessary that Christ himself shall mediate in his office of priesthood (*intervenire et fungi sacerdotis partibus*).[93] The heifer was taken outside the camp as a *signum anathematis*, just as also the beasts for expiation were burned outside the camp. This is a *figura*, whose truth was fulfilled in Christ, who suffered outside the gates of the city. It was, in regard to the heifer, an image (*species*) of rejection; but the Israelites were shown that her blood was nevertheless not accursed but holy and of a sweet savour, for it was to be sprinkled on the altar. Similarly with Christ. He was made a curse for us 'because he bore on the accursed cross our sins and was the expiatory sacrifice. But this detracted in no way from his purity, in no way from his sanctity being the sanctification of the whole world'.[94] Therefore Paul called his death the sacrifice of a most sweet odour.

The sprinkling of the blood was united with the sprinkling of the water by the instruments of sprinkling, the cedar-wood, the hyssop, and the scarlet thread, being thrown into the fire which burnt the heifer. This was a visible *symbolum* to the people that not only had they themselves been washed in the water but their stains had been obliterated by the offering of the sacrifice, by the sprinkling of the blood. John tells us that every part of this ceremony is to be found in Christ – *this is he that came by water and blood*.

The regulations for purification after touching a dead body are

[91] OC 24,333; CTS Mo 2,39.
[92] OC 24,333-4; CTS Mo 2,39.
[93] OC 24,334; CTS Mo 2,39.
[94] OC 24,334; CTS Mo 2,40.

first explained as death being 'a mirror of the curse of God';[95] but
the rite is also a sign, a mode of signifying that we become unclean
when we have fellowship with the unfruitful works of darkness
(Eph.5.11). This somewhat obscure connection is arrived at by
the "unfruitful" works of Eph.5.11 being the dead works of
Heb.6.1, and where, therefore, we catch up again with the
concept of death: 'a corpse, bones, a sepulchre, these represent
whatever we are by nature (*afferimus ex utero*); for, until we are
regenerate and God quickens us by his Spirit and by faith, we are
dead while we live'.[96] It is of this that the ceremony was intended
to remind the Israelites.

XI *Another Appendix: On keeping themselves clean by concealing their
uncleannesses.*

Deut.23.9-14.
The same purity is to be observed by soldiers in camp as by the
whole people in peace. It may be more difficult to preserve
standards under such circumstances, 'but God never relinquishes
his rights'.[97] The point of the regulations for latrines (so to say)
was not simply a care for hygiene or decency but to train the
people to hate uncleanness of any sort.

XII *Another Appendix: [On fleeing all corruptions, adulterations, and
falsifications.]*

Deut.22.9-11; Lev.19.19, 23-25, 27-28; Deut.14.1-2.
This Appendix is concerned with *simplicitas*, simplicity or
single-mindedness, in opposition to adulteration and additives.[98]
The reason why these passages are placed under the First
Commandment is that in it *simplicitas* is commanded: 'thou shalt
have no other god'. Each precept enjoins singleness – one type of
seed for a vineyard, one kind of beast yoked together at the
plough, one sort of cloth in garments, any domestic animal to be
mated only with its own kind. In these everyday matters the
people 'were kept firmly in purity, so that they should not

[95] OC 24,335; CTS Mo 2,42.
[96] OC 24,335; CTS Mo 2,42.
[97] OC 24,338; CTS Mo 2,45-6.
[98] OC 24,339; CTS Mo 2,48.

become used to corrupted customs and so go on to introduce
foreign rites or, with perverted curiosity, desire mixtures which
at last might touch the worship of God'.[99] For 'men become in
some degree defiled so soon as they degenerate from
simplicity'.[100] Therefore, God's purpose was 'that by cultivating
natural simplicity in their entire life they might keep themselves
pure and sound from all outward defects'.[101]

At the end of the exposition of Deut.22.9-11 comes a statement
that will be repeated in the next two sections: 'the people was
surrounded with barriers or fixed boundaries, lest they should
profane themselves with alien vices and imitate the nations from
whom they had been separated'.[102] Similarly the "circumcision"
of trees (Lev.19.23-25), a *symbolum* of their adoption and a
reminder that the fruit was only for God's children and that all
food needs to be sanctified, is a wall erected by God 'to separate
his people from the Gentiles'.[103] And the tonsuring and scars
(Lev.19.27-28) had the same end, 'to separate his people from
heathen nations by putting a barrier (*obstaculum*) between
them'.[104] What it came to was that God did not wish his people to
practise these customs 'so that they might learn, like children on
the first elements, that God would be pleased with them only if
they were entirely unlike the uncircumcised foreigners and at the
opposite pole from imitating them'.[105]

XIII *Another Appendix: On Clean and Unclean Beasts.*

Lev.20.25-26; 11.1-47; Deut.14.3-20.

Once again, the reason for this differentiation lay in the
separation of the people from the Gentiles. It taught them 'to
study purity',[106] both in regard to holiness of life and also to
purity of worship. The regulations belong therefore to the First
Commandment. But they also pre-dated the giving of the Law,

[99] OC 24,340; CTS Mo 2,48-9.
[100] OC 24,340; CTS Mo 2,48.
[101] OC 24,340; CTS Mo 2,49.
[102] OC 24,340; CTS Mo 2,49.
[103] OC 24,341; CTS Mo 2,50.
[104] OC 24,341; CTS Mo 2,50.
[105] OC 24,341; CTS Mo 2,51.
[106] OC 24,345; CTS Mo 2,58.

for we can see that Noah was aware of the distinction between clean and unclean beasts (Gen.7.1-8); but he was aware of it 'by secret instinct' or perhaps by tradition. The identities of all the animals is not known to us nowadays and all we can do is to go by the given indications about cloven hoofs and chewing the cud and so on. The distinctions were not made on grounds of hygiene but were 'a part of the infant teaching (*paedagogiae*) under which God kept his ancient people'[107] – this 'practically primitive and savage' people.

On this subject, Calvin departs from his usual practice and, after a short apology, indulges in allegory, a course he can follow because the allegory 'has been handed down to us from the old writers'.[108] 'By the cleaving of the hoof is denoted prudence in "dividing" the mysteries of Scripture and by chewing the cud earnest meditation on the heavenly teaching'.[109] He cannot accept that "dividing" will mean drawing the spiritual senses (*mystici sensus*) out of the literal, but prefers a simpler interpretation, that Scripture 'is not divided by anyone who is only carnally minded, for only the spiritual man "divides" all things, as Paul says (I Cor.2.15). "Chewing the cud" is also necessary for spiritual food to be well digested and distributed. Many swallow Scripture without it doing them any good, for they neither sincerely desire it to do them good nor seek to refresh their souls with it as food, but are content with the empty delights of mere knowing and care nothing about studying to form their lives'.[110] This allegory is permissible by "probable analogy" between animals and men on the basis of Peter's vision (Acts 10.9ff.).

The *quaestio* is posed, 'How God could pronounce unclean what he had created,'[111] and which he had at first declared to be "very good"? *Solutio est,* that no animal was ever unclean in itself. The differentiation was purely a matter of command and obedience, that 'the people might detest what had been forbidden'.[112] Putting it another way, 'it is only transgression that

107 OC 24,346; CTS Mo 2,60.
108 OC 24,345-6; CTS Mo 2,61. See pp. 76-7.
109 OC 24,347; CTS Mo 2,61f.
110 OC 24,347; CTS Mo 2,62.
111 OC 24,348; CTS Mo 2,63.
112 OC 24,348; CTS Mo 2,63.

defiles; the animals never changed their nature, but it was in the will of God to decree what he wished to be lawful or unlawful'.[113]

Now, although *the kingdom of God is not meat and drink* (Rom.14.17 – a verse Calvin often has on his lips), this ceremony of eating the clean and refusing the unclean was intended to teach the Jews 'how abominable is the inward pollution of the heart; so that little by little they might be led by such elementary training (*elementis*) towards spiritual teaching and learn that nothing defiles a man save what comes out of his mouth (Matt.15.12)'.[114]

Lev.11.4, *ye shall not eat of them that chew the cud, or of them that divide the hoof*, causes Calvin again to glance towards allegory. 'Moses teaches here that a semi-cleanness or a mutilated cleanness is not to be forced on God. If anyone wishes to make chewing the cud a symbol of inward purity and dividing the hoof of external, his judgment is perhaps probable. As this distinction has come into mind, I wanted to mention it, leaving it an open question for the reader, although I myself do not enjoy these clever speculations'.[115] What is certain is that God requires complete cleanness in his people, without any adulterating defilements. And this is the heart of the rest of his comment, although he gives a good deal of space to asking why swine flesh, such good food and very cheap, was prohibited, and to laughing at the allegories of Hesychius.

XIV *Another Appendix: On Things Accidentally Unclean.*

Deut.14.21; Ex.22.31; Lev.17.15-16.

Calvin explains the details of these prohibitions and again refers them to the category of holiness and avoidance of ritual uncleanness. These, too, are a mark of distinction between the Jews and the Gentiles, who were allowed to eat whatever they liked.

XV *Another Appendix: On Marriage with Unbelievers.*

Deut.21.10-13.

This is stricter than a general command not to intermarry with

---

[113] OC 24,348; CTS Mo 2,63.
[114] OC 24,348; CTS Mo 2,63.
[115] OC 24,348-9; CTS Mo 2,64.

Gentiles, for it is a matter of women taken as spoil in a war. It would be better if the women were left alone; but because soldiers who take a town will usually give way to lust and capture women to carry them off as their wives or concubines (for this is not dealing only with rape), God is indulgent with his people so that they may remember their adoption as God's children and not dishonour themselves 'but even in the heat of lust retain some care for godliness'.[116] The reason for this prohibition lies in the need to keep God's people pure and uncorrupt, separated from the Gentiles. If a Jew marries such a captive, she is to become herself a Jew, lest her heathen ways lead her husband astray.

4 Judicial Appendices.

(1)   Deut. 18.19; 13.5.

Under the first of these passages Calvin moves over from the ceremonies of the First Commandment to the penalties for transgressing or failing to perform them. He makes the distinction between the Commandment and its ceremonies that the Commandment is both perpetual and common to Jews and Christians whereas the ceremonies were temporary and (by inference) belonged to the Jews only. But there is a sense in which they belong to Christians also, in that their spirit is always in force: 'God made use of the ceremonies in the old time as temporary helps. Their use has now ceased but their utility remains; for they show very well how God is to be rightly worshipped and served; the very essence (vis) of godliness shines in them'.[117] And he goes on to speak of them in sacramental terms: 'Therefore in the commandment is contained the whole *substantia*, whereas in the outward practices is, as it were, the *forma*, to which God bound only his ancient people'.[118]

The penalties are comprehended and arranged under the title of *Appendices Forenses* or *Politicae*, *politicae* in this context bearing the sense of "disciplinary". In them 'God orders the punishment to be dispensed if the religion has been violated'.[119] But then Calvin

[116]   OC 24,353; CTS Mo 2,71.
[117]   OC 24,354; CTS Mo 2,73.
[118]   OC 24,354; CTS Mo 2,73.
[119]   OC 24,354; CTS Mo 2,73.

shows that he is not making the break between State law and
Church law that is so easily made in the modern world. For he
goes on to use *lex politica* to mean State law, to which he assigns a
religious use: 'Political laws are not only concerned with earthly
affairs, that men may cultivate mutual equity among themselves
and follow and observe what is right, but they exist that men may
be trained in the veneration of God'.[120] This he confirms by
appeal to Plato and 'every profane author who has ever
existed',[121] so that the point can now be taken as universally
agreed. The *leges politicae* we are dealing with here, however, are
those decreed by God, the Lord of his people Israel (for in any
State, laws are made by the rulers). His Commandments were the
rule and standard; the ceremonies were the practical application
and interpretation of the Commandments. But something else
was necessary; a continual reminding and exhorting to obedience,
in fact, 'a daily preaching' by the Prophets, and on top of that, the
threats of punishment for disobedience.

Before we continue with Calvin's exposition, we must state a
problem. Did the *leges politicae* cease with the ceremonies to
which they were related or, if not, how are they still in force? That
they and at least some of their penalties are not in the power of the
Church is quite clear; but if it is the duty of the Christian State to
train its citizens in the veneration of God, are the *leges politicae* to
be taken into the laws of that State? Putting this historically, we
are asking about the relationship of the Mosaic Law with the laws
of the European States. We shall, in what follows, see Calvin
taking some political laws as still in force, others not. The further
question has then to be asked whether it is the Old Testament
political law that he is concerned to enforce or a medieval
interpretation or even a medieval law apparently identical with
the Mosaic Law.

Calvin interprets Deut. 18.19 and 13.5, taken in juxtaposition,
not of a man who spreads one particular, perhaps slight, error,
but of a false prophet who deliberately attempts to subvert the
Church 'and so eradicate godliness'.[122] Such men are to be put to
death. Should toleration be shown to a false prophet? Not at all,

[120] OC 24,354; CTS Mo 2,73.
[121] OC 24,354-5; CTS Mo 2,73.
[122] OC 24,355; CTS Mo 2,75.

'in a well ordered State (*politia*) profane men who overturn religion should certainly not be tolerated'.[123] In this discussion, which he argues passionately and at length, Calvin is no longer talking about "the ancient people" but about the duty of the magistracy "today". He therefore has to raise the *quaestio: 'An haec lex ad Christi regnum, quod spirituale est ac remotum a terrenis imperiis, pertineat'* – 'Does this law refer to the kingdom of Christ, which is spiritual and separate from earthly kingdoms?' And some good men will answer in the negative. 'But I deny that the nature of an earthly judge's work is changed because it is directed (*consecrant*) towards promoting the kingdom of Christ'.[124] He bases his argument on the change in the relationship between Church and State which has taken place between New Testament times and his own. The anti-Christian, persecuting State has been replaced by States that have embraced Christianity and therefore have a duty to 'care for the safety of the Church and the defence of godliness'.[125] Christ would certainly have us to imitate his gentleness, but to let poor souls be destroyed by 'ungodly, wicked, cruel impostors'[126] without lifting a finger would be the height of treachery and cruelty. He ends, however, with the caution that, not only is the sentence of capital punishment to be passed (in this context) only on authors of apostasy, but the cases are to be tried with the utmost care and under strict legal forms.

(2)   Deut.17,12-13.

The same punishment is decreed for disobedience to Priests. It is not clear whether Calvin was applying this to his contemporary situation, with pastors understood for Priests.

(3)   Deut.13.6-11.

The scope of this judicial law is now widened to take in every one of the people individually as both under the law and responsible for its observance. The two provisos are repeated: the judgment is relevant 'only where religion is rightly settled';[127] and the death penalty is applicable only to those 'who uproot godliness to such an extent that the worship of God is adulterated

or pure doctrine abolished'.[128] Individuals must also be responsible for the observance of the law, at whatever cost to themselves
and their feelings; 'pure zeal must not be weakened by humane
feelings when it sees the holy Name profaned. Christ confesses
none as his disciple who does not, if necessary, disregard his
father and mother and children.'[129] God and his honour are to be
set above all earthly ties.

Those who denounce a capital sin must be willing to go the
whole way and to be themselves the executioners, to the extent of
throwing the first stone. An excellent system, which taught
accusers to be cautious and moderate.

(4)   Deut. 13.12–17.

This passage deals with the destruction of apostate cities and is
therefore an extension of the three earlier Appendices. To wish
apostasy to escape unpunished is 'an impure softness',[130] for the
fearfulness of the punishment shows the atrocity of the crime.
Then Calvin drops into the first person: 'Since we were created to
no other end and live for no other reason than that God should be
glorified in us, let the whole world perish rather than that men
should enjoy the earth's nourishments only to contaminate it with
sacrilege'.[131] But such severity as is commanded here should
never be used except when the religion from which the city has
apostasized can be shown to be both the established religion and
also *solide probata*, proved on sound grounds. And again, the two
extremes of laxity and hastiness are to be avoided and the case
judged diligently and fairly.

The words *the inhabitants of that city* are taken to include women
and children. The excuse that babies were innocent of apostasy is
rejected as an arguing against God's decision: 'because our
feelings cry out against it, we must reverently accept the heavenly
judgment instead of subjecting it to our own laws'.[132] Calvin
finds further justification for the passage in his doctrine of
predestination: 'God never suffered any infants to be killed save

[128]   OC 24,359; CTS Mo 2,81.
[129]   OC 24,360; CTS Mo 2,82.
[130]   OC 24,362; CTS Mo 2,85.
[131]   OC 24,362; CTS Mo 2,85.
[132]   OC 24,363; CTS Mo 2,87.

those whom he had already reprobated and destined to eternal death'.[133]

(5)   Ex.22.18;   Lev.20.6,27;   Num.15.30–31;   Lev.20.1–5; Ex.12.15,19.

The previous judgments had related to apostasy from true religion; the present one, on not suffering witches to live, concerns the purity of religion itself. Perhaps strangely, in view of the practice of various contemporary forms of witchcraft, Calvin expounds this place largely historically, with only general applications. It is a fearful sin to call in the help of the devil in personal quarrels or in seeking some sort of knowledge, and it was equivalent to divorce from God: 'the moment our eyes rove hither and thither, instead of being fixed on God alone and being content with him, we break that sacred marriage with which he has bound us to himself'.[134]

This section ends with the insertion of an exposition of the punishment for eating leavened bread during the Passover celebrations. It should have been given a section of its own, but its brevity made that impracticable.

(6)   Deut.17.14–20.

The atmosphere abruptly changes as Calvin treats of the 'priestly kingdom' in the promised land. It is difficult to see why he placed this passage among the Judicial Appendices, for it contains no overt threats of punishment. The sum of his exposition is that God alone is the king over his people and that any earthly king they may appoint will be his subject no less than will the rest of the people. The initial stage of government by judges was a further mark of differentiation from surrounding nations, who had their kings. Once this mark was removed, the danger of assimilation was increased. The *quaestio* is posed as to the consistency of the system of kingship being chosen by the people's wrong-headed whims and yet that 'the kingdom was the chief glory of the people, a pledge of the special grace of God and therefore of salvation and complete happiness'.[135] *Respondeo*, what was wrong was the people's rashness and haste; they were too precipitate. It had been God's purpose *ab initio* (from all

[133] OC 24,363; CTS Mo 2,87.
[134] OC 24,366; CTS Mo 2,91.
[135] OC 24,369; CTS Mo 2,95.

eternity?) to set up an image (*effigiem*) of Christ in David, but the people wanted to imitate their Gentile neighbours as quickly as possible. It is this which is censured. When he gives them kings, God nevertheless reserves the supreme kingship to himself. To keep the kings humble and mindful of their subordinate position, their power is circumscribed by certain practical limitations, like a moderate possession of horses, wives, and treasure. They were also to be custodians of God's Law, both learning and observing it themselves and also seeing that the people were taught it.

(7)   Deut.20.1-4.

In their wars the Israelites are to fight *sub Dei auspiciis*, under the over-all command of God, trusting in his aid and following him as their commander-in-chief. (This passage also does not seem well-placed).

(8)   Num.10.1-10.

The two silver trumpets were blown for three purposes, to assemble the people for meetings, to call them to arms, and to proclaim sacrifices and feasts. They were like a heavenly proclamation and taught the people always to hearken to God's voice. Their "Taratantara" ('a coined word which some use, but I render it "with jubilation"')[136] in battle was an external *symbolum*, the reality of which was 'that they may fight in God, follow him as their commander, and place all their strength in his grace'.[137]

Our condensation of Calvin's exposition of the First Commandment will have shown the reader how he went to work and the nature of his scheme. The rest are treated in a similar way, the second at greater length, the others much more briefly. An outline of Commandments 2-7, 9-10 and the suffixes will be found in the Appendix to this chapter.

The Eighth Commandment

1.   Ex.20.15; repeated Deut.5.19.

'Since love is the end of the Law, it is here that we must look for a definition'.[138] We must remember that Calvin views the Law as a prohibition to which corresponds a positive command. The opposite of stealing, then, is not simply not stealing but loving,

---

[136]   OC 24,374; CTS Mo 2,104.
[137]   OC 24,375; CTS Mo 2,105.
[138]   OC 24,669; CTS Mo 3,110.

and that in a completely practical way. It is this understanding that saves Calvin's exposition of the Commandment from being a typical lawyer's product, concerned only with rights and possessions. But once it is established that love is at the heart of his interpretation, then even rights and possessions appear in this light. That everyone should have his own rights is 'the rule of love',[139] as is not doing to another what we do not wish to be done to ourselves. Negatively, this will lead to a wide interpretation of theft, that it is not only blatant stealing but 'getting rich at another's expense, accumulating wealth by illicit tricks',[140] even 'being more attentive to personal advantage than to fair dealing'.[141] On the other hand, the commandment teaches us that God is not satisfied merely that we should refrain from all forms of actual stealing. He has bound men into a mutual relationship, 'so that they should take pains to be useful to others, to look after them, and to help them'.[142]

2. Exposition of the Commandment

(1) Lev.19.11,13.

This is a clarification of the scope of stealing, that it includes cunning and fraud as well as violence. The second verse gives an example of this, when a master postpones paying his servant's wages. As a *summa*, Calvin makes the affirmative 'cultivating humanity, so that none is oppressed, or is injured by a mean manner of payment (*ex maligna solutione*)'.[143]

(2) Deut.24.14-15; 25.4.

Again on payment of wages, at first repeating the former prohibition. Servants are not to be treated as slaves, and masters must not treat them in a mean or niggardly manner. Moreover, we must note that this command is not "political", i.e. social, but completely "spiritual", binding men's consciences before the heavenly judgment seat of God. A poor servant may not be in a position to sue his master in the courts, but God will require the unfairness at the hand of the master.

[139] OC 24,669; CTS Mo 3,110.
[140] OC 24,669; CTS Mo 3,110.
[141] OC 24,669; CTS Mo 3,110-1.
[142] OC 24,669; CTS Mo 3,111.
[143] OC 24,670-1; CTS Mo 3,113.

(3)   Ex.22.21–24; Lev.19.33–34.

What of those who have none to speak for them, the foreigners, poor widows, fatherless children? The command is to be fair to all without any exception. They have one who cares for them and who can fearfully avenge their wrongs.

(4)   Deut.10.17–19.

A confirmation of the previous passage.

(5)   Lev.19.35–36; Deut.25.13–16.

Passages on fair trading practices. Here Calvin the lawyer comes to the fore: 'The corruption which leads to subverting judgments or which vitiates all contracts by weakening rectitude, leaves nothing safe; false weights and measures remove and abolish all lawful ways of transacting business. And when the rights of selling and buying are corrupted, the society of men is in a sense broken up'.[144] He goes on to confirm this from Roman law as well as from the Bible.

(6)   Deut.19.14.

To remove land-marks is a form of theft. Again Calvin appeals to Roman Law.

(7)   Ex.22.26–27; Deut.24.6,10–13, 17–18.

Calvin's emphasis on these passages about the payment of loans and the respect for workmen's tools is on the defence of the poor against the rich. The poor are in God's care and anyone who treats them badly will be held answerable to God. The phrase *it shall be unto righteousness for thee before Jehovah thy God* (Deut.24.13), used by the opponents of "by faith alone" to prove the value of works for justification, is expounded by Calvin in his usual way. It is indeed an act of righteousness, even though there will be unrighteousness mixed in it; but justification concerns the whole life, whereas this is only one act of righteousness, and that one which might be performed by, say, a glutton or an adulterer. Even this work of kindness needs God's mercy and sanctification.

(8)   Ex.22.25; Lev.25.35–38; Deut.23.19–20.

The first part of this comment declares the positive injunction to be liberal towards the needy. The second part consists of a quite long *locus* on usury. We may note that it is not initially treated in terms of economics or even of general economic ethics, but the giving of interest free loans is based on 'the rule of love', for the

[144] OC 24,675; CTS Mo 3,120.

sake of the poor. Later, however, when the discussion is broadened into answering the *quaestio* 'Whether usury is wrong in itself', the basis becomes a matter of what is just and fair. So far as the rich are concerned, lending on interest is certainly allowable. The rule of love still holds, but it applies to the oppression of the poor. Those who engage in usury must not do to the other what he would not have him do to himself.

(9)   Deut.22.1-3; Ex.23.4.

We come to ways in which we can help our neighbour. Negative abstention from ill-doing is not enough; we must also do good. These injunctions apply to enemies as well as friends. The sum of it is 'that believers should imitate their heavenly Father in doing good'.[145]

(10)   Num.5.5-7.

This command to make restitution, says Calvin, refers to undetected thefts. Without restitution, confession of sin is hollow.

(11)   Ex.23.8; Lev.19.15; Deut.16.19-20.

Bribery of judges is a deadly poison and completely destroys all rectitude. That judges should not accept any gifts is obvious and has been known in all ages.

(12)   Ex.23.3,6.

Whereas the previous passage was general and referred by implication to favour shown to the rich, this refers to the poor. Sometimes the poor are more litigious than the rich and their very wretchedness 'may get round incautious judges and make them forget the point at issue'.[146] God may befriend the poor, but he certainly does not want them unfairly favoured at the expense of the rich.

3 Political Appendices.[147]

(1)   (a)   Ex.22.1-4.

In this group of Appendices Calvin has arranged what we may call common-sense laws governing the orderly running of society. They are not so precise and absolute (*perfecta*) as those already considered, but show a certain relaxation because of the

[145] OC 24,684; CTS Mo 3,134.
[146] OC 24,688; CTS Mo 3,139.
[147] OC 24,688; CTS Mo 3,140.

hardness of the people (cf. Matt. 19.8). It is significant that he immediately turns to non-Jewish law, which was borrowed, he says, from the Mosaic. He therefore discusses the present passage on the killing of a burglar by day or by night with cross reference to Greek and Roman law.

(b)   Ex.22.9.

This verse regulates law suits with, not merely the losing of the case but an actual penalty, if the suit fails.

(c)   Ex.22.5-8 10-13.

Various agricultural frauds and grounds for damages.

(d)   Ex.22.14-15.

The question of harm happening to a horse while it is borrowed. The damage must be made good. The same rule applies to anything borrowed.

(e)   Lev.24.18,21

If a man causes damage to anyone's property, he shall make it good.

(f)   Ex.21.33-36.

And this shall be so if the damage is caused by carelessness.

(g)   Deut.23.24-25.

Calvin takes these verses to refer, not to harvesters in a vineyard, but to weary and hungry travellers. Nevertheless, he says, 'they must not take too much license, only what humanity demands'.[148]

(h)   Lev.19.9-10; 23.22; Deut.24.19-22.

A similar injunction, this time on gleaning a corn-field, with a similar caveat.

(2)   Deut.15.1-11.

At the end of every seven years, debts are to be forgiven. This is an act of humanity, but it was peculiar to the Jews. 'We are no longer bound by this law today, nor is it right that we should be'.[149] But the spirit of the law is still in force, that we should not be grasping in the matter of debts, especially towards the poor. The words in v.6, *Jehovah thy God blesseth thee* . . . reminds them of the Covenant, by which they were made heirs of the land of Canaan; but this 'flowed entirely from the primary fount of God's

[148] OC 24,695; CTS Mo 3,150.
[149] OC 24,697; CTS Mo 3,154.

grace'.[150] The richness of the blessing would be related to their richness or meanness towards the poor. If they were mean, the land also would cease to be rich towards them and become barren.

(3) Ex.21.1-6; Deut.15.12-18.

Slavery among the children of Israel is to be different from that which is practised by the Gentiles, in that freedom is to be given after seven years. The exception is of a slave who has been given a wife by his master; if he goes free, his wife and children stay with the master. Calvin the man calls this unnatural, 'an ungodly violation of marriage',[151] 'a foul barbarity'.[152] Calvin the lawyer admits the justice of it; the woman had been the master's slave; to take her away would have been spoliation of the master's possessions. 'Thus in this respect the sanctity of marriage yields to the rights of the individual (*iuri privato*)'. This is one of the ordinances given on account of the people's hardness of heart.

(4) Lev.25.39-55.

The exposition on the treatment of Hebrew slaves is based on the twin concepts of God's ownership and grace. That masters are commanded to treat their slaves humanely and more like hired servants is no more than secular philosophers had enjoined. So much, then, is self-evident. But the reason given in Leviticus is that all the Jews are God's slaves, acquired by his liberating them from the bondage of Pharaoh. Therefore, for another to make a Jew his perpetual slave is an infringement of God's rights over the person. That God permitted a temporary enslavement was 'by indulgence';[153] the qualification that the slavery was temporary was a *symbolum*, to remind them of God's grace in redeeming them. This *lex politica* is no longer in force, but, by *anagogē* we must hold that 'the condition [of slaves] must not be worse among us who have been redeemed by the blood of Christ than it was among the people of old'.[154]

(5) Lev.25.23-34.

Not only were the Jews God's possession, but so also was the land. This fact governs the laws on land tenure and sale. The land

[150] OC 24,699; CTS Mo 3,157.
[151] OC 24,701; CTS Mo 3,160.
[152] OC 24,701; CTS Mo 3,160.
[153] OC 24,704; CTS Mo 3,165.
[154] OC 24,704; CTS Mo 3,165.

belonged to God as his free-hold property. The Jews were simply his tenants, his guests, dependent on his will: 'Canaan is called God's land as if he were asserting his single direct ownership (*directum dominium*), as they say'. He at once explains his meaning more clearly when he says that the children of Israel sojourned there as his guests. For, although their condition was that of rightful and perpetual owners, yet, in regard to God, they were nothing but tenant farmers (*coloni*), merely permitted to live there (*precario tantum illic quiescebant*)'.[155] If a man sold his land, he was to that extent expunging the memory of the Covenant, for 'the land of Canaan was a pledge, or symbol, or mirror, of the adoption on which their salvation was founded'.[156]

(6)   Deut. 20.19-20.

This law on limited deforestation is treated under the Eighth Commandment because the felling of fruit trees is a depriving men of their food. What is true of war-time is true no less of peace-time, and what is true of the wanton destruction of fruit trees is no less true of all destruction and devastation of the land.

(7)   Deut. 21.14-17.

The law on the sale of captive wives comes under this commandment rather than the Seventh because it is a question of equity and not chastity. The woman has lost 'a unique treasure', her chastity; she must be repaid with 'an inestimable good', her liberty.[157]

The second part of this section concerns fairness in inheritance for sons of more than one wife. Calvin shrewdly observes that under polygamy it was common for a man to favour the son of a second wife, 'and this was clearly a kind of theft'.[158]

(8)   Deut. 20.5-8.

In war-time, relaxations were to be made for certain men – those who had built a new house, planted a new vineyard, newly married a wife, and those who were 'timid and soft-hearted'. This may seem remote from *Thou shalt not steal*, says Calvin. But he sees it as a question of people being fairly allowed to enjoy their possessions; to forbid them is undoubtedly a form of stealing.

---

[155] OC 24,706; CTS Mo 3,169-70.
[156] OC 24,706; CTS Mo 3,169.
[157] OC 24,709; CTS Mo 3,173.
[158] OC 24,709; CTS Mo 3,174.

Even the indulgence for the timid 'depends on equity, which dictates that we must abstain from all unjust oppression',[159] and to press someone beyond their capacity is an unjust oppression. (9)   Deut.25.5-10.

In the final passage, on 'raising children to his brother', the children are considered as property which a man would have possessed had he not died, and to whom also he can therefore leave his name and his goods. 'And so, unless a relative shall help the dead man, it would not only be inhumanity but also a kind of theft'.[160] The word "relative" should be stressed, for Calvin argued strongly that the Law did not refer to actual brothers and therefore command incest.

The Sum of the Law

Deut.10.12-13; 6.5; Lev.19.18.

For the whole sum and direction of the Law Calvin goes at once to the New Testament, to 1 Tim.1.5: *The end of the commandment is love out of a pure heart, and of a good conscience, and of faith unfeigned*, and to Matt.22.37: *Thou shalt love the Lord thy God . . . and thy neighbour as thyself.* The latter teaches that 'all the perfection of righteousness delivered in the Law consists in two parts, cultivating true piety towards God and living harmlessly with men, following the rule of love'. [161] The other passage says in effect the same thing, for the word "faith" there also comprehends love for God. Therefore the statement (*sententia*) of Christ is that the Law demands nothing but the love of God and our neighbours. And so he arrives at a definition: 'for right living, nothing is required save *pietas* and *iustitia*, godliness and righteousness'.[162]

In Deut.10.12 two important words are used – "fear" and "love". As the Lord, God has the power and authority to be feared; as Father, he asks to be loved. Hence, to keep the Law, we must gird ourselves with this combined fear and love: 'He must be harder than iron who is not charmed by such sweetness. For he

---

[159]   OC 24,711; CTS Mo 3,176-7.
[160]   OC 24,712; CTS Mo 3,178.
[161]   OC 24,721; CTS Mo 3,191.
[162]   OC 24,721; CTS Mo 3,191.

invites us and exhorts us to love him for no other cause than that he himself loves us'.[163] A grudging, gloomy, coerced obedience does not please God, for he loves a cheerful giver.

But how difficult it is to subdue 'the depraved motion of the flesh'![164] The best runners make little progress in this spiritual race, and none can claim he has got anywhere near the goal set by the Law.

Thou shalt love thy neighbour as thyself says everything necessary about the Second Table. We are prone to self-love; in fact, 'φιλαυτία so blinds us that it is the mother of all evils'.[165] We are forgetful and neglectful of our brethren. But in this verse God tears out this deep and innate vice. In explanation, Calvin criticises the scholastic doctrine that the love of the neighbour is based on the primary love of self, which is therefore necessary. Not so; God does not stir up a fire which is already far too hot. What he does is to 'transfer to another the love which is in us':[166] 'he turns us, and puts our neighbour in our place'.[167]

And who is my neighbour? Not only those with whom we come into contact, but all people without any exception; 'for the whole human race forms one body, of which individuals are the members and who must therefore keep a mutual conjunction among themselves'.[168]

[163] OC 24,723; CTS Mo 3,193.
[164] OC 24,723; CTS Mo 3,194.
[165] OC 24,724; CTS Mo 3,195.
[166] OC 24,724; CTS Mo 3,195.
[167] OC 24,724; CTS Mo 3,195.
[168] OC 24,724; CTS Mo 3,195-6.

Appendix

In this outline of Commandments 2-7, 9-10 the headings in square brackets are mine, as are also the subject-titles following the passage references.

Second Commandment[1]
Ex.20.4-6; repeated Deut.5.8-10.
1. [Introduction, expounding the two passages.]

2. Exposition of the Second Commandment.
   [A. Introduction][2]

(1) Ex.34.17; Lev.19.4; 26.1; Ex.20.22-23.
   On physical images.
(2) Deut.4.12-19, 23-24; Ex.34.14; Deut.11.16-17; 8.19-20.
   Revelation by the Word.
(3) Deut.16.22; Ex.23.24.
   Repetition.
(4) Deut.12.4-14, 17-18, 26-27.
   Lawful worship and superstitious rites.
(5) Deut.14.23-26.
   Tithes.
(6) Ex.20.24-25; Deut.27.5-7.
   Altars.
   [B. The Tabernacle.][3]
(1) Ex.25.1-22; 35.4-19.
   Offerings for the building of the Tabernacle.
(2) Ex.25.23-30.
   Construction of the Table, etc.
(3) Ex.25.31-40.
   Candelabra, etc.
(4) Ex.27.20-21; Lev.24.1-4.
   Significance of oil and light.
(5) Num.8.1-4.
   Continued.

[1] OC 24,375-560; CTS Mo 2,106-407.
[2] OC 24,382ff.; CTS Mo 2,115ff.
[3] OC 24,398ff.; CTS Mo 2,141ff.

(6) Ex.26.1-37.
Construction of Tabernacle.
(7) Ex.27.1-8.
Construction of Altar.
(8) Ex.27.9-19.
Court of Tabernacle.
(9) Ex.29.36-37.
Sin offering.
(10) Ex.30.1-10.
Altar of incense.
(11) Ex.30.34-38.
Sweet smelling spices.
(12) Ex.30.17-21.
Laver of brass.

[C. The Priesthood.][4]
(i) (1) Ex.28.1-43.
General explanation of this type of Christ.
(2) Ex.29.1-35.
Consecration of Priests.
(3) Lev.6.19-22.
Priest's offering at his consecration.
(4) Num.8.5-19, 23-26.
Cleansing of Levites and their duties.
(5) Num.3.5-10.
Ministry of Levites and their obedience to the chief Priests.
(6) Ex.30.22-33.
Oil for anointing Priests, Altar, etc.
(7) Lev.8.1-3.
Rite of anointing Priests.
(8) Lev.21.1-6, 10-12.
Prohibitions to Priests.
(9) Deut.31.9.
The book of the Law.
(10) Lev.10.8-11.
Prohibition of wine to Priests.

[4] OC 24,424ff.; CTS Mo 2,187ff.

(11) Lev.21.vv.7-8, vv.13-15, v.9.[5]
Marriage of Priests.

(12) Lev.21.16-24.
Physical defects in Priests.

(13) Lev.22.1-16.
Uncleanness in Priests.

(14) Ex.20.26.
Modesty of Priests.

(15) Num.6.22-27.
Priestly blessing.

(16) Num.35.1-8.
Cities for Levites and cities of refuge.

(17) Num.18.1-7, 22-23.
Warnings to Priests and Levites.

(18) Num.4.4-20, 24-28, 31-33.
Various duties of Levites.

(19) Lev.17.1-9.
Sacrifices to be offered by Priests.

(20) Deut.17.8-11.
Priests the interpreters of the Law.

(ii) [The Rights of Priests.][6]

(1) Num.5.9-10.
Offerings to the Priests.

(2) Num.18.8-19; Lev.6.16-18, 26-29.
Further gifts and offerings.

(3) Num.5.8.
Trespass recompense.

(4) Lev.7.6-10, 14, 31-36.
Further offerings.

(5) Num.18.20-21, 23-24; Lev.27.30-33; Deut.14.22,27-29; 12.19; 26.12-15.
Payment of tithes.

---

[5] Before these verses the Latin prints a new title, *On the High Priest*. But as this seems to apply only to the one section and breaks the sequence, I have omitted it.

[6] OC 24,471ff.; CTS Mo 2,265ff. Although no sub-title is given at this point, Calvin indicates a new section with, 'I will now begin to treat of the rights [of the Priests]' (OC 24,471; CTS Mo 2,265).

(6) Num.18.25–32.
    The tenth of the tithe.
(7) Deut.18.1–8.
    The lot of the Priests and Levites.
(iii) [Sacred Offerings.][7]
    (1) Lev.24.5–9.
        Offering of bread.
    (2) Ex.29.38–46.
        Sacrifices.
    (3) Num.28.1–15.
        The same continued.
    (4) Num.28.16–31.
        Sacrifices during the Passover and the First Fruits.
    (5) Num.29.1–39.
        Sacrifices during other feasts.
    (6) Lev.16.1–34.
        The yearly atonement.
    (7) Lev.1.1–17.
        Sacrificial regulations.
    (8) Lev.2.1–16.
        Regulations for offerings.
    (9) Lev.3.1–17.
        Further regulations.
    (10) Lev.4.1–35; Num.15.22–29.
        The sin offering.
    (11) Lev.5.1–13.
        Sin offerings.
    (12) Lev.5.14–19.
        Continued.
    (13) Lev.6.1–7.
        Continued.
    (14) Lev.6.8–15, 23–25, 30.
        Further regulations.

---

[7] OC 24,487ff.; CTS Mo 2,291ff. Although no sub-title is given at this point, Calvin indicates a new section with, 'I now arrive at the third part of external worship, and this will lead us to the end of the exposition of the Second Commandment. We shall now treat of Sacred Offerings' (OC 24,488; CTS Mo 2,291).

(15) Lev.7.1-5.
The Trespass offering.
(16) Lev.7.11-18; 22.29-30; 19.5-8.
Peace offerings.
(17) Lev.7.19-25, 28-31., 37-38.
Further regulations.
(18) Num.15.1-16.
Summary of regulations.
(19) Lev.22.17-25; Deut.17.1.
Offering to be perfect.
(20) Deut.23.18.
Prohibitions.
(21) Lev.22.26-28; Ex.22.30; 23.19; 34.26; Deut.14.21.
Prohibitions.

3. Political Appendices of the Second Commandment.[8]
(1) Ex.23.24; Deut.12.1-3; Ex.34.13; Deut.7.5; Num.23.52; Deut.16.21.
Destruction of heathen altars and places of worship.
(2) Ex.34.11-12, 15-16; Deut.7.1-4; Ex.23.31-33.
Warnings against alliances with Canaanites.
(3) Deut.7.16-26.
Canaanites to be destroyed.
(4) Deut.25.17-19.
Against Amalekites.
(5) Deut.23.3-8.
Against Ammonites and Moabites.
(6) Deut.17.2-5,7.
Capital punishment against idolaters.

Third Commandment.[9]
Ex.20.7; repeated Deut 5.11.
1. [Introduction, expounding the two passages.]

2. Exposition of the Third Commandment.[10]

[8] OC 24,545ff.; CTS Mo 2,386ff.
[9] OC 24,559-576; CTS Mo 2,408-432.
[10] OC 24,561ff.; CTS Mo 2,410ff.

(1) Lev.19.12; Ex.23.13; Deut.6.13; 10–20.
Not to swear falsely but truly by God's name.
(2) Deut.23.21–23.
On vows.
(3) Lev.27.1–25, 27–29.
On redeeming vows.
(4) Num.30.1–16.
On observing vows.

3. Political Appendix of the Third Commandment.[11]
Lev.24.15–16.
Capital punishment against cursers of God.

Fourth Commandment.[12]
Ex.20.8–11; repeated Deut.5.12–15.

1. [Exposition of the two passages.]

2. Passages relating to the exposition of this Commandment.[13]
Lev.19.30; 26.2; Ex.23.12; Lev.23.3; Ex.31.12–17; Ex.34.21;
Ex.35.1–3;   Lev.19.3.
Various regulations on the Sabbath.

3. Appendices to the Fourth Commandment.[14]
(1) Ex.23.10–11; Lev.25.1–7, 20–22.
Directions on the Observance of the Sabbath.
(2) Lev.25.8–13.
The Jubilee.
(3) Lev.23.1–44.
Festivals.
(4) Ex.23.14–17; 34.22–24; Deut.16.1–2,5–17; Ex.34.20.
Festivals.

[11] OC 24,573ff.; CTS Mo 2,431ff. Although Calvin put this sub–title in the plural, there is only one Appendix. (But see OC 24,573 n.2).
[12] OC 24,575–602; CTS Mo 2,432–472.
[13] OC 24,581ff.; CTS Mo 2,440ff.
[14] OC 24,583ff.; CTS Mo 2,445ff.

The Second Table, of which this is the First Commandment and
the Fifth of the Law.[15]

Ex.20.12; repeated Deut.5.16.

1. [Introduction, expounding the two passages.]

2. Exposition of the commandment.[16]

Lev.19.3.

3. Appendices of the Fifth Commandment.[17]

(1) Ex.21.15,17; Lev.20.9.

Capital punishment against cursers of parents.

(2) Deut.21.18–21.

Capital punishment against rebellious son.

(3) Ex.22.28; Lev.19.32; Deut.16.18; 20.9.

Respect for authority.

Sixth Commandment.[18]

Ex.20.13; repeated Deut.5.17.

1. [Introduction, expounding the two passages.]

2. Exposition of the Commandment.[19]

(1) Lev.19.17.

Hatred against the brother.

(2) Lev.19.18.

Revenge.

(3) Lev.19.14.

Injuring the disabled.

3. Ceremonial Appendices of the Sixth Commandment.[20]

(1) Deut.21.1–9.

Expiation for murder.

(2) Deut.12.15–16,20–25; Lev.17.10–14; 7.26–27; 19.26.

Prohibition to eat blood.

---

[15] OC 24,601–12; CTS Mo 3,5–19.
[16] OC 24,606; CTS Mo 3,12f.
[17] OC 24,605ff.; CTS Mo 3,13ff.
[18] OC 24,611–42; CTS Mo 3,20–68.
[19] OC 24,613ff.; CTS Mo 3,22ff.
[20] OC 24,615ff.; CTS Mo 3,25ff.

4. Political Appendices of the Sixth Commandment.[21]

(1) Lev.24.17, 19–22; Ex.21.12–14, 18–32.
Penalties for taking life.

(2) Deut.17.6; 19.15.
On witnesses.

(3) Deut.22.8.
Fenced roof.

(4) Deut.24.7.
Capital punishment against slave-traders.

(5) Deut.21.22–23.
Burial of the executed.

(6) Deut.25.1–3.
Punishment to be moderate.

(7) Deut.24.16.
Capital punishment for own sin only.

(8) Deut.20.10–18.
Moderation in war.

(9) Deut.23.15–16.
Hospitality for runaway slaves.

(10) Deut.22.6–7.
Sitting birds not to be taken.

(11) Ex.23.5; Deut.22.4.
Humanity to animals and help for neighbour.

(12) Num.35.9–34; Deut.19.1–13.
Cities of refuge.

Seventh Commandment.[22]
Ex.20.14; repeated Deut.5.18.

1. [Exposition of the two passages, followed by exposition of Lev.18.20.]

2. Appendix of the Seventh Commandment.[23]
Lev.18.22–30.
[The passage is printed on its own, without comments.

---

[21] OC 24,619ff.; CTS Mo 3,33ff.
[22] OC 24,641–668; CTS Mo 3,68–110.
[23] OC 24,643ff.; CTS Mo 3,71. Although the sub-title is in the plural, there is only one Appendix. But OC 24,643–4 prints it differently, giving Lev.18.20 without a title and omitting "Judicial" in the next title.

Apparently Calvin intended it to be taken as part of the next section.]

3. Judicial Appendices.[24]

(1) Ex.22.19; Lev.20.13, 15–16.

Capital punishment against bestiality.

(2) Lev.19.29.

Prohibition of "prostituting thy daughter".

(3) Deut.23.17.

Prohibition of whoredom and sodomy.

(4) Lev.20.10; Deut.22.22–27.

Capital punishment or penalties for forms of adultery.

(5) Lev.19.20–22.

Penalty and offering for a form of adultery.

(6) Ex.21.7–11.

Regulations for divorce of slave-concubine.

(7) Ex.22.16–17.

Seducer to marry the girl.

(8) Deut. 24.5.

Newly married man not to go to wars.

(9) Num.5.11–31.

Trial by ordeal of unfaithfulness in wives.

(10) Deut.22.13–21.

Regulations on accusations of unchastity.

(11) Deut.24.1–4.

Regulations on divorce.

(12) Lev.18.19; 20.18.

Regulations on intercourse during menstruation.

(13) Lev.18.1–4,6–18; Deut.22.30.

Incest and degrees of consanguinity.

(14) Lev.20.11–12,14,17,19–24.[25]

Penalties for various forms of adultery.

(15) Deut.25.11–12.[26]

Penalty for obscene action.

[24] OC 24,645ff.; CTS Mo 3,72ff.

[25] There is a muddle about titles here. Before this section the Latin has the sub-title: *These are Judicial Appendices.* The French omits this and the next. I suggest that the French is correct and that the two titles were written by Calvin on two separate papers containing the section, merely as a guide to the printer, who, however, put in the titles also.

[26] See former note.

(16) Deut.22.12.
Chastity in dress.

Ninth Commandment.[27]
Ex.20.16; repeated Deut.5.20.
1. [Introduction, expounding the two passages.]
2. Exposition of the Commandment.[28]
Ex.23.1-2,7; Lev.19.16-17.
On false reports, detractions, and carping criticisms.
3. Appendix.[29]
Deut.19.16-21.
Judgment on false witnesses.

The Tenth Commandment.[30]
Ex.20.17; repeated Deut.5.21.
Exposition of the two passages.

The Sum of the Law.[31]

The End and Use of the Law.[32]
[Not an exposition of any passage, but a doctrinal *locus communis*. It covers the same ground as *Inst.*II.vii, to which Calvin refers us at the end.]

The Sanctions of Promises and Threats.[33]
1. Lev.18.5; Deut.27.11-26.
Cursings against law-breakers.
2. Deut.11.26-32.
The blessing and the curse.
3(a) Lev.26.3-13; repeated Deut.28.1-14.
Blessings upon the obedient.
(b) Deut.7.9-15.
The same.

[27] OC 24,713-8; CTS Mo 3,179-86.
[28] OC 24,714ff.; CTS Mo 3,181ff.
[29] OC 24,717f.; CTS Mo 3,185f.
[30] OC 24,717-20; CTS Mo 3,186-9.
[31] OC 24,721-4; CTS Mo 3,190-6.
[32] OC 24,735-8; CTS Mo 3,196-201.
[33] OC 25,5-58; CTS Mo 3,201-89.

(c) Deut.12.28.
The same.
4(a) Lev.26.14–45.
Threats to the disobedient.
(b) Deut.28.15–29.
The same.
(c) Deut.28.30–48.
The same.
(d) Deut.28.49–57.
The same.
(e) Deut.28.58–68.
The same.
7. Deut.4.25–31.
Threats and a promise.
8. Deut.29.10–21.
The people to enter into Covenant with Jehovah.
9. Deut.29.22–28.
Threat against them if they forsake the Covenant.
10. Deut.30.1–10.
Promise of mercy upon repentance.
11. Deut.30.15–20.
The choice before Israel of life or death, blessing or cursing.

Chapter Five

The Exposition of Prophecy

1 Interpreters of the Law

In Chapter Two we explained Calvin's concept of the office and task of the Old Testament Prophet: 'The fourth stage came with the Prophets "through whom God published new oracles – yet not so new but that they flowed from the Law and had reference to it" (*Inst.* IV.viii.6). In regard to doctrine the Prophets were only interpreters or expounders of the Law. Their sole original contribution consisted of predictions of the future'.[1] This must now be expanded a little, so that we may go on to see how his concept of the Prophet's office determines his exposition of the prophecies themselves.

The Law is the primary and fundamental Word of God in his Covenant with his people. Having once established the relationship, 'I will be your God; you shall be my people', God supplied the Law to teach the Truth, to train in righteousness, to convict of unrighteousness, and, especially by its ceremonies, to lead to assurance of forgiveness and regeneration. The Law therefore stood to the man of the Old Testament as the Word of God in a special sense. Nothing was to be added to it, nothing taken away. All subsequent teachers, whether Priests or Prophets, were themselves under the supreme authority of the Law. Calvin frequently insists on this subjection as the necessary condition for the authority of the message which the Prophets have to deliver to the people. 'There is a necessary connection between God demanding obedience to nothing but his Law and his will that his Prophets should be heard. *To hear*, he says, *the words of my servants the Prophets, whom I send to you* (it is in in the

[1] p.67

176

second person). There might seem to be a contradiction here. If God's Law was sufficient, what was the point of hearing the Prophets? But there is perfect agreement – the Law alone was to be heard and yet also its interpreters the Prophets. God did not send his Prophets to correct the Law, to alter anything in it, to add to it or to take away from it. What, then, was the use of prophecy? To make God's Law clearer and clearer and also to accommodate it to the use of the people'.[2] This relationship becomes a principle of criticism: 'He says, *he shall have returned his pledge to the debtor.* This is not to be taken generally; it depends on a precept of the Law. We have very often said that the Prophets were interpreters of Moses. They therefore frequently touch briefly on what Moses expresses more clearly. If we wish to read them with profit, we must determine the meaning of the Law and then accommodate what we read in the Prophets to the teaching contained there'.[3]

The office and task of the Prophets is treated most comprehensively in the Preface to *Isaiah*, which begins with the title-like phrase *De Officio Prophetarum*: 'On the office of the Prophets it is usual for commentators to write long essays. But I prefer to summarise and say that we should relate the Prophets to the Law, from which they drew their teaching like streams from a spring. They made it their rule and so may justly be called and declared its interpreters; in nothing were they independent. Now, the Law consists chiefly of three parts: first, the doctrine of life; secondly, threatenings and promises; thirdly, the Covenant of grace, which is founded in Christ and comprehends within itself all the special promises . . . The Prophets, therefore, explain the teaching more copiously and interpret more fully what is summarised in the two Tables and show what the Lord especially demands of us. Next they accommodate to their own age and describe specifically the threatenings and promises which Moses promulgated in general. Lastly, they express more openly what Moses says more obscurely about Christ and his grace and bring forward fuller and richer testimonies of the free Covenant'.[4] Thus, the Law, to which they were bound, is here summarised as three-fold: It contains the *doctrina vitae*, by which Calvin means, as we saw in

[2] OC 38,517; CTS Jer 3,313f.
[3] OC 40,428; CTS Ezek 2,223.
[4] OC 36,19; CTS Isa 1,xxvi.

the preceding chapter, the declaration of the holy will of God and its consequent demand of holiness and righteousness of life in God's Covenant partner, deterrent threats against those who transgress it and promises to those who observe it, and the Covenant of grace which is established in Christ and which comprehends the special promises, that is, the heavenly promises in distinction to the general, earthly promises of the second heading. This is the brief given to the Prophets.

Their own task was correspondingly three-fold; but in each instance it represented both a clarification and an application, as we shall see. First, he goes on to say that the Law is 'the perpetual rule of the Church' and is 'to be observed by every succeeding age'.[5] But the Jews were 'a primitive and untamed people',[6] not only rebelling against God by transgressing the commandments but also neglecting the teaching of the Law in favour of some extraneous way to knowledge or safety. This point Calvin is making under the form of the forbidding the people to consult soothsayers or diviners. Prophets were given precisely to make such a course unnecessary, for, as interpreters of the Law, they would teach the people all the truth that they needed. He therefore quotes Deut.18.15, *The Lord thy God will raise up unto thee a Prophet from the midst of thee, of thy brethren, like unto me; unto him thou shalt hearken,* changing "Prophet" into the plural, in accordance with his exegesis of that passage: 'the expression a Prophet is used by *enallage* for a number of Prophets'.[7] (*Enallage* in this instance is the use of one number for another.)

It would be easy from a reading of the expositions to infer that for Calvin the role of the Prophet was largely denunciatory. He will use such phrases as 'the Prophets were heralds of God's vengeance' (*vindictae Dei praecones*),[8] or 'the Prophet's duty is to convict sinners, to threaten them, and to cite them to God's judgment seat'.[9] But this is only when the Prophets he is expounding are themselves denunciatory. The negative, denunciatory side of the Prophets' message is adventitious, provoked

[5] OC 36,19; CTS Isa 1,xxvii.
[6] OC 36,19; CTS Isa 1,xxvii.
[7] OC 24,271; CTS Mo 1,434.
[8] OC 37,600; CTS Jer 1,243.
[9] OC 40,473; CTS Ezek 2,286.

by the sin and rebellion of the people. For Calvin the real task of the Prophet is the teaching of the will of God expressed in the Law. The definitive clause in the passage in the Preface to *Isaiah* is *solaque eius doctrina sint contenti*[10] – that the Jews should not seek wisdom or guidance from soothsayers and such, but 'should be content with God's teaching alone'. To supply them with his teaching, he would raise up Prophets 'through whom he would open his mind'.[11] This is to be taken exclusively. Just as the Law is the unique expression of God's will, so the teaching of the Prophets is the sole true interpretation of the Law: 'When therefore the Lord promised Prophets, through whom he would open his mind and purpose, he commanded the people to be satisfied with (*acquiescere in*) their interpretations and teaching'.[12] Quoting Mal.4.3: *Remember the law of Moses my servant, which I commanded him in Horeb, for all Israel*, Calvin glosses it as 'He recalls them to the unique Law of God and commands them to be content with it'.[13] But contentment with the Law does not make the Prophets redundant. What the Law teaches in summary form the Prophets, as its legitimate and authorized interpreters, treat more fully. Thus, in their teaching on morality, 'the Prophets bring nothing new, but only explain things in the Law which had been misunderstood',[14] things like the use and value of ceremonies, which the people performed as outward exercises without inward repentance and affection. Similarly with the Second Table, which was the source of all their exhortations to righteousness and denunciations against 'injustice, violence, and fraud'.[15]

The general threats and promises of the Law are applied in particular situations by the Prophets. Where Moses will predict a general threat (e.g. 'God will pursue you in battle – foreign enemies and domestic quarrels will harass you – your life will hang as on a thread – you will tremble at the sound of a falling leaf' – a series of paraphrases), the Prophets will particularize, naming

[10] OC 36,20; CTS Isa 1,xxvii.
[11] OC 36,20; CTS Isa 1,xxvii.
[12] OC 36,20; CTS Isa 1,xxvii.
[13] OC 36,20-1; CTS Isa 1,xxviii.
[14] OC 36,21; CTS Isa 1,xxviii.
[15] OC 36,21; CTS Isa 1,xxviii.

the enemies (e.g. the Assyrians or the Babylonians) and the actual afflictions which will befall the people. Where Moses gives no more than a general list of blessings, the Prophets will promise the actual event occurring at a certain time, as, for example, the return from captivity after seventy years.

The third concern of the Law is "the free Covenant", *gratuitum foedus*, which preceded the Law and to which the Law is annexed. The Prophets are bound equally to the Covenant, but they advance beyond the Law in clarity of statement. The clarity consists in the clearer and more definite delineation of the Mediator of the Covenant – we remember from our Chapter Two the metaphors of the sketch and the finished portrait and the gradual illumination of the people by the Sun of righteousness. So now Calvin says that when the Prophets recall the people to the Covenant and try to comfort them in their afflictions, 'they put forward the coming of Christ, who was the foundation of the Covenant and the bond of the mutual uniting between God and the people; for this reason the whole (*omnis summa*) of the promises are to be referred to him'.[16] Thirdly, then, the office of the Prophets is to 'make more and more manifest'[17] the Christ who is the Mediator of the Covenant, through and in whom God says, 'I will be your God', and through and in whom the people are able to be his people; and to make him more and more manifest in the midst of particular situations like the destruction of Jerusalem and the Exile.

The principle of criticism mentioned earlier – determining the meaning of the Law and accommodating to it what we read in the Prophets – has now been explained; and so Calvin can end this section by saying, 'Anyone who grasps this will easily understand what he should look for in the Prophets and what is the purpose of their writings'.[18]

2 Covenant and Election

The general context in which each of the Prophets stands, whatever his dates, is the context of the Covenant and the Law.

[16] OC 36,22; CTS Isa 1,xxix.
[17] OC 38,517; CTS Jer 3,314.
[18] OC 36,22; CTS Isa 1,xxix.

This means the context of the God who chooses the Jews and is the Lord over them on the one hand and the context of the Jews who, although they are chosen and blest, are ungrateful and break the Covenant with the Law.

The Covenant, we saw, was not merely an agreement between two parties but was a complete and mutual union; complete in that God entered it with his whole self and for all eternity, and that he demanded of the Jews that they also should give themselves wholly to him in every generation. It was such a union that God willed that his existence and the existence of the Jews should be one for ever: 'It was his will to be called the God of Israel. What likeness is there between God and men? Yet, as if he descended from his heavenly glory, he bound to himself the seed of Abraham, that he might also mutually bind himself. Therefore God's election was like the joining of a mutual bond, so that he did not will to be separate from the people'.[19] By entering into such a binding union God in no way surrendered his Lordship. Indeed, the essential significance of the Covenant was that God should be the King ruling over his people and caring for their welfare and that the people should submit themselves to his rule: '*Let there be no strange God in thee* (Ps. 81.9). Here is propounded the leading article of the Covenant and almost the whole sum of it – that God alone must have the preëminence'.[20] Alongside this is placed the more intimate and familiar image of God the Father: '*That they may know thy way upon the earth* (Ps.67.2). By *the way of God* is meant his Covenant, which is the source or spring of salvation and by which he revealed himself in the character of Father to his ancient people'.[21]

The foundation of the Covenant was the love, the grace, the mercy, of God, choosing a people who had nothing to commend them. Before he chose them they had been merely one among many Gentile nations: 'he recalls them to the first origin or fountain of their race. But we must notice that God speaks variously of the origin of the people. Sometimes he reminds them what Abraham's condition was before he had stretched out his hand and so to say dragged them up out of hell into life, as it is said

[19] OC 38,158; CTS Jer 2,168.
[20] OC 31,763; CTS Ps 3,318. Ps.81.10 in Calvin.
[21] OC 31,618; CTS Ps 3,3. Ps.67.3 in Calvin.

in the last chapter of Joshua, "Thy father Abraham was worshipping idols when God adopted him . . . " God here pronounces that the Jews originated from the land of Canaan, from their Amorite fathers and Hittite mothers'.[22] And on Joshua 24.2: 'He reminds them that their fathers had dwelt in Chaldaea, worshipping the common idols, just like the rest. Hence we infer that Abraham, sunk in idolatry, was so to say dragged up out of hell'.[23]

On God's side the Covenant springs from his loving-kindness and mercy: 'God keeps his Covenant and mercy to all that love him (Dan.9.4). We must next notice that he adds the word "mercy" to "Covenant". He does not set these two words Berith and chesed in opposition but conjoins Pact and mercy; and the statement (it is hypallage, as they say)[24] ought to be resolved as: the Covenant of God is gratuitous; or, it flows from the fount of his mercy. What, then, is the Pact or Covenant and the mercy of God? The Covenant which proceeds from God's mercy; that is, the Covenant which is not grounded in the worth (dignitas) of men nor depends on their merits, but which has its cause, its stability, its accomplishment, and its fulfilment in the grace of God alone. This should be noted, for those who are not well versed in the Scriptures might ask why Daniel makes a distinction between mercy and Pact, as if, when God enters into an agreement with men, it were only a mutual bargain (stipulatio), so that God's Covenant simply depended on man's obedience. This question is resolved when we grasp that there is an hypallage in the words. And this way of speaking occurs frequently in Scripture. As often as God's Covenant is treated, there is also added mercy, or goodness, or disposition to love (propensio ad amorem). Therefore Daniel avows in the first place that the Covenant which God made with the Israelites was gratuitous, since it had no other cause or origin than the free goodness of God'.[25]

The passage continues with an emphasizing of the word "keeps"; that God is faithful to his promise to be the God, King,

[22] OC 40,335; CTS Ezek 2, 94-5.
[23] OC 25,563; CTS Josh 272.
[24] Hypallage: used here, as in Quintilian, for metonymy; "mercy", a noun, being placed for the adjective "gratuitous".
[25] OC 41,133-4; CTS Dan 2,146f.

Father of this people, not for a little while but for ever. On their side, however, the people, unworthy at the outset, fall further and further away from obedience. If now and then they repent and return to the keeping of the Covenant, it is only temporary and before long they are as bad as ever or even worse. This, of course, is the continual accusation of the Prophets and Calvin expounds it in the categories that are characteristic of his theology – obstinacy, stupidity, hypocrisy, inexcusability, and the like. All these words occur in the expositions time without number. The emphasis is not laid on the individual moral faults or the failures in religious observance, but these are traced back to their source in an inward rejection of God and his rule. Thus he takes up and glosses Jeremiah's words 'Neither said they – that is, they did not think within themselves', and comments: 'When he said "They did not say, Where is Jehovah?", he means that he was present with them or near them, but that they were blind; and therefore that they could not plead ignorance . . . Why then were they so wrong, or rather mad, as to go after idols? Because they did not want to make any effort or apply their minds to seek or to think of God . . . Therefore, lest the Jews should offer any such excuse, the Prophet here shows that they had not just been mistaken or deceived somehow but had been carried away by malice to follow a lie, because they had deliberately despised God and did not wish to seek after him, although he was near enough to them'.[26]

From the inward rebelliousness came the continual treachery of neglecting or deserting the Covenant while demanding that God should observe his side faithfully; and from the treachery came the idolatry, the Sabbath breaking, and the transgression of the Second Table. And along with all this, the obstinacy in continued sin, the obstinacy of a continual self-righteousness that nurtured itself on the observance of the ceremonies of the Law without a corresponding righteousness of life and claimed to represent the genuine family of Abraham, the people chosen by God.

It is at this point that a distinctive line of thought in Calvin shows itself particularly strongly, a line of thought which was perhaps originally based on Rom. 9.1ff., and which is expressed in

[26] OC 37,501; CTS Jer 1,77.

the first edition (1540) of his commentary on that epistle but is vastly expanded and worked out thoroughly in the definitive edition of 1556. The breaking of the Covenant by the unfaithfulness of the people and the consequent repudiation of the people by God, who nevertheless remains faithful to his promise to be the God of the family of Abraham for ever, is expounded in the light of God's eternal decrees of election and reprobation.

First, Calvin has no doubt about the rejection of the people. Examples of this are numerous. Thus, on the two "visions" of the potter and the pots in Jer. 19.1-3 and 18.1-6: 'The main object of the two visions is the same: the Jews thought they were exempt from the common lot of men because they had been chosen as a peculiar people. Indeed, their boasting of that inestimable privilege would not have been empty had there been mutual agreement between God and them. But they were Covenant-breakers; their boasting that God was bound to them was empty and foolish. What right had they to claim it? God had indeed adopted the whole race of Abraham; but there was an agreement included: *Walk before me and be perfect* (Gen. 17.2). When they had all become apostates, the Covenant was abolished so far as they were concerned. They could not therefore, take God to court, so to say, for breaking his Covenant with them, for he owed them nothing. They were strangers, for through their wickedness and perfidy they had departed from him'.[27] When Calvin says that the Covenant was abolished (elsewhere, that God abolished the Covenant),[28] this is never intended absolutely. The qualification will always be added that it was, as in the quotation above 'as far as they were concerned'. For Calvin follows the distinction made in Gal. 4.22-27 between the children of the flesh and the children of promise; the promise was not given, the Covenant was not made, with the physical descendants of Abraham, but with those of them who could justly also be called his spiritual descendants, in other words, with those who faithfully endeavoured to observe the Covenant on their side – that is, to allow God to be their God and strive to be the faithful people of God. There was, therefore, a remnant with whom God maintained his Covenant.

But the existence of the remnant depended, not on their

[27] OC 38,318-9; CTS Jer 2,430.
[28] OC 38,203; CTS Jer 2,243.

acceptance of the Covenant, but on the Covenant itself. For the Covenant was the declaration of a decision of God to unite himself with this people, this people with himself, in perpetuity. And the decision was made from all eternity. It was impossible that God should be unfaithful to his word or that his determination should fail to be effected. The grace of God, when it encounters the unfaithfulness of man, is not overcome and abolished but stands firm and is effected in some unexpected manner – 'God had secret methods'.[29] The unfaithful man betrays, by his continuing unfaithfulness, the fact that he is rejected, reprobate, by the eternal decision of God. In regard to the Covenant and the people, God's faithfulness is maintained in the existence of the faithful remnant, those whom he had chosen: 'Hitherto [Ezekiel] had regarded the people as a complete body, and this was lost. Therefore he set nothing before them but despair. But now he turns to the remnants of grace, as Paul says (Rom.11.5), and on this basis promises that God would remember his Covenant; though he would not restore the whole people indiscriminately. For the universal body had to perish; and a little handful only was saved. We therefore know that the promise was not common to all the sons of Abraham, his off-spring according to the flesh, but belonged to the elect alone'.[30]

The Covenant, therefore, was made, not with the race of Abraham as a whole, but with those of them, a mere handful, Calvin often says, who had been chosen by God and who shared the faith of Abraham. The remainder were 'destroyed';[31] on them 'God executed terrible vengeance';[32] 'God would destroy them and blot them out from the midst of his people'.[33] This sort of expression is to be taken as referring, not to temporal sufferings or even to the loss of their identity as Jews, but to eternal damnation. Just as the Covenant established union with God and therefore eternal life, so it was eternal death to be rejected from union with God. The temporal sufferings, particularly those

[29] OC 38,203; CTS Jer 2,243.
[30] OC 40,392; CTS Ezek 2,172f.
[31] OC 43,423; CTS Mi 3,390. Mic 7.14.
[32] Mic 7.18. OC 43,430; CTS Mi 3,402.
[33] OC 40,314; CTS Ezek 2,65.

centering round the sack of Jerusalem and the Exile, were, so to say, preliminary warnings from God.

It is on the basis of the remnant that Calvin explains the threats and promises in the Prophets. The threats are addressed to the whole people and meet with derision or neglect from the vast mass of the "irreclaimable" and with repentance from the few faithful. The promises, however, are spoken as an aside to the faithful only, to encourage them in the midst of the sufferings which they share with the rest of the people. Thus, on Hab.1.11, *Then shall [the Chaldaean's] mind change:* 'He had hitherto addressed that people beyond hope, but he now turns to the remnant. For there were always in that people some faithful, even if few, whom God never neglected, for whose sake he repeatedly sent his Prophets. Although the multitude profited nothing, the faithful were aware that God did not threaten in vain and were therefore kept in his fear. This is why the Prophets were accustomed, when they had spoken in general, to come to the faithful and, as it were, to comfort them apart and privately. And this distinction should be noted, as we have said elsewhere; for while the Prophets denounce God's anger, their word is directed indiscriminately to the whole body of the people; but when they add promises, it is as if they called the faithful to a private conversation and spoke in their ear what the Lord had commanded them'.[34] And on Hos.6.4, *O Ephraim, what shall I do with thee? O Judah, what shall I do with thee?*: 'The Prophets had to do with the whole people; they had to do with the few faithful. . . When therefore the Prophets rebuked the people, they addressed the whole body. But as there was also some remaining seed, they put in, as I have said, consolations; and they put them in so that God's elect might always rest on his mercy and thus patiently submit to his rod and continue in his fear, knowing that in him there is sure salvation. Therefore the promises which we see inserted by the Prophets among threats and rebukes should not be referred to all in common, or indiscriminately to the multitude, but only to the faithful, who were then few, as we have said.'[35] For, as he says a little later, 'the faithful behold the light of life even in the deepest abyss of death; for by faith, as we have said,

[34] OC 43,505; CTS Mi 4,34-5.
[35] OC 42,325; CTS Mi 1,224.

they penetrate beyond this world. But at the same time they come to God in serious penitence, while the ungodly remain in their obstinacy'.[36]

3 The Word of God

The teaching of the Prophets, no less than the Law, is the Word of God, the declaration of his inner mind and purpose: 'Jeremiah calls the counsel of God metaphorically his "thoughts", the sure and steadfast counsel which he declared by his Prophets . . . Whatever, then, the Prophets announced in his name flowed from his secret purpose; and this was the same as if he had opened his heart to us . . . I call the teaching "God's mouth". And this, he says, proceeded from the depth of his heart'.[37] The prophecies are not only the Word of God because they are true interpretations of the Law, which is the Word of God, or as if the light of the Word in the Law is reflected on to their moon. They are the Word of God because God himself spoke them to the Prophets and the Prophets faithfully transmitted them to the people.

In an earlier chapter we spoke of Christ as the *doctor* or teacher of the writers of the Old Testament. This concept seems to play little part in the expositions themselves, where the emphasis is overwhelmingly on the activity of the Holy Spirit. In fact, however, it is the presupposition, necessary but usually unspoken, to his understanding of the Old Testament prophetic office, depending as that does on his doctrine of the prophetic office of Christ. In the Preface to *Isaiah*, from which we have been quoting, he says of the verse, *he will raise up a Prophet*: 'as it is interpreted by Peter, the passage refers properly and above all to Christ, because he is the Head of the Prophets, and they all, together with their teaching, depend on him and with one accord are directed towards him'.[38] Where, then, Calvin speaks of the Prophets being taught by the Holy Spirit, we should take it that he means that they were taught by Christ through the Spirit.

That they were taught by the Spirit is stated so often in all the

[36] OC 42,325; CTS Mi 1,224-5.
[37] OC 38,429; CTS Jer 3,174-5.
[38] OC 36,20; CTS Isa 1,xxvii.

expositions as to be a common-place. As was said in Chapter Two, the more detailed way in which Calvin has expressed this has often caused him to be misunderstood as holding a doctrine of the verbal inerrancy of the Bible. So strongly and so often does he speak of the Holy Spirit dictating to the Prophets what they are to say that such a misunderstanding is easily committed. But if we correct this view, we must be careful not to fall into the perhaps even worse misunderstanding of watering down Calvin's doctrine of Scripture as the complete Word of God.

We may now see how this stands in the Prophets. The Latin word *dicto*, which so easily suggests its English derivative "dictate", is often used in a quite general sense of "declare" and even "suggest". There are several places where Calvin couples the two ideas. Thus: 'Without doubt [Jeremiah] here speaks by the impelling (*instinctu*) of the Holy Spirit, as if he were saying that he was not putting forward what he had conceived in his own mind but what had been dictated (*dictatum fuit*) by the Spirit of God. To sum up, this indignation is to be referred to his teaching, as if he said, "If I am treating you very vehemently, do not think it is that I am a man corrupted with anger and forgetful of moderation; it is that God's Spirit seizes and impels me (*rapit me et impellit*)".[39] Or: 'Here the Prophet narrates that he dictated (*se dictasse*) to Baruch, a servant of God, all that he had earlier taught. And without doubt God was at that moment suggesting (*suggesserit*) things that might otherwise have been blotted out of the Prophet's memory. For we cannot on every occasion recall everything that we have said in the past. Therefore out of so many words the greater part would have fled from the Prophet if God had not dictated (*dictasset*) them again to him. Therefore Jeremiah stood between God and Baruch, because God by his Spirit first spoke the words (*praeivit*) and steered [governed? *gubernavit*] the Prophet's mind and tongue. And the Prophet, with the Spirit as his leader and master, recited what God was commanding . . . We see, therefore, that he did not dictate (*dictasse*) at will anything that came into his mind, but that God suggested (*suggessisse*) what he wanted Baruch to write down'.[40] On Ezek.19.1–4, "dictate" and "suggest" are used as near synonyms: 'There is, in my judgment, a tacit oblique

[39] OC 37,653; CTS Jer 1,331.
[40] OC 39, 118; CTS Jer 4,329.

antithesis between this song, which God dictated (*dictavit*) to them by his Prophet, and the general complaints which were continually sounding on all their lips . . . The Prophet therefore obliquely rebukes them when he says that this sad song had been suggested (*fuisse suggestum*) by God'.[41] Lewis and Short does not give anything so strong and precise as "dictate" for *suggero*; in this sort of context it would normally mean something like "hint" or "intimate" or "suggest". Nevertheless, this would be too weak here. Calvin meant very much more than that God suggested to the Prophets that they should say this or that and then the Prophets put it into their own words.

Certainly, he makes it clear that he did not think the Prophets lost their individuality or their natural qualities when they were under the sway of the Spirit. Thus on Jer.6.2-3, (*I have likened the daughter of Sion to a quiet and delicate maiden. The shepherds with their flocks shall come upon her, they shall pitch their tents against her round about . . .* ') Calvin says: 'The place where the Prophet was brought up was in sheep country, and he kept many forms of speech from his early upbringing. God does not strip his servants of everything that is in their mind (*omni sensu*) when he promotes them to teaching his people. The Prophet is here speaking out of what he knew as a little child and a boy'.[42] *Sensus* is a wide-ranging word; the meaning of this passage is that God does not replace their minds, formed by education and environment, with a new intelligence clean and unformed. It is rather that the man, just as he is, with his own language and idiom, is taken over by the Spirit to be his instrument.

On the other hand, the Prophet is but a man and man is not capable of speaking God's Word. He must be taken over, possessed, by the Spirit and used as an instrument. Yet even so, Calvin continues on a moderate course, emphasizing the Prophet's human individuality and weakness, and rejecting any idea that he was so taken over as to cease to be himself. Thus, on Ezek.3.14 (*And the Spirit lifted me up and appropriated* (sumpsit) *me; and I went bitterly, in the indignation of my spirit, and the hand of Jehovah was strong upon me*): 'He confirms what we saw a little earlier, that he was driven (*actum fuisse*) by God's Spirit, so that he

41 OC 40,460; CTS Ezek 2,268.
42 OC 37,643; CTS Jer 1,315.

was in a sense outside himself – yet not what heathen writers call ἐνθουσιάσμος. Their "prophets" were men ravished and transported (*abreptitii*); the devil so wrought with them that they became insane. Therefore the Prophet does not mean that he was ravished and transported, for God's Prophets were always sober and sound in mind (*sedatae et compositae mentis*). He meant that he was so guided and governed by the Spirit of God that he was unlike himself and had no earthly thoughts (*spiraret terrestre*)'.[43] In the quite long comment that follows he twice says that God "renewed" the Prophet, that God 'separated him from ordinary life, to represent something heavenly',[44] that Ezekiel felt the moving (*agitatio*) of the Spirit. Calvin even applies to him the word he had used pejoratively of the heathen prophets, *abreptus*, "ravished" or "transported". The present passage is the opening account of a *visio*, and therefore of an extraordinarily intense experience, transcending the usual course of a Prophet's work. Yet even in this experience, Calvin insists that the Prophet is not somehow re-placed by the Spirit, as if he were a mere human shell filled with the Divine. 'He was not completely divested of all sense. Therefore, although he was entirely consecrated to God and did not fail in diligence and readiness, yet he still kept something human – hence "bitterness of spirit" . . . there was a tacit antithesis between that movement by which he was transported (*motum illum, quo abreptus erat*) and his own feeling, which, if not quite wrong, yet was very remote from the grace of the Spirit'.[45] The end of the matter was that the Prophet 'signified that he was so restrained by the secret impulse of the Spirit that he did nothing humanly, did not submit to himself or his own wishes, did not even follow his own counsel, but was only directed towards rendering obedience to God'.[46]

That Calvin combined an absolute belief in the operation of the Holy Spirit on the Prophets with such a steady acceptance of their humanity that he feels free to criticise them when necessary we may further illustrate from Jeremiah. In chapter 15.10, 15–18 Jeremiah protests his innocence and bewails his lot as a Prophet to

[43] OC 40,86; CTS Ezek 1,144.
[44] OC 40,86; CTS Ezek 1,144.
[45] OC 40,86-7; CTS Ezek 1,145.
[46] OC 40,87; CTS Ezek 1,145.

a rebellious people, expressing sentiments that Calvin considered unworthy of a Prophet. Nevertheless, he was restrained and guided by the Holy Spirit, so that ultimately God's Word was spoken and not man's. 'There is no doubt that when the Prophet saw that his labour was not so beneficial and fruitful as he had wished, he suffered in a human way. Yet at the same time we must note that he was so restrained by the secret bridle of the Holy Spirit that he did not burst out intemperately, as many do. He was directed towards the right end, so that even his griefs should always look towards his object, that his labour might be useful to the people'.[47] That Jeremiah cried out 'My mother!' and as good as blamed her for giving him birth was 'a sign of an intemperate feeling'.[48] But his purpose was to benefit the people, who had been slandering him as 'a man of strife'. That he prayed for vengeance on his enemies (v.15) demands more explanation. A distinction must be made, first, between public and private feelings, and second, between 'the passions of the flesh, which never observe moderation, and the zeal of the Spirit'.[49] Jeremiah as a man was sorry for the people: 'but he was, so to say, released from all human feeling and stripped of that which disturbs us and draws us away from moderation . . . In short, whenever the Prophets are carried away by so much fervour, we should realise that they are full of the Spirit of Christ; and since they are thus filled, we should also know that they direct all their heat against the reprobate, but in such a way that they may take care to collect all that can be saved'.[50] On v.18 Calvin speaks more strongly about Jeremiah's human weakness. 'But now he confesses his weakness; and there is no doubt that he was often torn between two opposing thoughts and feelings. This must necessarily happen to us, for the flesh always wars against the Spirit. For although the Prophet brought nothing human when he declared the teaching of God, yet he was not completely stripped of sorrow and fear and the various feelings of the flesh. For in regard to the Prophets and Apostles we should always distinguish between the teaching itself, which was pure of all stain, and their

[47] OC 38,217; CTS Jer 2,267.
[48] OC 38,218; CTS Jer 2,269.
[49] OC 38,224; CTS Jer 2,278.
[50] OC 38,224; CTS Jer 2,279.

own persons (to use the common phrase), that is, themselves. And they were not so perfectly renewed but that some residue of the flesh remained in them. Thus Jeremiah in himself (*privatim*) was seized with anxiety and terror and felt tired of it all and would have been glad to have shed such a heavy load from his shoulders. He did indeed suffer these feelings; but it was only in himself; his teaching was completely free from such a fault, for the Holy Spirit directed his mind and all his senses and his tongue, so that there might be nothing human there'.[51] In himself Jeremiah was 'swayed by many thoughts which smacked of the weakness of the flesh and were not without fault'.[52] Afterwards he will say that Jeremiah in a sense vacillated or wavered in face of the wickedness of the people and was not so steadfast in doing his duty as he should have been.

Calvin's view of the dictation of the prophecies by the Holy Spirit must therefore take into account his ready acceptance of the continuing humanity of the Prophets. This is why also, although he will usually try to reconcile inconsistences, he can accept errors by Biblical authors – the mistaken reference to Jeremiah instead of Zechariah, for instance, in Matt. 27.9. His comment on that verse is as follows: 'How the name "Jeremiah" crept in here I must confess I do not know and I do not much care. "Jeremiah" was certainly put in error for "Zechariah"'.[53] Similarly, we may point to the different literary styles of the writers: 'Whether you read David, Isaiah and their like, whose style flows smoothly and happily, or the herdsman Amos, Jeremiah and Zechariah, whose rougher style has something rustic in it, everywhere the Spirit's majesty will be prominent' (*Inst*.I.viii.2).[54] He is far from complimentary to Ezekiel, although he excuses his style on the grounds that the exiles' knowledge of their mother tongue had degenerated under the foreign influence of Babylon: 'We have said that our Prophet was more verbose than Isaiah or even Jeremiah himself. For he had got used to (*assueverat*) the form of speaking then current among the exiles. He is therefore not at all precise or polished. But we must consider that he was

[51] OC 38,231; CTS Jer 2,290.
[52] OC 38,231; CTS Jer 2,291.
[53] OC 45,749; CTS Harm 3,272; CC Harm Gospel 3,177.
[54] OS 3,73[3ff].

accommodating his discourse to learners, for he had to do with a people not only primitive and dull but also obstinate. They had almost degenerated from their own language, as they had from purity of belief. The Prophet therefore deliberately foreswore elegance of language'.[55] The style was not artificially shaped by the Spirit as he dictated but was the expression of the way the writer thought and was the product of his upbringing. Certainly, that upbringing was at every point determined by God's providence, so that each writer acquired his writing style in order that he might, in course of time, be able to preach and write what he was commanded to write. Certainly also, each style was fitted for that people at that time and the cruder styles were accommodations to the contemporary primitiveness or back-wardness of the people. But this does not alter the fact that the style, like the capability of having little slips of memory and of being exasperated and frustrated, was human. The writers did not lose their humanity when they became the amanuenses of the Holy Spirit. These are the literary analogues to the human weaknesses of the Prophets. The problem it creates in regard to dictation can be put very bluntly: The Holy Spirit, being all-wise, does not make mistakes in facts or make pronouncements unworthy of himself or of his creatures. But, acording to Calvin, such mistakes could happen and such pronouncements be made. Therefore, such places in Scripture may not be ascribed to the Holy Spirit. In other words, Calvin's strong statements about dictation must be qualified by his equally clear statements about the humanity of the Biblical writers.

All that being said, however, the overwhelming emphasis in all Calvin's exposition is not on the humanity but on the divinity of the prophetic writings. Whether he meant that every word in Hebrew or "Chaldee" was dictated by the Spirit or that every thought was put into the writer's mind together with an ability to express it perfectly, there can be no doubt that Calvin believed that what was said came from God in such a sense that the Holy Spirit was its author.

The solution of the problem posed by Calvin's doctrine is of purely academic interest. Even were it solved, nothing would be

[55] OC 40,83; CTS Ezek 1,139.

added to our knowledge of his view of Holy Scripture. We already know that he believed everything in Scripture to have been "spoken" by God and gave Scripture the reverence and obedience due to God's Word and that at the same time he treated it as literature with the limitations as well as the glories of other literature and attempted to understand it by the various methods of literary criticism.

4 Christ in the Prophets

So far we have made no reference to the Prophets taking up and applying to their own generation the fact that Christ is the foundation of the Covenant, the seed in whom all the families of the earth should be blessed (Gen. 22.18, Gal. 3.16). As we saw, Calvin uses this expression of Christ; and he continues to use it very occasionally in his expositions of the Prophets. But a Christological interpretation of the promises occurs less often than a straight historical exposition of the circumstance of the promise. The passage quoted earlier from Habakkuk 1.11, for example, goes on only to deal with the retribution which will be visited upon the Chaldeans for their arrogance. The faithful are therefore comforted with the assurance that God, and not the King of Babylon, rules the world and that he will have the final say. Even such a verse as Jer. 23.3; *And I will gather the remnant of my sheep out of all countries into which I have driven them, and will bring them again to their folds; and they shall be fruitful and increase*, a verse which one might well have expected to be related to Lk. 15.3–7 and Jn. 10.1–18, is interpreted only of the Exile and the return. It is not treated as an analogue or as a type; indeed, there is no mention of Christ apart from the incidental 'Christ seemed by his coming to have completely abolished the Covenant by which God had adopted the children of Abraham'.[56] Yet from time to time Calvin shows, even when there is no Christological interpretation, that this is precisely what he is thinking of. As: 'Yet all the same Jeremiah presupposed this principle, "The grace of God cannot be wholly destroyed". For he had chosen the race of Abraham, from whom the Redeemer of the world would at

[56] OC 38,404; CTS Jer 3,132.

length be born'.[57] This last clause is not incidental but the basis and meaning of the two previous clauses. "God's grace" and "the Redeemer of the world" are indissolubly joined; the race of Abraham was chosen in order that the Redeemer, "the seed", should be born of it. This place is the more significant in that the verse does not seem, according to Calvin's usual practice, to demand a reference to Christ.

Sometimes his careful observance of the historical context leads him into conflict with traditional Christian interpretation. Jer.3.16 does not predict the kingdom of Christ, but 'refers to that divorce or division which had for a long time existed between the kingdom of Judah and the kingdom of Israel'.[58] Elsewhere he criticizes "the Christians" for being too rigid in their interpretation of prophecy, 'for, passing over the whole intermediate time between the return of the people and the advent of Christ, they have too violently twisted these prophecies to spiritual liberation'.[59] Here he is clearly not criticizing Christological interpretation as such but the uncritical application of it as a principle on any and every occasion. He himself, when he judges that the context demands it, will interpret prophecies with direct reference to the incarnate Christ. It is clear that, although he may feel the force of traditional interpretations, the decisive criterion is the context, with the rider that it is also the context viewed in the light of subsequent history.

Quite often he will say that a passage can only be interpreted of Christ because it does not fit the known facts in regard to what it seems to be saying. Jer.50.5: *They shall ask the way to Sion with their faces towards it: Come and join yourselves to Jehovah with an everlasting Covenant, which shall not be blotted out in oblivion.* But, runs Calvin's argument, the Covenant promised the Jews earthly blessings in the land. These earthly blessings were not fulfilled after the Return; only a small number returned, 'they were harassed by many troubles; God afflicted their land with sterility; they were worn down by various savage wars'.[60] The "everlasting Covenant" must refer to Christ and 'this prophecy can only be

[57] OC 38,202; CTS Jer 2,243.
[58] OC 37,564; CTS Jer 1,183.
[59] OC 38,414; CTS Jer 3,149.
[60] OC 39,397; CTS Jer 5,131.

explained of Christ's spiritual kingdom'.[61] In Dan.9.24 (*Seventy weeks are determined upon thy people, and upon the holy city, to finish transgression, and to make an end of sin, and to expiate iniquity, and to bring in everlasting righteousness, and to seal up the vision and prophecy, and to anoint the holy of holies*) he takes the Christological reference as self-evident: 'Everyone knows that here is promised something more excellent than existed under the Law. It follows that the prophecy can only be taken of the advent of Christ and the entire renewal (*reparatione*) of the Church of God'.[62] The predictions therefore vary, both in nature and in time, and may be put into three periods: First, the contemporary or near contemporary, that is, almost always, relating to the Exile and the Return. Secondly, in the intervening time from the present, or from the Return, to the Incarnation. Thirdly, from the Incarnation to the Second Coming.

In the second, there may be predictions of what would happen to the Jews for the five hundred years or so between the Return and the coming of Christ. This appears very strongly in Daniel, some parts of which are nothing but an extended narration of classical history. Thus the visions in Dan.11.2-32 give rise to a very long account of the appearing and fall of empires and kingdoms, so that lectures 56-60 read more like history lessons than Biblical expositions.[63] Calvin himself was aware of the fact: 'I do not refer to the details here. I could detain you for three, no, many days, even months, with recounting the history'.[64] The purpose of the predictions in Daniel is to teach the Prophet, and through him the people, 'what various changes would happen before the advent of Christ . . . God therefore very relevantly shows his Prophet these Four Monarchies, lest the faithful should waver when they see the world so often shifting and disturbed and all but changing its form and nature'.[65]

It is the third period which is decisive. Everything was in a state

[61] OC 39,397; CTS Jer 5,131.

[62] OC 41,172; CTS Dan 2,203.

[63] If Calvin lectured extemporarily, his ready command of historical detail and of even secondary names shows that he knew his classical historians extraordinarily well. But perhaps this would be worth testing carefully.

[64] OC 41,78; CTS Dan 2,67.

[65] OC 41,87; CTS Dan 2,80.

of suspense until the Incarnation of Christ. The Covenant, the Law, the proclamations of the Prophets were in themselves temporary, waiting for the coming of the one from whom they themselves had come. When Christ came (Calvin usually speaks of his "advent" or his "appearing") the temporary ceased and became in him eternal. The stage of suspense ended in eternal finality. 'But the Prophet says, *And it shall be in the extremity of days, that the mount of the house of Jehovah shall be set in order on the top of the mountains* (Micah 4.1). Without doubt, by the "extremity of days" the Prophet means the advent of Christ: for then it was that the Church of God was built anew. In short, it was Christ who brought in the renovation of the world, and his advent is rightly called the new age . . . As Christ, then, brought in the fulfilment of all things by his coming, the Prophet rightly says that these would be the last days when God would restore his Church by the hand of the Redeemer'.[66]

But Calvin interprets the predictions about Christ in a number of ways. Most obviously, it will refer to Jesus Christ himself. Thus the classic places like the Suffering Servant of Isa.52.13–53.12 or the Righteous Branch of Jer. 23.5-6 are interpreted directly of him. But Christ and the Gospel of Christ are inseparable; Christ and his Church are inseparable; and the kingdom of Christ may not be limited to the period of his earthly life. Therefore, prophecies of Christ are sometimes referred to him indirectly, to the Gospel or Church directly, and prophecies of his kingdom are sometimes referred to the time between the Ascension and the Second Coming and sometimes to his kingdom before the Incarnation; for the people of the Covenant were the kingdom of Christ in as true a sense as the Christian Church, and the history of that people was the history of the kingdom. This is set out very clearly and decisively on Ezek.17.22: '*Thus says the Lord Jehovah, I will take from the top of the tall cedar and will tear off a tender twig from its head and will set it and I will plant it upon a high and lofty mountain.* Here the Prophet begins to treat of the restoration both of the nation and kingdom. This prophecy therefore without doubt refers to Christ; because, although partly God had pity on his people, when they were

[66] OC 43,339-40; CTS Mi 3,250f.

given the liberty of returning by Cyrus and Darius, yet what is read here was never fully manifested except in Christ. It is true . . . that, when the Prophets promise the restoration of the Church, they do not restrict their discourse to Christ's person but begin with the return of the people. For that was the prelude of the full and solid liberty which was at length revealed in Christ. And Christian writers have erred in urging so strictly that anything said about the restoration of the Church can only be understood of the person of Christ . . . But as often as the Prophets hold out the hope of liberty to the elect and the faithful, they embrace the whole of the time from the return of the people, or from the end of the Exile, to the end of the kingdom of Christ. When, therefore, Christ's kingdom is treated, we must place its beginning in the Temple, which was built after the people's return at the end of seventy years; and then we must place its end, not in Christ's Ascension, nor yet in one or another century, but in the whole progress of his kingdom, until he shall appear at the last day'.[67]

The unity of the Head and the Body, Christ and his people, supplies a ground of hope and encouragement to the pilgrim Church. Where Daniel says that *in the days of these kings the God of the heavens shall raise up a kingdom which shall never be dissipated . . . and it shall stand for ever* (Dan.2.44), Calvin comments: 'It is important to note what is the perpetuity of the kingdom of which Daniel speaks. It should not be restricted to the person of Christ, but belongs to all the godly and the whole body of the Church . . . The perpetuity of Christ's kingdom, therefore, is twofold, apart from his person. First, in the whole body; for although the Church is often dispersed so that nothing appears in men's sight, it never entirely perishes, but God guards it by his hidden and incomprehensible power, so that it will survive until the end of the world. Then there is the other perpetuity in individual believers, for they are born again of incorruptible seed and begotten anew by the Spirit of God . . . We must hold, therefore, that whenever Scripture affirms Christ's reign to be eternal, this is to be extended to the whole Body of the Church and should not be applied only to his person'.[68]

[67] OC 40,417; CTS Ezek 2,207.
[68] OC 40,607-8; CTS Dan 1,188.

The prophecies of Christ are always grounded in the Covenant, the Law, and the Kingdom; they are always, that is to say, an unfolding of their meaning. The Christ they promise 'sets up again his Covenant and so perpetually establishes it';[69] it is 'a new Covenant, which God has made by the hand of Christ';[70] but 'its origin is the old Covenant which had been abolished by the fault of the people. Thus we see that the new Testament flows from that Covenant which God made with Abraham and afterwards confirmed by the hand of Moses'.[71] Therefore he would be *the messenger of the Covenant*, for it is necessary that the Covenant should be confirmed in him . . . We know that the office of Christ consists only in confirming and sealing to us God's Covenant, not only by his teaching but by his blood and the sacrifice of his death'.[72] Again, Christ 'the end of the Law', is 'the soul of the Law';[73] 'if the Law is separated from Christ, it is like a dead letter; Christ alone gives it life'.[74] Hence Christ is promised as the one who would fulfil the Law and so 'in our flesh win righteousness for us' by his obedience, the obedience even to death: 'He does not say "the Son" but "my servant", that we may not only view him as God but may grasp his human nature, in which he performed that obedience by which we are acquitted before God. The foundation of our salvation is that he offered himself as a sacrifice'.[75] The corollary of this promise is the abrogation of the ceremonies of the Law which, being figures of the reality, are rendered unnecessary by the presence of the reality itself.

The prophecies of the kingdom of Christ embrace all three, Covenant, Law, and Kingdom. God made such a Covenant with the race of Abraham that he was and remained the superior partner, the Lord whom the people must obey. He gave the Law as the way in which he, the Lord, would rule over his people. And the Davidic kingdom was set up as an earthly image of his kingship over his people. In all three, therefore, the concept of

[69] OC 40,395; CTS Ezek 2,177.
[70] OC 40,393; CTS Ezek 2,173.
[71] OC 40,393; CTS Ezek 2,173
[72] Mal 3.1. OC 44,461; CTS Mi 5,569.
[73] OC 36,492; CTS Isa 2,322.
[74] OC 40,395; CTS Ezek 2,176-7.
[75] OC 37,265; CTS Isa 4,129.

king and kingdom is predominant. But the kingship was, as we saw in Chapter Two, established in order to be a type or figure of Christ. Accordingly, the prophecies of the kingdom are usually based on King David or one of his descendants. Thus Jer.33.15: *In those days and at that time I will cause the branch of righteousness to sprout unto David.* 'It is necessary to consider the nature of Christ's kingdom. We know it is spiritual. But it is painted for us under the image of an earthly and civil rule. For whenever the Prophets speak of Christ's kingdom, they set before us an earthly image, because spiritual truth without *figura* could not have been sufficiently understood by the primitive people in that childhood'.[76] The earthly image is the kingdom, whether in the reign of David himself or of any of his descendants, down to the ill-fated and final Jehoiachin.

On the first mention in the Psalms of the kingdom, Calvin lays down his general principle of interpretation. 'That David prophesied of Christ is quite plain from the fact that he knew his own kingdom to be only a shadow (*umbratile*). And in order to learn to refer to Christ whatsoever David in olden times sang about himself, we must hold this principle that occurs everywhere in all the Prophets, that he, with his successors, was made king, not so much for his own sake, as to be the image of the Redeemer. We shall very often have to repeat this; at present I would briefly inform readers that (because that temporal kingdom was an earnest to the ancient people of the eternal kingdom which at length was truly established in the person of Christ) those things which David declares about himself are not violently or allegorically twisted to Christ but were truly foretold of him'.[77] This typological treatment is, indeed, very common in Calvin's expositions of the Prophets. Perhaps invariably when good King David is mentioned by any Prophet Calvin will make the reference to Christ; similarly with the good kings Josiah and Hezekiah; even the less good or quite wicked descendants of David serve to point negatively to Christ in the sense that the particular promise cannot be said to refer to them and must therefore refer to Christ. Thus, when Jeremiah was commanded,

[76] OC 39,67; CTS Jer 4,253.
[77] OC 31,42-3; CTS Ps 1,11; CP 32.

Go down to the house of the king of Judah (22.1ff.), Calvin comments:
'he speaks of the king *sitting upon the throne of David*, but not for the
sake of honour . . . but rather to underline the guilt of the king;
for he occupied the sacred throne of which he was quite unworthy
. . . We know that the throne of David was more eminent than
any other; for it was a priestly kingdom and the image of that
heavenly kingdom which was afterwards fully revealed in Christ.
As, then, the kings of Judah, David's descendants, were images of
Christ, less tolerable was their godlessness when they forgot their
vocation and ceased to imitate their father David and became
wholly degenerate'.[78] In their case, it was the office and not their
own person which was the direct type.

Again, as with prediction in general, the promises of an eternal
Kingdom could, if they were to be fulfilled, be referred only to
Christ, since the dynasty of David lasted for only a few
generations. After asserting that David was a type of Christ, so
that God 'engraved on him a living image of his only-begotten
Son',[79] he goes on to ask how the prophecy, *there shall not be cut off
from David a man who shall sit upon the throne of the house of Israel*,
agrees with the historical facts; 'for from the time that Jeremiah
promised such a state, there has been no successor to David. It is
true that Zerubbabel was the leader of the people, but he lacked
royal title and glory. There was no throne, no crown, no sceptre,
from the time when the people returned from their Babylonian
exile. Yet God testified by the mouth of Jeremiah that there
would be a continual succession of David's descendants to govern
the people. He does not say they would be mere chieftains, but he
adorns them with the title of king. "There will ever remain a
successor to occupy the throne" he says. Now, we have already
said that there was no throne; but we must keep to what Ezekiel
says, that an interruption of the kingdom was not contrary to this
prophecy of the perpetuity of the kingdom or the continual
succession, for he foretold that the diadem would be cast down
until the legitimate descendant of David should come. It was
therefore necessary that the diadem should fall and be cast to the
ground, or be transformed, as the Prophet says, until Christ

[78] OC 38,372; CTS Jer 3,76.
[79] OC 39,70; CTS Jer 4,257-8.

should be manifested . . . To summarise, whenever the Prophets declare that David's kingdom would be perpetual, they do not promise a continuous succession without any interruption; but it ought to be referred to that perpetuity which was at length manifested in Christ alone'.[80] But at this point he gives a twist to his argument by combining typology with the contemporaneity of Christ's eternal kingdom. 'It is not necessary or expedient to introduce an *anagogē* from the return of the people to the liberation revealed through Christ, as interpreters usually do. It ought to be considered as the one benefit of God, that he brought back his people from exile that they might at length enjoy peaceful and solid happiness when David's kingdom should again be established'.[81] David's earthly kingdom was therefore not the sign of an absent and future kingdom of Christ but the figure of the present and eternal Kingdom. Types, like Sacraments, contain the reality they signify.

The commentary on the Psalms abounds in examples of typology based on David. But Calvin is very selective in his use of typology. Often he will expound a psalm historically which seems to lend itself to typology. If we go through the earlier psalms, the second is thoroughly "Messianic", and indeed is applied to Christ in several places in the New Testament. Calvin therefore also interprets it of Christ. Nevertheless, he does not cut it off from its historical context. It is a song of David, in which (and this is Calvin's introductory summary) 'David boasts that his kingdom, although it be assailed with a huge multitude of enemies and mighty power, shall notwithstanding be perpetual, because it is upheld by the hand and power of God. He adds also that it shall be enlarged, even to the uttermost coasts of the earth, in spite of his enemies. He therefore exhorts kings and other rulers to lay down their pride, and with meek hearts to take the yoke that the Lord lays upon them, because it is in vain for them to struggle to shake it off'.[82] So far, not a word about Christ. If he had left it there, it would have been a purely historical summary. But he adds the one sentence: 'Moreover, this figure contains a

---

[80] OC 39,70–1; CTS Jer 4,258–60.
[81] OC 39,71; CTS Jer 4,260.
[82] OC 31,41; CTS Ps 1,9; CP 1,30.

prophecy concerning Christ's kingdom that was to come'.[83] The actual exposition gives more than this apparent after-thought promises, for it is concerned almost entirely with Christ and his kingdom. The transition that Calvin makes is by a "figure". David and his kingdom, real historical entities, are nevertheless "figures" which in themselves are not the reality. Thus Calvin says: 'But now it is high time to come to the substance of the figure. For, that David prophesied of Christ, appears certain from this, that he knew his own kingdom was but as a shadow. And that we may learn to refer to Christ whatsoever David in times past sang of himself, this principle . . . is to be held, that he, with his posterity, was created king, not so much for his own sake, as to be the image of the Redeemer'.[84] He goes on to say that these Christological interpretations are not 'violently or allegorically wrested to Christ'[85] but are the true sense.

But compare Ps.2 with those on either side of it. Ps.1 is about the godly and the wicked and there is no Messianic prophecy in it: we are therefore not surprised to find in Calvin's comments no reference to Christ apart from a generalization. But Ps.3 is summarised thus: 'David being driven from his kingdom, although utter despair of all things weighed him down, calls notwithstanding upon God, and supports himself with His promise against his great terrors, and against the workings and cruel assaults of his enemies; yea, and against even death itself, which then thrusts itself before his eyes. In the end he rejoices on behalf of himself and the whole Church for the happy issue of all'.[86] It would not be out of the way to apply this psalm Christologically, taking, by Calvin's own method, the sufferings of David as a figure whose substance was concentrated in Gethsemane, the Cross, and the Resurrection. But in Calvin's exposition, not a word about Christ.

The next psalm after the second to be given a Christological interpretation is the eighth. This is in reference to verses 4-6, which are quoted in Hebrews: *What is man, that thou art mindful of him, and the son of man that thou visitest him. For thou hast made him*

[83] OC 31,41; CTS Ps 1,9; CP 1,30.
[84] OC 31,42-3; CTS Ps 1,11; CP 1,32.
[85] OC 31,43; CTS Ps 1,11; CP 1,32.
[86] OC 31,52; CTS Ps 1,27; CP 1,42.

little inferior to God [I quote Calvin's version], *and hast crowned him with glory and honour*, and so on. He expounds it of men in general and treats the New Testament application of it to Christ and his humiliation and exaltation at first as a difficulty to be resolved. The solution, however, brings out clearly his own fundamental Christological interpretation. The psalm is speaking of perfect man, man before the Fall; what it says does not apply, except in a small degree, to man as he now is. But on Christ as man the Father bestowed 'the fulness of all gifts'.[87] Therefore, this is true primarily of Christ and, inasmuch as they draw these gifts from him, of his people in him.

Again, no more Christological interpretations until Ps.16,10: *For thou wilt not leave my soul in the grave; neither shalt thou put thy holy one to see the corruption.* This verse Calvin steadfastly interprets of David in particular and of all the saints in general. He takes the Apostolic reference of it to Christ as merely indirect: 'That Peter in Acts 2.30 and Paul in Acts 13.33 assert that this prophecy was fulfilled in [Christ's] person alone, take like this: He was completely and utterly exempt from the corruption of the grave that he might, gradually and each according to his measure, call his members into his society'.[88]

His sobriety in exegesis will come out in places that had traditionally been given a direct and perhaps imaginative reference to a New Testament event. Ps.72, for example, with the verses 7-11 engendering 'Hail to the Lord's Anointed, Great David's greater Son', which fix a Messianic interpretation in the minds of generations of church-goers, is treated cautiously. The initial summary interprets it of the Davidic kingdom and the Church, but without mention of Christ; and the exposition of the rubric *Of* [or *For*] *Solomon*, expressly says: 'Those who would interpret it simply as a foretelling of the kingdom of Christ, seem to twist the words violently'.[89] He himself expounds the psalm of Christ, not directly but through the figure or type of the kingship of David and Solomon. The more fanciful relations get short shrift. It is nonsensical to equate *The kings of Tarshish and of the isles*

[87] OC 31,93; CTS Ps 1,104; CP 1,93. In Calvin, vv.5ff.
[88] OC 31,157; CTS Ps 1,231; CP 1,170.
[89] OC 31,664; CTS Ps 3,100.

shall bring presents: the kings of Sheba and Seba shall offer gifts with
Matt.2: 'It goes without saying how stupidly this verse has been
twisted under the Papacy. They chant it of the philosophers or
magi who came to worship Christ. Fancy making the philosophers kings in a trice at their own will and switching round the
corners of the globe, making the south or the west into the east!'[90]
The psalm, he says, has to be taken as a prophecy of Christ
because what it promises is too great for any earthly kingdom and
was not in fact fulfilled in the Davidic kingdom.

5 The Historical Context.

One of the outstanding features of Calvin's exposition of the
Prophets is his historical treatment. He is careful to observe their
historical context, establishing from internal and sometimes
external sources the dates of the Prophets and their historical
circumstances. Thus he speaks at some length on the date of
Ezekiel, discussing the Jewish method of dating from Jubilees, the
opinion of 'the majority of commentators', who follow "the
Chaldee Paraphrast", another view which Jerome rejected and
which Calvin adopted, and finally, on the basis of Ezek.1.1, II
Kings 24.15, Lev.25, II Chron.35.18, II Kings 23.23 and 36, II
Kings 24.8 and II Chron.34.14, comes to a solution satisfactory to
himself. The dates of Hosea also are worked out precisely[91] and
fully, but Joel's are dealt with summarily: 'it is better to leave the
time when he taught undecided. As we shall see, it is of no great
importance. Not to know the time of Hosea would be a great loss
to readers, for there are many places which can not be explained
without a knowledge of the history'.[92] We note that the dating is
always tied to the understanding of a Prophet; this, indeed, is
carried so far in Micah as to be used only, or mainly, for purposes
of application: Micah 1.1: 'First, this inscription indicates the time
at which Micah lived and during which God used his labours.
And this should be noted, for his sermons would nowadays be
useless, or at least frigid, unless we knew his dates and could

[90] OC 31,668-9; CTS Ps 3,111.
[91] OC 42,199-201; CTS Mi 1,37-40.
[92] OC 42,515; CTS Mi 2,xv.

thereby compare and contrast the men of his age and of our own. For when we understand that Micah condemned this or that vice . . . we are able to apply what he said more easily to ourselves, inasmuch as we can view our own life as it were in a mirror'.[93]

He therefore interprets their teaching in relation to the historical context; and this is why he has to make the conscious transition from their times to "our own day". There are extended expositions without frequent application, however, and in these passages the Prophet's teaching becomes what we might call historical theology. Application is not detached from its historical origin. Even in such a passage as Isaiah 53, which Calvin interprets directly of the Cross and Resurrection of Christ, we are never allowed to forget that, although we might seem to have passed over into the New Testament, these are still the words of a Prophet preaching to the Jews just before the Exile. At the outset of the passage, after his preliminary exegesis, he sets it in context: 'He speaks therefore of the prosperity of the Church; but as this did not appear he directs them to the supreme King, by whom all things were to be restored, and bids them to wait for him. And here we should carefully observe the contrasts the Prophet makes: the mightiness of this King whom the Lord will exalt is opposed to the wretched and debased state of the people, who were nearly in despair'.[94]

6 Visions.

Besides straightforward prediction and typology, we have also to consider visions, which we have already looked at in Chapter Three. This word he applies broadly. It includes revelations through dreams (e.g. 'Daniel's vision, concerning the Four Empires' was a dream),[95] the narration of fictional events, and the viewing of present or future events set before the Prophet directly by God. A vision is 'a crude symbol',[96] 'a sign or symbol',[97] and

---

[93] OC 43,281; CTS Mi 3,151.
[94] OC 37,251-2; CTS Isa 4,106.
[95] OC 41,37; CTS Dan 2,8.
[96] OC 40,74; CTS Ezek 1,126.
[97] OC 40,196; CTS Ezek 1,304.

as such it is analogous to Sacraments in that it demands explanation; that is, the sign must be accompanied by the Word: 'Here we must note that signs without a word (*voce*) are mere games. If the vision only had been set before the Prophet's eyes, without a word (*vox*) of God to follow, what profit could there have been? But when God confirmed the vision by his Word (*sermone*), the Prophet could relate empirically that he had seen the glory of God'.[98] The distinction between the narration of fiction and the narration of what is seen in a trance is not easy to draw. But examples of the former are the marriage of Hosea and the marred girdle of Jeremiah. It seemed impossible to Calvin that Hosea, a Prophet, should have married an unchaste woman; such an action would have been unendurable in one whose office was to teach the people the ways of righteousness and, moreover, at variance with St Paul's requirements for a bishop ('and no doubt the same was required at that time in the Prophets').[99] Calvin gives the arguments on both sides, but is firm that this is a *visio* – in this case a fictional narrative. Hosea is therefore enabled to maintain his honour and dignity among the people. Calvin moves from the drama to the art gallery in expounding this: '"The Lord places me here as on a stage (*in theatro*) to explain to you that I have married a wife, a wife habituated to adulteries and whoredoms, and that I have begotten children by her". All the people knew that he had done no such thing; but the Prophet spoke like this to set before their eyes a painting – in colour (*pictam tabulam*). Such then was the vision, the figure; not that the Prophet knew it by a vision, but the Lord had bidden him to relate this so to say parable, that is, similitude, that the people might recognise, as in a living picture (*in viva pictura*) their wickedness and unfaithfulness. Finally, it is an *hypotyposis*, in which not only is the reality explained in words but it is set before our eyes in, as it were, a visible form'.[100] The very accumulation of nouns shows what he had in mind – vision, figure, parable, similitude, living picture, visible form, *hypotyposis* (interestingly enough, this word reminds us that we are on the fringe of the *umbra* metaphor, for it means 'a general representation, an outline, *adumbratio*').

[98] OC 40,63; CTS Ezek 1,110.
[99] OC 42,203; CTS Mi 1,43.
[100] OC 42,204; CTS Mi 1,45.

On Jer.13.1-9, he first explains the meaning of the prophecy and goes on to give his reason for taking the story as a *visio*: 'But without doubt a vision is here narrated and not an actual event – some think Jeremiah went [to the Euphrates]. What can be more absurd? He was, we know, day by day performing his office of teacher among his people. Had he undertaken so long a journey, and that twice, he would not have returned for several months . . . We know that this form of speaking is common and usual enough in the Prophets, and they narrate visions as actual events'.[101]

In neither of these instances was the story or event given to the Prophet as a direct revelation from God to him privately but was a message conveyed by the Prophet (of course, under the inspiration of the Holy Spirit) by visual means.

It is in Ezekiel and Daniel that the third class of *visiones* is most prominent. Here we see Calvin struggling courageously with an unfamiliar and uncongenial form. He sometimes confesses his bewilderment but accepts the fact that the passage is part of Holy Scripture, dictated by the Holy Spirit and given for the Church to understand and use: 'We must now investigate a vision whose obscurity so deterred the Jews that they forbade even attempts at explanation. But God appeared to his Prophet either in vain or fruitfully. To suppose the former is absurd. Therefore, if the vision is useful, it is necessary for us to understand it at least partially. If any one object that the vision was given to the Prophet and not to the rest, the cavil is easily resolved. The Prophet wrote what we read here for the common use of the whole Church. If any one asks whether the vision is clear, I avow it to be very obscure and I do not profess to understand it. Yet, it is not only lawful and useful but also necessary to enquire into what God has set before us. We should indeed be disgracefully lazy if we deliberately shut our eyes and paid no heed to the vision'.[102]

We will follow through his exposition of Ezek.1.4-28.

He first considers the general intention of the vision. It was twofold: to furnish Ezekiel with authority, and to fill the people with terror. But to this it must be added that the visible does not contradict but agrees with the teaching in the vision: 'We must

---

[101] OC 38,154; CTS Jer 2,161.
[102] OC 40,29; CTS Ezek 1,62.

hold that there is an analogy or similitude between this vision and the Prophet's teaching (*doctrina*)'.[103]

Next, for the significance of the details of the vision. Of the four beasts he mentions six interpretations and rejects each with varying degrees of scorn. 'All these, then, I reject. And now we must see what the Prophet really means'.[104] He approaches carefully from the general intention he has already decided on: 'God shortly indicates by this symbol for what purpose he sent his Prophet. For the visions have as great a similitude with the *doctrina* as possible'.[105] On this basis he says that the tempest is the judgment of God and that God is seen on his throne. The four beasts are, as chapter 10 shows, cherubim. There are four and not the two overshadowing the Ark of the Covenant, as one would expect, because, although Ezekiel is indeed alluding to the Sanctuary, where God was enthroned, he had to accommodate what he says to "the rudeness of the people", whose religion had so degenerated that they did not understand the purpose and significance of the Sanctuary. Therefore the image of the four beasts was based on the Sanctuary but it was adapted for the sake of the people. Of course, 'he did not manufacture anything out of his own head, for I am now speaking of the purpose of the Holy Spirit'.[106] But why did God want to make the two cherubs four? 'To teach us that his power is spread throughout all the regions of the world; for we know that the world is divided into four parts'.[107] The fact that these were Angels is a reference to God's universal providence, for it is through his Angels that God works in the world. Why did each beast have four heads? To show that Angelic power resides in them all; and here Calvin slips over from the animals who were the cherubim to the animate part of the creation and so, since this is "a part of the whole", to all creation: 'God by his Angels works not only in man and other living things, but in all creatures. But because inanimate things have no motion in themselves . . . God sets before the people under the animals the image of all things'.[108] Calvin then explains literally

[103] OC 40,29-30; CTS Ezek 1,63.
[104] OC 40,30; CTS Ezek 1,64.
[105] OC 40,30; CTS Ezek 1,64.
[106] OC 40,31; CTS Ezek 1,65.
[107] OC 40,31; CTS Ezek 1,65.
[108] OC 40,32; CTS Ezek 1,66.

('I am not fabricating allegories, but only embracing the literal sense')[109] the meaning of each beast. Man holds the first place, for he was made in the image of God; the lion is king of wild beasts; the ox represents domesticated animals; by the eagle, a royal bird, is meant all birds (he obviously means that with the king of birds go all his subjects, the other birds). In other words, we have here four representatives of all earthly living creatures, and by synecdoche, of all the creatures and elements. Hence we see that God is ruler over all in every part of the world and that he works by means of his Angels.

We come to the wheels, which Calvin takes to signify changes and re-volutions: 'for we see the world continually changing and putting on, so to say, new appearances, just as if a wheel has made a revolution'.[110] But the wheels are connected with the Angels, meaning that changes do not come about by chance but by the agency of the Angels and therefore, of the God who employs the Angels. That there were wheels within wheels denotes that the changes in the world are not orderly and simple but highly complex and apparently in disorder. Hence the Stoic belief that events came *ex causarum connexione* – from the inter-combination of causes. On the contrary, although the changes (*conversiones*) that occur are interwoven, their setting in motion (*agitatio*) depends on the Angels, whom God guides according to his will. The *eyes* in the wheels show that nothing happens by *blind* chance.

What will surely strike anyone who reads this account (and it will be even clearer if we go on to read the exposition of the whole vision) is not the ingenuity with which Calvin arrives at his conclusion, but the conclusion itself. The vision has become a straightforward statement of Calvin's doctrine of providence, and in the process it has lost, if not its poetry (for there is a certain splendid poetry in that doctrine), yet its Road to Xanadu quality and become rational and plain. But then, Calvin insisted that the Prophet had been rational at the times of the vision and had never fallen into an ecstasy, had never been ἐνθουσιάσμος. We find just the same sort of interpretation of the continuation of this vision in Ezek. 10.1ff.

[109] OC 40,32; CTS Ezek 1,66.
[110] OC 40,32; CTS Ezek 1,67.

In Daniel the situation has changed. Whereas, according to
Calvin, Ezekiel 'threatens final slaughter against the people
because they did not cease to heap iniquity upon iniquity and
more and more inflamed the vengeance of God',[111] the task of
Daniel was to encourage the people during their long captivity,
but at the same time to warn them that they must not
misunderstand what Isaiah and the other pre-Exilic prophets had
said about their splendid future when they should return, for God
had many severe trials in store for them over many centuries.
Through visions, then, God showed Daniel, and through him the
people, the relevant history of the world up to the advent of
Christ. This last phrase is highly important: 'God wished only to
indicate to his Prophet what was going to happen up to the first
advent of Christ',[112] he says in a passage we are about to consider.
If Calvin's sensible, reasonable approach prevented him from
entering more fully into the riches of apocalyptic, it also saved
him from the extravagance of applying Daniel's visions to the
contemporary theological or political enemies of the Reformed
Churches or of mankind.

Chapter 7 tells of Daniel's vision of four great beasts coming up
from the sea, a lion, a bear, a leopard, and "a fourth beast,
dreadful and terrible". This, says Calvin, begins a new section.
Before it, Daniel's mission had been to heathen kings; now he
begins to teach the Church. God forewarns his people of the trials
that they must undergo before Christ comes to save them and so
foretells the domination of four empires. This was addressed not
only to the Jews but also to us today, for it not only proves the
genuineness of the prophecies, which were fulfilled to the letter as
we can see, but shows that we also have severe trials before us.

The vision begins, then, with a storm at sea, 'as if all the winds
were meeting in one general conflict',[113] an image of what was
soon to befall the captives, who would return to their own land
and find troubles and persecution awaiting them instead of the
rest and happiness they thought they had been promised. They
must therefore brace themselves to further struggles. And the

[111] OC 40,24; CTS Ezek 1,55.
[112] OC 41,50; CTS Dan 2,26.
[113] OC 41,39; CTS Dan 2,10-1.

same will be true of their descendants for many generations. For four hundred years the Jews will be persecuted by foreign tyrants.

As for the details, there are disagreements among commentators. The first beast, the lion with eagle's wings which became a man with a man's heart (7.4), Calvin takes, in agreement with "all", to be the Assyrian-Chaldaean empire. The lion had wings to show the swiftness of the growth of this empire; but that the wings were plucked off means that God checked their continual victories. When the lion was taken up from the earth, it signified that this empire came to an end, although the people were not completely destroyed. The strong, swift lion became just a man, like any other man. 'This, in my judgment, is the simple meaning of the Prophet'.[114]

The bear that raised itself on one side and had three ribs in its mouth between its teeth (7.5) signified without doubt the Persians. 'We know the bear to be an ignoble and ugly animal, slothful and lazy and yet very fierce. If we compare the bear with the lion, we say the appearance of the bear is ugly and gloomy, but the lion is beautiful, even if formidable. He compares the Persians to a bear on account of their barbarity'.[115] They are uncivilized; 'they lived in their caves like wild beasts'.[116] They overcame the Chaldaeans and became the dominant power. That the bear had three ribs between his teeth meant that the Persians overcame many nations.

When he came to the leopard, or panther, with four heads and four wings (7.6), Calvin was furnished with more authorities and was able to write in greater detail. The animal certainly represents Alexander, that man so swift in execution, drunk with ambition, and, with him, his successors. The four heads and the four wings are interpreted variously, 'but a simpler meaning is . . . that Alexander had scarcely enjoyed his victories when he died, quite unexpectedly, and after his death every one seized a portion of the prey for himself '[117] (he means that the four heads and wings are those who seized a portion for himself). Thereupon he proceeds to explain at length and in detail what happened when Alexander

[114] OC 41,41; CTS Dan 2,15.
[115] OC 41,42; CTS Dan 2,15.
[116] OC 41,42; CTS Dan 2,15.
[117] OC 41,44; CTS Dan 2,18.

had died, ending with the remark that this is only an outline and promising a fuller treatment under Chapter 11.

The fourth beast, with great iron teeth and ten horns, is more difficult to interpret. Some say it means the Pope, others that it is the Turks; 'I have no doubt that in this vision the Prophet was shown the figure of the Roman Empire'.[118] Again Calvin restricts the prophecy to the period between the return from the Exile up to and including the apostolic age. He therefore relates the rise of the Roman domination in the Middle East; that is, Rome in its role of tyrant over the Jews. That the beast had ten horns is not to be taken precisely, for "ten" often means "many" in the Bible. It therefore signifies the many provinces into which the Empire was divided. But then in the vision another horn grew up, a little one, and in front of it three of the former horns were plucked out; *and in this horn were, as it were, the eyes of a man, and a mouth speaking great things*. We must remember, says Calvin, that 'God wished only to indicate to his Prophet what was going to happen up to the first advent of Christ. This is where all those who under this vision want to embrace the perpetual state of the Church to the end of the world go wrong'.[119] The little horn therefore represents the Caesars, from Julius onwards. Calvin leaves the *terminus ad quem* vague, only insisting that 'we must grasp the purpose of the Holy Spirit. He leads the faithful right on to the beginning of the kingdom of Christ, that is, to the preaching of the Gospel, which happened under Caligula, Claudius, Nero, and their successors'.[120] This horn is called little because, although Julius Caesar made himself dictator, he did not take the rank of king and the senate always retained something of its majesty. That three of the former horns were removed is not difficult to explain. It cannot mean that Rome had lost part of its Empire, for at this period (i.e. the early preaching of the Gospel) the Empire was still intact. It is a reference to Augustus' assuming extra powers to himself over the senate and the army and thus taking power from the republic. The eyes of a man in the horn signify that the Caesars were content with power without the trappings of royalty and so seemed to be merely men and no more. This is

[118] OC 41,46; CTS Dan 2,21.
[119] OC 41,50; CTS Dan 2,26.
[120] OC 41,50; CTS Dan 2,27.

apparent in the behaviour of Julius, Augustus, and Tiberius. The mouth which spoke great things stands in contrast to the human eyes. The Caesars conducted themselves as mere men but spoke as dictators whom none was to gainsay.

We have gone far enough through the exposition of this vision. All that follows is of the same nature. The faithful Jews are forewarned of the troubles that they must face until the kingdom of Christ is set up, that kingdom which is governed by the Gospel. The grotesque imagery dissolves into common-sense ancient history, as thoroughly as if Picasso's *Guernica* should be suddenly metamorphosed into a set of newspaper photographs of that stricken city. And yet this is not entirely fair. Certainly the historical passages could well have stood in a text-book of ancient history; but even here the mystery is preserved; no longer the mystery of the pictorial but that of a history which is the activity of God bringing to pass the incarnation of Christ and the proclamation of the Gospel.

In most visions the Prophet is addressed either by God himself or by an Angel of God. These are always interpreted by Calvin as pre-Incarnation appearances of Christ. We have already considered this subject in connection with the exposition of narrative and need not go over the same ground twice. One quotation will recall the points noticed there and put them in the context of the Prophets.

Ezek. 1.26 *And above the firmament* – or rather, expansion, as we said – *which was over their head, as the vision* – or aspect – *of a throne in the likeness of a sapphire stone; and upon the likeness of the throne the likeness of the aspect of a man upon it above.* 'Now, it may be asked why God put on the form of a man, both in this place that is, in this vision, and in others like it. I readily accept the judgment of the fathers who say that this was a prelude of his mystery which was at length revealed and which Paul extolled when he cried "Great is this mystery, that God was at last manifest in the flesh". Jerome's statement is crude and dangerous, that this was spoken of the Father himself. For we know that the Father never put on human flesh. If he had said simply that God was represented here, there would be nothing absurd in it; just remove all mention of the Persons and it will be entirely true that the man seated on the throne was God . . . But John said in chapter 12 [v. 41], that when

Isaiah saw God sitting on a throne it was the glory of Christ that he saw and of him that he was speaking. And so what I have already quoted from the fathers is very apt, that whenever God appeared under the appearance of a man, some obscure token (*specimen*) was given of the mystery which was at last revealed in the person of Christ'.[121]

7 Application of prophecy

As with narrative, it is the application of a passage to the readers or hearers that is most prominent in Calvin's exposition of the Prophets. The applications are directed commonly towards three parties, the Papists, "us", and preachers or teachers.

The Prophets' polemic against the hypocrisy and disobedience of the people lent itself easily to application against the Romanists. This sort of warfare was not, of course, peculiar to Calvin or to the other Evangelicals; the Romanists also found plenty of verses to use as ammunition. But here we are concerned only with Calvin. The root of the matter for him was obedience to God's will as it is stated in Scripture. On Jer.7.21-24 he discussed the nature of superstition and how it differs from true worship: *For I did not speak to your fathers and I did not command them in the day on which I led them out of the land of Egypt, concerning burnt offerings and sacrifices; but rather I commanded them this word, saying, Hear my voice, and I will be your God, and you will be to me a people, and you will walk in all the way that I shall command you, that it may be well with you.* From this it is clear that the basis of true religion is obedience to God's expressed will; and conversely, a religion invented by men and apart from the will of God is only superstition: 'true religion can always be distinguished from superstitions by this mark: If the truth of God governs us, our religion is good; but if anyone follows his own ideas (*sensum*), even if there is a general consensus of opinion, then that is fabricating superstition. Nothing of this will please God'.[122] But the Papists do not have a single eye to the truth of God expressed in Scripture: 'they esteem the teaching of the fathers and the perpetual consensus of the Catholic Church, as they call it, more

---

[121] OC 40,53-4; CTS Ezek 1,97.
[122] OC 37,692; CTS Jer 1,395.

than the Law, and the Prophets, and the Gospel'.[123] Hence, with this divided vision, their worship becomes an admixture and therefore superstition. Calvin goes so far in this passage as to make *Scriptura sola* the ultimate barrier between the two sides: 'This one passage could put an end to all our present-day contentions in the world. For if the Papists admitted that obedience is more to God than all sacrifices (I Sam.15.22), we could easily come to agreement. They might go on to argue over individual articles; but agreement would be reached if they would subscribe simply and unreservedly (*absque controversia*) to the Word of God'.[124] Or again, on Jer.18.18, where Calvin brings in the argument levelled against the Reformers since the fifteen-twenties: 'it seems quite absurd to them and even intolerable when we ask for a hearing and wish the controversies which trouble the world today to be determined and removed by the Law and the Prophets, and the Gospel. "What! So the Church's decrees are to be reduced to nothing, are they? The Scripture is a wax nose; it has nothing sure or consistent (*firmum*); it can be twisted into any direction, and hypocrites always abuse the Word of God. Therefore it follows that there is nothing certain, nothing clear in Scripture"'.[125] But 'we, on the contrary, say that perfect wisdom is embraced in the Law, the Prophets, and the Gospel. Therefore if we were [all] to hearken to the voice of God, it would be easy to settle all the disputes . . . For he himself has spoken and has not spoken in secret, that is, in riddles and obscurely. There is nothing more clear than his teaching, if only men are not blind through malice'.[126]

The individual applications against the Papists stem from this point. The objectionable ceremonies and the pomp of their worship ('they think that a great part of holiness consists in the splendour of vestments');[127] the foundation of antiquity instead of "the Law, the Prophets, and the Gospel"; the imitation of the Church fathers, faults as well as virtues; the perversion of the doctrine and the discipline of Scripture, as in the sacrament of

[123] OC 37,692; CTS Jer 1,396.
[124] OC 37,692; CTS Jer 1,396.
[125] OC 38,311; CTS Jer 2,419.
[126] OC 38,426; CTS Jer 3,168.
[127] OC 42,240; CTS Mi 1,99. Hos 2.13.

penance; all these charges, each of them brought many times throughout the expositions, are symptoms of the inward disease of disobedience.

No less common are the applications to "us", which will sometimes mean Geneva in particular, sometimes the Evangelical Christians. The lesson to be gathered will, of course, depend on the passage under consideration. Most common are encouragement (if God worked so wonderfully then, will he not help us now?), the need for continual renewal of repentance and faith, warnings against the sins so prevalent among the Jews and Israelites, hypocrisy, disobedience, idolatry, ingratitude, spiritual adultery. And continually the refrain that however bad the people of the Old Covenant may have been, "we" are far worse, for "we" have a clearer light than they: 'there is a great difference between us, who have been taught the true and lawful worship of God intimately and over a long period, and those unhappy people who were blind in darkness. For our wickedness is much more atrocious and deserves heavier punishment. We may also add that if God bears with us for a time, the whole time of his patience will have to be accounted for. There is no day in which God does not call us to wake up; and thus "he rises up early" and shows what concern he has for our salvation. But if we remain sunk in sloth, this threatening hangs over our heads today – especially if we consider how much nearer God comes to us than to the olden people. Hence we may learn how much less tolerable is our ingratitude'.[128]

For preachers and teachers the applications are plain. Jer.3.15: *And I will give you pastors according to my heart, and they shall feed you with knowledge and understanding* – that is, skilfully and wisely (*scienter et prudenter*). 'Hence we learn that the Church cannot long stand unless it is governed by faithful pastors who will show the way of salvation. The safety of the Church consists in God's raising up true and sincere teachers to proclaim his doctrine . . . It therefore follows that the Church of God is not only begotten by the activity of holy and godly pastors but that its life is also cherished, nourished, and strengthened by them to the end'.[129] The foundations of the office of teacher are first that he shall have

[128] OC 38,110; CTS Jer 2,90–1.
[129] OC 37,563; CTS Jer 1,181.

been obedient to the call of God and not taken on the task at his own will, and secondly that he shall declare only what is given him to teach: 'those who are called to the office of teaching are not adorned with royal power, to proclaim whatever they please, but they are pastors in the train of God (*post Deum*)'.[130] Elsewhere he will call them God's heralds:[131] but although God 'would have them to be heads, or leaders, or standard-bearers, yet he himself wills always to keep his own rank'.[132]

Again, it is necessary, if a teacher is to perform his task faithfully, that he shall set God's will and purpose before him as his sole intention, for otherwise he will soon capitulate in the face of opposition: 'The Prophet declares the source of the great courage with which he and other servants of God need to be endowed in order to withstand courageously all attacks. It comes from God's help. By trusting in him, he declares that he holds his ground against all the attacks of the world. Endowed with sublime fortitude, he despises all opposition . . . and paints, so to say, a picture of the situation of all ministers of the Word; that, turned away from the world, they turn wholly towards God and are entirely focussed on him. There will never be so grave a conflict but they will win it by trusting in this leader'.[133] For ministers must make no mistake; if they are faithful, they will suffer for it in one way or another. Therefore they must be ready to fight, not only in defence but in attack: 'Those who are sent to teach the world are sent to the battle. It is therefore not enough to teach faithfully what God commands, unless we also fight'.[134] They are not to despair, even if the whole world is against them; and if they see no fruit for all their labour, they are still not to despair: 'We are here taught that although ministers of the Word may think they are labouring in vain, while they are singing a ballad to the deaf, as the proverb goes, they ought not to desert from the course of their vocation. For there will always be some who will really show, after a long time, that they had been

---

[130] OC 38,280; CTS Jer 2,371.
[131] Hos 5.8. OC 42,307; CTS Mi 1,198.
[132] OC 38,280; CTS Jer 2,371.
[133] OC 37,221; CTS Isa 4,56-7.
[134] OC 43,330; CTS Mi 3,234. Mic 3.8.

divinely and wonderfully saved and do not perish with the rest'.[135]

Calvin is not usually associated with any *via media*, but it is precisely this that he enjoins to ministers, after the example of Daniel declaring Nebuchadnezzar's dream: 'nothing is more difficult for ministers of the Word than to maintain this mean (*mediocritatem*). Some are always thundering under pretext of zeal, and forget that they are men; they show no sign of benevolence but just creak and croak mere bitterness. So they have no authority and all their admonitions are odious. And they expound God's Word haughtily and insultingly, inhumanely frightening sinners without any sign of sorrow or συμπαθείας. Others, who are lazy, no, who are unfaithful flatterers, bury even the grossest crimes; their excuse is that neither the Prophets nor the Apostles were so fervent that their zeal drove out all human affections. Thus they delude unhappy men and destroy them by their flatteries. But our Prophet, like all the others, here shows the middle course (*mediam rationem*) which God's servants ought to take'.[136]

We continue to consider Daniel, but under another aspect. These lectures have a quality of their own and, indeed, an historical importance only slightly shared by the other sets. And it is in regard to their importance as documents relating to the contemporary history of France that I wish to consider them now.

Calvin began to lecture on Daniel on June 12, 1559 and ended some time in the first fortnight of April 1560. During these ten months the religious and political situation in France moved into an alarming new phase. The Evangelicals had been persecuted with now more, now less, consistency and severity for some twenty-five years. During that time their numbers had grown to such an extent that they had now organised themselves on a national basis. In May 1559 (just before the lectures started) they had held their first national synod in Paris and had issued their own Confession of Faith. There were therefore now two powerful bodies in France calling themselves the true Church of God. The power of the government – in other words, of the

135 Zeph 2.3. OC 44,31; CTS Mi 4,234.
136 OC 40,667; CTS Dan 1,270.

monarch, Henry II – was whole-heartedly behind one of these bodies and as strongly against the other; but this other had the considerable support of leading noblemen. When the king died after an accident early in July, his heir was a boy of fifteen whose feebleness of mind made a regency necessary. The proper person to take charge of affairs was the King of Navarre, next in succession after Henry and his sons. He and his brother, the Prince de Condé, were Evangelicals of a sort – their wives were sincerer and firmer than they. Far from taking charge, however, the supine Navarre allowed the uncles of the young king's wife (Mary, later Queen of Scots) to assume power. They continued the persecuting policy of Henry II. The thoughts of some of the evangelical nobles and gentry began to turn to resistance, even armed rebellion.

In the autumn of 1559 (that is, about mid-way through these lectures) Calvin was sounded out about his views on resistance. His teaching on submission to lawful authority was clear and had been stated in its final form as early as 1536. It was not lawful for private citizens to resist even the most tyrannical ruler; but it was the duty of those in whom constitutional power was vested to put things right, if necessary even by the extreme step of deposing a ruler. The sort of people he had in mind as possessing such power were princes of the blood and the Three Estates. Precisely such a situation had now arisen. A large part of the people was suffering under oppression. In two of their adherents the Evangelicals possessed the means to curb or even break the tyranny, for the King of Navarre and the Prince de Condé were princes of the blood. But they had let their opportunity slip, and now the most that Calvin would sanction was that the Evangelicals should display their considerable political and military power and so by a bloodless coup displace the existing regency so that Navarre might take his rightful place as Regent.

But about this time a man turned up in Geneva with the scheme, for which he claimed influential backing in France, of seizing the person of the King in order thereafter to claim his support and authority. Calvin would have nothing to do with what he considered a completely immoral and irresponsible plot. However, this man managed to enlist a few volunteers in Geneva, and the attempt was made in March 1560. It failed and the Evangelicals were worse off than before.

This story forms the background to the lectures on Daniel. Moreover, it seems very likely that Calvin chose Daniel to lecture on at this point because it was so apposite to the situation in France. He could proclaim in the authoritative form of a commentary on Scripture what he was emphasizing in many letters to French nobles and commoners and churches at this time. Although, ouside the preface, there is no open reference to France in the lectures, yet if we read between the lines, it is impossible to doubt that in recounting the history of the Jews in Babylon, he was tacitly applying it to the persecuted churches in his own country.

The first half of the book of Daniel relates both the sufferings of the godly under the tyrants and also the judgment of God on kingdoms and rulers. Here, surely, was an opportunity for Calvin to threaten the wrath of God upon the French tyrants with the dreadful warnings of the fates of Nebuchadnezzar and Belshazzar; an opportunity also for him to incite the French Evangelicals to rebellion as the instrument of that divine providence and vengeance. Threaten the judgment of God he does, but without ever naming the French. And far from inciting rebellion, he preaches patience, suffering, martyrdom, as the course for the persecuted to follow.

His dedicatory letter, addressed 'To all sincere worshippers of God who desire the kingdom of Christ to be rightly constituted in France', sets the tone and gives a prospectus of how he will interpret and apply the book. 'Nothing can be more opportune than the publication of these lectures on the prophecies of Daniel. For I can show you, my very dear brethren, as in a mirror those ancient examples by which God wishes to strengthen the minds of his people whose faith he puts to the test in our own day by all sorts of conflicts, according to his marvellous wisdom. For he would not have them sink when they are smitten by storms and tempests – or at least, even if they should totter, not to fall completely . . . Here, as in a living image, we can see that when God spares and even tolerates some wicked men, he is trying his servants like gold and silver. So we must not think it hard that we are cast into the furnace of trials while the ungodly enjoy peace and quiet'.[137] Calvin can see very well the agonized objection that God is not intervening when French Evangelicals are cast literally into the burning fiery furnace or figuratively into the den of lions. No, God does not always stretch out his hand from heaven to preserve his people; but it should be enough for us to know 'that he has sworn to be the faithful guardian of our lives when we are in peril . . . And what we must look at, is not the outcome only, but how bravely those holy men gave themselves up to death in order to assert God's glory'.[138]

The discussion, in the preface, on the second half of the book is addressed, plainly enough, to both the Evangelicals and their rulers. The prophecies show the rise and fall of empires up to the time of Christ. But what was true then is true now. 'God shows that all earthly power which is not founded on Christ is frail and transitory. A quick destruction is threatened to all kingdoms which obscure the glory of Christ by raising themselves too high. Those kings who now rule great dominions will learn at last by sad experience the terrifying judgment that is theirs unless they submit freely to the rule of Christ . . . They call themselves Christian kings and boast that they are great defenders of the Catholic faith. But if you apply the true and genuine definition of the kingdom of Christ to such weak emptiness it is easily refuted. The throne and sceptre of Christ is the preaching (*doctrina*) of the Gospel'.[139] This sounds inflammatory enough, not much different from Papal bulls releasing subjects from their allegiance to their rulers. But strong as are the condemnations of tyrants, with tacit reference to the regency in France, the message to the Evangelicals is equally clear and strong: They must obey the powers that be in everything lawful; if they are faced with the choice of obeying the power or obeying God, then they must obey God – and be ready to suffer for it; but on no account may any of those who are private citizens attempt to take power into their own hands. His final words are full of stern foreboding, nerving them to perseverance: 'If the conflict has to go on longer (and I prophesy that harder battles than you think are still to

137 OC 18,615; CTS Dan 1,1xiv-1xv.
138 OC 18,616; CTS Dan 1,1xvi.
139 OC 18,617; CTS Dan 1,1xvii.

come) remember, in whatever assaults the madness of the ungodly vents itself, if they summon up all the powers of hell, remember that it is the heavenly judge of the race who has marked out the course you are to run. Obey his rule cheerfully and readily, for he will supply his people with strength to the very end'.[140]

[140] OC 18,623-4; CTS Dan 1,1xxv.

Conclusion

I Pet.1.12: *Unto whom it was revealed, that not unto themselves, but unto us they did minister those things, which are now announced unto you by them that preached the Gospel unto you . . .*

'We see what magnificent praises they gave to the kingdom of Christ, how earnest they were in glorifying it, how whole-heartedly they urged men to seek it. But death prevented their seeing it for themselves. We may well say that they laid the table for others later to dine on the feast. They indeed tasted by faith that which by their hands the Lord gives us to be enjoyed; they indeed were partakers of Christ, the substantial food of the soul. But this verse speaks of the manifestation of the reality. And we know that the prophetic office was, so to say, enclosed within limits, so that they should feed themselves and others in hope of the Christ who was to come. They therefore possessed him only as hidden and as it were absent. Absent, not in power or grace, but as not yet manifest in the flesh; so that his kingdom also was hidden as yet under coverings. When he came down to earth, he so to say opened the heavens to us, so that we might have a closer view of the spiritual riches which were shown to them in figures and at a distance. Therefore this enjoyment of Christ revealed indicates the difference between us and the Prophets'.

'Almighty God, who hast left nothing undone to help us in the course of our faith, grant (because such is our sloth that we move hardly a step even at thy urging), grant, we pray, that we may strive to make better use of those helps that thou hast set before us, that the Law, the Prophets, the voice of John Baptist and at last the teaching of thy only-begotten Son may arouse us better to run more quickly to himself and to journey steadfastly on that course and persevere until at length we possess the victory and reward of our calling, the eternal inheritance which thou hast promised, reserved in heaven for all who do not faint but wait for the coming of that great Redeemer. Amen.'

(Prayer to the final lecture on Malachi)

Bibliography of First and Revised Editions

Isaiah

Ioannis Calvini Commentarii in Isaiam Prophetam . . . Genevae, Ex officina Ioannis Crispini. M.D.LI.

Ioannis Calvini Commentarii in Isaiam Prophetam . . . Genevae, Apud Io. Crispinvm. M.D.LIX.

Commentaires sur le Prophete Isaie. Par M. Iean Caluin . . . a Geneve Par Adam et Iean Riveriz freres. 1552.

Genesis

In Primvm Mosis Librū, qui Genesis vulgo dicitur, Commentarius Iohannis Caluini . . . Oliua Roberti Stephani. M.D.LIIII.

Commentaire de M. Iean Caluin sur le premier livre de Moyse dit Genese . . . A Geneve chez Iean Gerard. M.D.LIIII.

Psalms

In Librvm Psalmorum, Iohannis Caluini commentarius . . . Oliva Roberti Stephani. M.D.LVII.

Le Livre des Pseaumes exposé par Iehan Calvin . . . Imprimé par Conrad Badius, M.D.LVIII.

Commentaires de M. Iean Calvin sur le livre des Pseaumes. Ceste traduction est tellement reveue et si fidelement conferée sur le Latin, qu'on le peut iuger estre nouvelle . . . Imprimé par Conrad Badius. M.D.LXI.

Pentateuch

Mosis Libri V, cum Iohannis Caluini Commentariis. Genesis seorsum: reliqui quatuor in formam harmoniae digesti . . . Genevae. Anno M.D.LXIII. Excvd. Henr. Stephanvs.

Commentaires de M. Iean Caluin, sur les cinq liures de Moyse. Genesis est mis à part, les autre quatre liures sont disposez en forme d'Harmonie . . . Geneve Imprimé par François Estienne. M.D.LXIIII.

Joshua
Commentaires de M. Iean Caluin, sur le livre de Iosué. Avec une preface de Theodore de Besze contenant en brief l'histoire de la vie et mort d'iceluy . . . A Geneve de l'Imprimerie de François Perrin. M.D.LXIIII.

Ioannis Caluini in librum Iosue brevis commentarius, quem paulo ante mortem absolvit. Addita sunt quaedam de eius morbo et obitu . . . Genevae ex officina Francisci Perrini. M.D.LXIIII.

Hosea
In Hoseam Prophetam, Io. Caluini praelectiones, a Ioanne Budaeo, et sociis auditoribus assiduis bona fide exceptae . . . Genevae, Excudebat Conradus Badius. M.D.LVII.

Leçons de Iehan Calvin svr le Prophete Hosee . . . A Geneve. De l'imprimerie de Conrad Badius. M.D.LVII.

Minor Prophets
Ioannis Calvini praelectiones in duodecim prophetas (quos vocant) minores . . . Genevae, apud Ioannem Crispinum, M.D.LIX.

Leçons et Expositions familieres de Iehan Caluin sur les douze petis Prophetes . . . A Geneve. Par Nicolas Barbier, et Thomas Courteau. M.D.LX.

Daniel
Ioannis Calvini Praelectiones in librum prophetiarum Danielis, Ioannis Budaei et Caroli Ionuillaei labore et industria exceptae . . . Genevae. M.D.LXI.

Leçons de M. Iean Calvin sur le livre des propheties de Daniel Recueillies fidelement par Iean Budé et Charles de Ionuiller, ses auditeurs . . . A Geneve M.D.LXII.

Jeremiah

Ioannis Calvini Praelectiones: in librum Prophetiarum Ieremiae, et Lamentationes. Ioannis Budaei et Caroli Ionuillaei labore et industria exceptae . . . Genevae apud Io. Crispinum. M.D.LXIII.

Leçons ou commentaires et expositions de Iean Caluin, tant sur les Revelations que sur les Lamentations du Prophete Ieremie . . . A Lyon, Par Clavde Senneton. M.D.LXV.

Ezekiel

Ioannis Caluini in viginti prima Ezechielis Prophetae capita Praelectiones, Ioannis Budaei et Caroli Ionuillaei labore et industria exceptae . . . Genevae, Ex officina Francisci Perrini. M.D.LXV.

Leçons ou Commentaires et Expositions de M. Iean Caluin, sur les vingt premiers Chapitres des Reuelations du Prophete Ezechiel: qui sont les dernieres Leçons qu'il a faites auant sa mort . . . A Geneve De l'Imprimerie de François Perrin M.D.LXV.

Corpus Reformatorum

Ioannis Calvini Opera Quae Supersunt Omnia. Ad Fidem Editionum Principum et Authenticarum . . . Ediderunt G. Baum E. Cunitz E. Reuss . . . Brunsvigae. 1863ff.

Vol. 23 Genesis; 24–25 Mosaic and Joshua; 31–32 Psalms; 36–37 Isaiah and Jeremiah 1-7; 38–39 Jeremiah 8ff. and Lamentations; 40 Ezekiel and Daniel 1-5; 41 Daniel 6ff. 42 Hosea – Joel; 43 Amos – Habbakuk; 44 Zephaniah – Malachi.

Calvin Translation Society

Genesis, 2 vols. tr. J. King. 1847,1850.
Pentateuch, 4 vols. tr. C. W. Bingham. 1852-55.
Joshua, tr. H. Beveridge. 1854.
Psalms, 5 vols. tr. J. Anderson. 1845-49.
Isaiah, 4 vols. tr W. Pringle. 1850-53.
Jeremiah and Lamentations 5 vols. tr. J. Owen. 1850-55.
Ezekiel, 2 vols. tr. T. Myers. 1849-50.
Daniel, 2 vols. tr. T. Myers. 1852-53.

Minor Prophets, 5 vols. tr. J. Owen. 1846–49.
Harmony of the Evangelists, 3 vols. tr. W. Pringle. 1845–46.
St. John, 2 vols. tr. W. Pringle. 1847.
Galatians, etc. tr. W. Pringle. 1854.
Philippians, Colossians, etc. tr. W. Pringle. 1851.

Calvin's Commentaries edited by D. W. and T. F. Torrance,
Edinburgh.
Harmony of the Gospels, III. tr. A. W. Morrison. 1972.
St. John, 2 vols. tr. T. H. L. Parker. 1959, 1961.
I Corinthians. tr. J. W. Fraser. 1960.
II Corinthians Tr. T. A. Smail. 1964.
Galatians – Colossians, tr. T. H. L. Parker. 1965.
Hebrews, etc. tr. W. B. Johnston. 1963.

Supplementa Calviniana. Sermons inédits. Neukirchen. 1936ff.
II. Samuel, ed. H. Rückert. 1936.
Psalms, ed. E. Mülhaupt. 1981.
Isaiah 13–29. ed. G. A. Barrois. 1961.
Jeremiah, Lamentations, ed. R. Peter. 1971.
Micah, ed. J.-D. Benoît. 1964.

A Commentary on the Psalms . . . vol. 1. Tr. Arthur Golding
(1571) revised and edited T. H. L. Parker, London. 1965.

Joannis Calvini Opera Selecta Ediderunt P. Barth G. Niesel. III–V
. . . Monachii MCMLVII – MCMLXII.

Iohannis Calvini Commentarius in Epistolam Pauli ad Romanos.
Edidit T. H. L. Parker, Leiden, 1981.

The Sermons of M. Iohn Calvin vpon . . . Deuteronomie . . . At
London, Printed by Henry Middleton for George Bishop. Anno
Domini 1583.

Biblical Index

INDEX OF MAIN TOPICS